To Joh
Kent

C000225360

About the Author

Doctor Grahame Howard was born in London in 1953
and his family moved to Norwich when he was four
years old. His childhood, particularly the eccentric
behaviour of his father, is recounted in his first book,
'The Tales of Dod'. He returned to London to study
Medicine at St Thomas' Hospital Medical School, from
where he graduated in 1976.

Following a series of junior doctor posts in London
and Cambridge he was appointed consultant Clinical
Oncologist in Edinburgh in 1986.

Kind regards
Grahame

Dedication

This book is dedicated to the patients it has been my privilege to treat and the colleagues who have helped me along the way.

Grahame Howard

THE MARBLE CORRIDOR

And Other Medical Tales

AUSTIN MACAULEY PUBLISHERS™

LONDON • CAMBRIDGE • NEW YORK • SHARJAH

A CIP catalogue record for this title is available from the British Library.

Disclaimer:
The characters and events described in this work are fictitious. Any resemblance to real persons, living or dead, is purely coincidental.

ISBN 978-1-78629-684-9 (Paperback)
ISBN 978-1-78629-685-6 (Hardback)
ISBN 978-1-78629-686-3 (E-Book)

www.austinmacauley.com

First Published (2017)
Austin Macauley Publishers Ltd.
25 Canada Square
Canary Wharf
London
E14 5LQ

CONTENTS

"Tomorrow to fresh woods and pastures new."
Milton. *Lycidas.*

PART I

THE MARBLE
CORRIDOR

The wailing started just as I had taken my first mouthful of bacon and egg and lasted for about five seconds. Ambulance crews would often sound their siren briefly as they approached the hospital to alert the staff in A&E that they had someone *in extremis* on board. Neil, having just finished his night on-call, looked up at me from his half-consumed plate of scrambled eggs and smiled. 'Here comes the crumble wagon. Sixty seconds till the first cardiac arrest of the day.' He looked at his watch and started an imaginary countdown. I began to eat more quickly.

We were in the doctors' mess where there was a pleasant early morning smell of fried bacon, toast and cigarettes. Neil, the medical senior house officer, was sitting opposite me, alongside the surgical registrar. Five minutes earlier, as I had joined them with my breakfast-laden plate, he had pushed the arrest-call pager across the table towards me. I had reluctantly accepted it and, with a mumbled, 'Thanks a lot,' dropped it into the pocket of my rather grubby white coat. There it joined my personal pager, a small pen torch, a list of useful phone numbers and drug doses, along with all the other paraphernalia essential to the smooth functioning of a junior doctor.

I loathed these long weekends of being first on-call. St Hilda's had around four hundred beds in total and, although only about sixty patients were directly under my care, I could be asked to see any of those inpatients with a medical problem if it were deemed to be necessary. I was also the first point of contact for GPs who wished to admit a patient from the local community. Just seven months after qualifying as a doctor, I was now gatekeeper of St Hilda's medical beds. Then there was the unplanned work which came through A&E. Men, women and children of all ages would walk, stumble or be carried through the ever open doors. In they came; some alone, others brought by relatives, friends or well-wishers; others plucked off the street by ambulance crews: a medley of tearful, wailing humankind. On Saturday night A&E could look like some battlefield dressing station, overflowing with civilian wounded, smeared with beer, blood and grime – a sickly smell of stale alcohol and vomit pervading every nook and cranny, every cubicle and cot.

However, that would be tomorrow. This was Friday morning, and I was now on duty until five o'clock the following Tuesday afternoon. For the first three of those days I was 'first on-call' and, as such, was a member of the cardiac arrest team. On Monday I would be able to pass the arrest-bleep over to Penny; but then there would still remain another twenty-four hours of being 'second on-call', and after that a normal day's work before I could hang up my pager. Four days when I had to be continuously and immediately available: potentially one hundred and four hours without a break.

Although on-call, and 'on-take' for emergency admissions, this did not necessarily mean having to stay awake for the whole of that time. Sometimes there were no out-of-hours calls at all and on such rare occasions one might enjoy an undisturbed night's sleep. More often than not, however, I would be wakened a few times, and it was usually necessary to struggle out of bed and see an emergency once or twice during the night. It was the uncertainty that I found hardest to cope with. You never knew what was going to happen; one moment you could be rushed off your feet, the next twiddling your thumbs – there was no way of telling. Some doctors revelled in this unpredictability – I detested it.

Standard fare for emergency admissions normally comprised patients with heart attacks, cardiac failure or exacerbations of asthma or chronic bronchitis. Those were the patients, often elderly, whom Neil dismissively described as 'crumble'. Then there were the more interesting diagnostic conundrums, such as diabetic patients whose blood glucose could be too high or too low, or someone having seizures for one reason or another. Then there were the overdoses. These were usually taken by young women on a Saturday night or early Sunday morning, when the highly combustible mix of alcohol and wayward boyfriends would explode resulting in a tearful half-attempt at suicide. The poisons taken depended on what was immediately available in the bathroom cabinet or bedside drawer, usually a cocktail of painkillers and sedatives.

Finally there were the cardiac arrests. Once given the arrest bleep, you were a slave to this until it could be

15

passed on to the next doctor on call. I knew colleagues who, when carrying this pager, would not risk opening their bowels in case it went off, literally, while their trousers were down. True cardio-pulmonary arrests, where a patient has been seen to collapse and stop breathing, were quite rare. Many arrest calls were put out when the inert body of a patient who had died in the night was discovered, often while the nurses made their early morning round at about 6 a.m. – the so-called cardiac-arrest round. Then there were those in A&E who were dead on arrival, but an arrest call was put out anyway, *just in case*. I was never sure what this was just in case *of*. On occasions there seemed to be some confusion between resuscitation and resurrection. We could sometimes achieve the former but never the latter. The problem was the unpredictability. It was either a feast or a famine but, busy or quiet, when on call it was impossible to settle to any other activity, such as reading or watching the TV, in case all hell suddenly broke loose.

'Five – four – three – two – one – and ...' Neil looked up from his wristwatch. Nothing happened. I smiled: perhaps the occupant of this particular crumble-wagon didn't need resuscitating. I took another mouthful of bacon and egg.

BEEP, BEEP – BEEP, BEEP. The pager in my left hand pocket erupted angrily; and from it a disembodied, switchboard-voice calmly announced, 'Cardiac arrest A&E – Cardiac arrest A&E.'

'Shit!' I took a final mouthful of buttered toast, scraped my chair back noisily on the parquet floor, and rushed towards the door of the mess. Before I was halfway there, Neil had set his coffee-cup down and calmly reached for my half-empty plate. 'No need to rush back, Grahame, we'll finish your breakfast for you.'

I ran along the great marble corridor, past the stout pillars and plinths on either side, to the north stairwell, my footsteps echoing loudly in the empty space. Once there, I leapt down the stairs, several at a time. One floor down, the door to A&E was being held open by a frightened, wide-eyed student nurse who had been stationed there to direct the arrest team as they arrived. 'Cardiac arrest – resuscitation room,' she called out, pointing towards two closed doors on which large red letters stated boldly: NO ENTRY – CLINICAL STAFF ONLY. Like a cinema usherette she continued to direct me with her left hand, while holding the door open with the right. 'Resuscitation room,' she repeated nervously.

Breathlessly, I slammed open the doors in question and raced through, leaving them to bang shut behind me. In the far left-hand corner of the brightly illuminated room there was a bustle of activity. Partially hidden by a half-drawn curtain, a gaggle of doctors and nurses were ranged about a trolley on which I could just discern the patient that was the focus of their attention. At the head-end of the trolley, nearest the wall, a young, shirt-sleeved A&E senior house officer was squeezing a black rubber bag the size of a rugby ball with one hand, while with the other he held a mask to the patient's nose and mouth. Hunched over the trolley, his back towards me, obscuring the casualty from view, was another doctor. He was the medical registrar who had been on call overnight and evidently had not yet been able to pass on *his* bleep. He was also wearing a grubby white coat and his shoulders heaved while he pumped up and down on the patient's chest. As I approached he ceased his compressions to allow a nurse to open the man's shirt (for I could now see that the centre of all this activity was a male) and apply ECG electrodes. Possibly in his sixties, the man had wiry grey hair, unshaven bluish cheeks, while around the mask covering the lower part of his face I could see deeply ingrained wrinkles. His eyes were open yet unseeing and his right arm hung limply from the side of the stretcher. His right hand, its fingers stained with nicotine, danced around loosely as the chest compressions recommenced.

'Can someone get a line in please?' The medical registrar was the senior doctor present and had taken charge of the situation. On seeing me he nodded, 'Are you the on-take medical houseman?'

'Yes,' I admitted.

'Good. Could you get a line in please?' I pushed my way to the opposite side of the trolley. Someone handed me a tourniquet which I applied to the patient's upper arm and after a few seconds I was pleased to see an inviting vein. A nurse offered me a Venflon, the needle used for inserting an intravenous drip. 'I'm Mark, medical registrar on call last night,' the white-coated doctor continued. 'Where's your reg?' Then, without waiting for a reply asked, 'Is that line in yet?'

'No.' My hands trembled as I pushed the needle through our patient's skin and, on removing the introducer I was relieved to see blood flow back and spill on to the patient's arm and on to the frayed white sheet covering the stretcher. 'Drip, please. I didn't look up but held out my left hand into which, as if by magic, appeared a plastic tube. 'Run through?' I asked.

'Yes. Dextrose saline,' came the proficient female voice on my left. I connected the plastic drip tube and secured the needle with tape. 'Switch on, please.' I directed this request to the voice on my left without lifting my head and removed the tourniquet. 'Is it running?' I asked.

'Yes,' the voice replied.

Mark had continued to pump the man's chest throughout this procedure. 'Drip running? Good! Get some bicarbonate up, please. Are those leads on?' After a brief pause, the voice replied, 'Bicarbonate up.'

'Electrodes connected. Monitor ready,' shouted the shirt-sleeved doctor to confirm that the ECG leads had been attached to the electrodes on the man's chest. On hearing this, Mark ceased his pumping and looked up. 'Right. Let's see if we have a rhythm.' We all turned our attention to the monitor mounted on the wall behind the stretcher. On the screen there had appeared a small green dot travelling from left to right leaving behind it a ghostly fading green line, rather like the disintegrating vapour trail left by a jet plane.

Mark looked towards the senior house officer, who was still squeezing the black rubber bag. 'Ron. Stop bagging now, please. Let's see what we've got on the monitor.' Mark peered intently at the small screen. The picture had changed and now the green line had peaks and troughs rather like a seismograph during a minor earthquake. 'Right! Ventricular fibrillation. We'll need to shock him. Continue resuscitation. Charge the defibrillator: two hundred joules, please.' This fluent sequence of instructions was directed to no one in particular, as Mark's attention was still concentrated on the little screen, but he knew someone would do his bidding; I was impressed that even in the heat of the moment this confident young man had the time to be courteous. A few seconds later the voice responded, 'Defib charged. Two hundred joules,' it said.

'Right. Stand back, everyone!' We all moved away from the sides of the trolley as Mark carefully placed the paddles on the patient's chest, one just right of centre and the other slightly lower down to the left. Like a snooker player attempting a difficult shot at full stretch, he looked down to check that neither he himself nor any part of his clothing was in contact with the trolley or the man, then pressed the red button on the back of the paddle in his right hand. The patient jerked and convulsed, arching his back before crashing back down on the trolley.

We all looked at the screen. There had been no discernible change. 'Right, we'll shock him again. Three hundred joules this time, please.' Mark repeated the procedure and on this occasion, as the patient settled back on the trolley, we heard a steady beeping sound: miraculously, the green line was altered to a regular recurring pattern; its shape, however, was grossly abnormal. Mark was the first to comment. 'Good! Sinus rhythm but with acute ischaemic changes. He's had a massive coronary.' He gave me an enquiring look.

'Where's your registrar? He should be here by now and taking over from me.'

'I don't know. Haven't seen him this morning, I'm afraid.' I replied.

'Okay. Well, at least you're here to help. You and I can deal with this. Then, turning his gaze to the junior A&E doctor, 'Ronnie, you'd better get back to casualty.'

Ronnie stood aside to let me take control both of the bag and of the mask covering the now blue nose and lips of our patient, and departed to deal with the other medical oddments in casualty. There, awaiting his attention, was an elderly man who probably had a fractured femur, a sixteen-year-old girl with abdominal pain, who was either severely constipated or pregnant, and two or three patients who had come to A&E in the early hours of the morning after an evening's drinking, with lacerations which needed suturing.

Mark continued to peer intently at the monitor. 'Can anyone detect a pulse? Could somebody check his blood pressure, please?'

I felt our man's neck for a carotid pulse. 'Nothing palpable, Mark.' Neither was there a measurable blood pressure.

'Right. Recommence resuscitation please, ladies and gentlemen.' Mark then turned to me, 'Here, Grahame, you take over with chest compressions and I'll ventilate. It gets a bit tiring after a while.' We swapped positions and I crossed the heel of both my hands over our patient's sternum and pressed. 'One, two, three, four,' I counted out loud, while pushing down on his chest. 'A bit slower, Grahame, and harder, please,' Mark instructed.

'Okay! One … two … three …' and so I continued.

'Bad sign if there's no output in sinus rhythm.' Mark sighed and just then the regular beeping noise became a constant high-pitched whine. He turned quickly to check the pattern on the monitor; the green line was now flat. 'Hello! He's gone into asystole.' Mark was not addressing anyone in particular, more thinking aloud. 'Okay, things not looking too good. Adrenaline please – in a cardiac syringe.' Mark palpated the man's chest, feeling for the fifth intercostal space. He then seized the loaded syringe and without hesitation plunged the long needle directly through the chest wall, aiming for our patient's heart. He pulled the plunger back and, gratified to see dark red blood enter the syringe, injected the adrenaline directly into our patient's left ventricle.

'Grahame,' he said without looking at me, 'this way we know the drug's where it needs to be – in the heart.' The green line developed some peaks and troughs as the drug took effect but still no pulse was detectable. We had now been trying to resuscitate this man for about forty-five minutes. 'He's clearly had a massive heart attack – you could see it on the cardiograph during that brief spell of sinus rhythm and now he's now in cardiogenic shock.' Mark was referring to the total absence of any detectable cardiac output, a condition incompatible with life. We continued our efforts, occasionally swapping roles, every now and again stopping briefly to assess whether there was any evidence of a spontaneous blood flow.

The green squiggles on the monitor grew gradually smaller and less frequent until the line once more became flat. 'I think we should try one more shock and if that doesn't work, we'll call it a day. Grahame, you can defibrillate this time.' So saying, Mark handed me the paddles. By now we had been resuscitating our patient for nearly an hour, during which time he had at no stage shown any sign of life, nor had a measurable cardiac output. The only reason we had continued for so long was because the ambulance crew had informed us that a witness had seen the man walking briskly along the street just before he collapsed, and there had initially been evidence of electrical activity on his cardiogram. I knew Mark was probably prescribing this one last shock in order to give me the experience, as none of us believed the patient's heart could now be restarted and we knew that, in effect, he was already dead.

'Four hundred joules, please.' I requested, looking at the nurse who was standing next to the defibrillator. A moment later I heard a voice say, 'Charged.'

'Stand back, please.' I carefully positioned the paddles and pressed the red button. The patient once more arched and lifted from the couch only to settle back down, this time for good. We all stood back and gazed at the monitor screen. The green line remained resolutely flat.

'Right. That's it, everyone. Turn the monitor off, please. Time of death,' Mark glanced at his wrist-watch, 'nine fifty-five. Thank you, everybody.'

I looked at the lifeless shell of the man who only an hour before had been a patient and, two hours before that, a living, sentient being. I found myself speculating about this patient and the events of his last morning. Perhaps he had overslept and then, with no time to shave, had dressed quickly and walked briskly to the bus stop, unaware that his life would end on the pavement in just a few minutes. A father? – maybe. A grandfather? – possibly. A husband, brother, clerk, businessman, labourer? I would never know. All I knew was that he had walked briskly to his death that summer morning.

Mark and I moved aside from the trolley and pushed through the curtains, carefully closing them behind us. 'Thanks for your help, Grahame. Clearly he'd had a massive heart attack and I suspect was probably dead on arrival. You have to attempt to resuscitate these patients though. You should try to attend the post-mortem.' So saying, Mark turned and walked purposefully in the direction of the wards.

'I will,' I called out to the disappearing figure.

I'd heard my pager beeping several times during the resuscitation attempt, so when Mark had left I went directly to the nurses' station where I picked up a phone and dialled zero. A cheery lady answered. 'Switchboard,' she sang.

'Grahame Howard here. You bleeped?'

'Ah, Doctor Howard, Doctor Liston's been looking for you. I'll put you through.' There was a click and then I heard an extension ringing. 'Endoscopy. Staff nurse speaking.'

'Hi. It's Grahame Howard. You bleeped me?'

'Yes, that was Doctor Liston. I'll hand you over.' There was a brief pause.

'Where on *earth* are you?' This was David Liston, the medical registrar on the team, my immediate senior and the doctor I would be on call with for the next ninety-six hours. 'Sorry, David,' I said, 'but there was a cardiac arrest in A&E.'

'You should have let the night team deal with that.'

'It was after nine, and I had the arrest bleep.'

'Okay. Never mind.' Liston continued in a calmer tone, 'Look, I'm in the endoscopy suite, the boss is elsewhere, and there's quite a big list. I suggest you do a quick ward round, discharge as many patients as you can and then come up here to help me.' He didn't wait for a response and with a click the line went dead.

St Hilda's was on the southern outskirts of London. It had an impressive, neo-gothic Victorian façade and, like so many hospitals of that period, its imposing front entrance opened directly on to a very grand main corridor. This thoroughfare ran the length of the hospital and was its main artery, the vessel that delivered life-blood to its various parts. Staff, patients, equipment; all the people and paraphernalia necessary for the functioning of the hospital, travelled its length. It formed the backbone of this great institution and attached to it, like so many ribs, were long Nightingale wards. This corridor, this marble edifice, lined on each side by imposing pillars and with its tall, arched cathedral-like ceiling, had borne witness to the injured from the Crimean and Boer Wars; had echoed during the war to end all wars, to the cries of neurasthenics with 'shell shock' and to the blinded and limbless from the Western Front. Then, just a generation later, it had witnessed the burned pilots and broken civilians of the London blitz. Doctors in tailcoats and top hats, with fob watches to take a pulse, had once paraded along this very line; and the blood-soaked aprons of surgeons, dextrous and quick, before anaesthetics could dull the agony of their labours, had dripped on to this very floor. Every few yards these memorable figures were immortalised in marble and set upon plinths, observing their successors traverse the same promenade.

I made my way along this corridor; now bustling with staff and patients of the modern day, past the scrutiny of those marble pioneers, to the two medical wards at the corridor's most southerly tip.

'Morning, Sister.' I smiled at Jenny, the sister in charge of the men's ward.

'Doctor Howard. You're late! Where *have* you been? It's after ten and we're on-take.' Her rebuke delivered, I was then greeted with a sweet smile of welcome.

'I know. Sorry, but there was an arrest in A&E. Can we do a quick notes-round please? I need to get to endoscopy as soon as I can.'

Jenny was one of the younger ward sisters. She was probably in her late-twenties and as such several years older than me, but we were close enough in age to have a good rapport. She was attractive rather than pretty and her tidy appearance radiated both authority and confidence. Initially, she gave the impression of being rather prim and stern – something of a martinet – but, like so many women in positions of responsibility, underneath this starchy veneer was a flirtatious young woman with a deep sense of humour.

We sat down at the tidy desk in her office and discussed the patients who were on the ward. Three were fit enough to go home. The rest were either stable, but awaiting further investigations, or on active treatment and not yet ready for discharge. I made a list of outstanding tasks in my little black notebook and then replaced it in the pocket of my white coat. 'Thanks, Sister,' I said preparing to leave. 'I'll be back as soon as the list is finished.'

'Before you go, there is *one* patient I'm a bit concerned about.'

'Yes. Who's that?'

'Mr Krakowski.'

'I know him. He's in for investigation of anaemia, isn't he?'

'Yes, that's right. There's nothing I can put my finger on, but I'm just not that happy with him. All his observations are okay, but I thought I should just flag him up. Perhaps you could have a quick look at him?'

'Of course, Sister. Do I need to see him now or can it wait till later?' I asked.

'Later will be fine. You'd better get off. Don't want to upset Liston so early in the weekend.' Jenny gave me a wry smile and I left to cross the corridor and repeat the process on the female ward.

My pager went off twice on my way to the endoscopy suite. The first call was a request to see a patient on the orthopaedic ward who was confused and consequently the surgical team wanted a medical opinion. The second call was from a GP on a home visit. He was with an asthmatic whose breathing was deteriorating and needed hospital treatment. I asked him to send the patient to A&E and added a note of these calls to my to-do list.

'You took your time!' Liston briefly looked up from the eyepiece of the endoscope he was holding, nearly the whole length of which was inserted into the stomach of a man lying on the couch next to him. 'I've just about finished the list. There's only one more.'

Having thus acknowledged my presence, Liston proceeded to continue the investigation, fiddling with the knobs on the handle that steered the instrument around the patient's upper gastrointestinal tract. David had recently passed the second part of the membership exam for the Royal College of Physicians and had now taken to writing MRCP after his name whenever possible. 'Where've you been?'

His question was rhetorical but I answered anyway, 'Just emptying the wards for the weekend.'

Having completed the procedure, Liston gently extracted the endoscope from his patient's stomach and handed it carefully to the attendant nurse. The man, who had been sedated, was now reasonably alert and Liston turned to him. 'That's much better,' he said. 'The ulcer seems to have healed up completely.' The patient tried to respond but only managed to cough and splutter. 'We'll need to check again in three months.' He stood up and then continued, 'The nurse will need to keep an eye on you for an hour or so, after which you can go home.' Liston strode across the room to a small table on which lay a pile of case notes and started to write in the topmost set.

David wasn't so bad but he had a justified reputation for being awkward and unhelpful on occasions. Certainly he had a brusque manner not entirely suited to the caring profession. Although only just over six feet he seemed taller since he was excruciatingly thin, so much so that you could see his shoulder blades through the back of his white coat. His thick blond hair fell in a wave over his forehead, below which his face was pinched and rather gaunt. I thought that maybe some of his perceived lack of commitment was that, slightly unusually he was married with two young children and spent more time with his family than did many junior doctors, most of whom considered the hospital to be their home.

'You can do this last one, Grahame.' Liston didn't look up from his writing. This was a bonus, opportunities to perform practical procedures being few and far between and to be grasped whenever they arose. 'Thanks,' I said picking up the last remaining set of case notes.

The next patient was already lying on the couch awaiting my attention. He had removed his shirt and was now wearing a white gown, tied at the back. He was a large and brawny man, probably in his early sixties, with broad shoulders and a considerable abdomen. His weather-beaten face was covered in blackheads and he had a lumpy, bright-red nose. These signs invariably shouted, 'DRINKER,' to the alert clinician. After introducing myself and explaining the procedure, I inserted a needle into the back of the man's large hand

and began slowly to inject the milky fluid that was diazepam. Ten milligrams was usually enough to stop the blink reflex, an indication that the patient was sedated enough to tolerate having a large tube pushed down his throat and into his stomach where it could then be steered about to inspect the interior. This man was wide awake and still telling me about his family in an animated fashion after having been given three times that dose. It was only when I had injected nearly forty milligrams that he sighed, snorted once and fell into a deep sleep. Fifteen minutes later, the investigation being completed, I withdrew the instrument. The problem now was that he was unrousable and snoring loudly.

'Must be a drinker. Observe the rhinophyma,' Liston said pompously, pointing at the man's strawberry-like nose. 'You'd better keep an eye on him till he comes round after that great whack of diazepam you gave him.'

'Beep – beep.' I dialled zero. The cheery switchboard voice informed me that the man I had accepted was now waiting in A&E.

'David,' I said, 'there's an asthmatic in A&E I need to see. Is it okay if I go now?'

'Yes. You go and sort him out. I'll call you later and we'll do a ward round of the day's admissions.'

Back in A&E, I knew immediately which cubicle my patient occupied by the loud wheezing audible from the end of the assessment area. The GP had written a comprehensive letter and there was no doubt about the diagnosis. Half an hour later, after an intravenous injection of aminophylline, he was beginning to breathe more easily and I filled in an X-ray request. I glanced at my watch. Five minutes to two. I hadn't stopped since leaving my breakfast in the mess five hours ago and reckoned if I rushed I might just make it to the canteen before it closed. I set off briskly along the corridor, dodging nurses, cleaners, and porters pushing wheelchairs or trolleys and skipping around the marble busts of toga-clad physicians.

'Beep – beep.' 'Hello. Doctor Howard. A&E for you,' the cheery voice sang and put me through again.

'Is that the medical houseman on take?'

'Yes,' I affirmed somewhat reluctantly.

'Hi. It's the A&E senior house officer here. I've got an elderly man in admissions with heart failure who needs your attention. Soon, please, as he's quite unwell.' Senior house officers, generally referred to as SHO's, were those junior doctors who had duly completed their year as a houseman and were now sampling a variety of different specialties before deciding on their preferred career. They were thus rather like a midshipman in the Royal Navy: not yet an officer but no longer an able seaman – neither fish nor fowl.

'I'll be right along.' I said and laid the phone down. After the briefest of hesitations, I turned on my heel, away from the canteen and back in the direction of A&E. I swung open the door to the assessment area. The nurse who had assisted me with the asthmatic looked at me, somewhat puzzled. 'He's not back from X-ray yet,' she said.

'No. I'm here to see someone else,' I explained. The SHO, who was sitting at a desk writing in a set of case-notes, glanced at me, 'Oh, good, Doctor Howard. Thanks for coming so quickly. He's in cubicle six. His daughter found him having trouble breathing earlier on this morning.'

I pushed back the curtains of cubicle six. There, semi-upright on a stretcher and gasping for air, was a plump, white-haired man. He was wearing pyjama trousers but was naked from the waist up and a few straggly grey hairs were visible between his small sagging breasts. On his face, held there by a length of green elastic, was an oxygen mask connected by plastic tubing to a bubbling humidifier attached to the wall behind him. From around the plastic mask came a fine cloud of water vapour, within which his head was enveloped. Sitting next to him, holding a large brown leather handbag firmly in her lap with both hands, was a worried-looking, slightly wizened middle-aged lady. Everything about her was neutral; the style and colour of her clothes, her demeanour and even her hat. She was definitely wearing a hat: I knew that because there was a small emerald green hatpin visible, as were a few brown feathers, but it was so nondescript and so moulded to the contour of her head that she might as well have not bothered to put it on.

'Mr Stewart?' I said looking at him. The man gasped and nodded his assent, clearly too breathless to respond.

'I'm Doctor Howard, the medical houseman.'

'I'm his daughter,' volunteered the lady. 'I found him like this when I went to give him his breakfast, first thing this morning. He's never been this bad before.'

'He's had heart problems in the past, has he?' I asked the daughter.

'Oh yes. But never this bad.' Then, after a pause, she added, 'I've got his tablets – here.' She rummaged in her bag and produced some small brown bottles. I looked at them and confirmed that they were standard medication for heart failure.

'I'd like to examine you,' I said loudly, in order to be heard above the hissing humidifier.

My patient had all the signs of congestive heart failure. An enlarged heart with a rapid pulse, crackles in his lungs signifying the presence of fluid where there should have been air, and grossly swollen ankles which felt like putty in which the indentations made by your fingers remained. He had what my Victorian predecessors, immortalised in the corridor above, would have called dropsy. I administered the 'crumble elixir' – as Neil had dubbed the combination of diuretic, aminophylline and morphine, and arranged for him to have a chest X-ray, a cardiogram, some blood tests and thence to be admitted. I decided I would review the results of these tests later, on the ward.

As the porters wheeled him off to X-ray, his daughter hesitated, then looked at me and asked timidly, 'Is it serious, Doctor?'

'Well, as I'm sure you realise, he's got bad heart failure. Normally it responds well to treatment, but we'll have to wait and see.'

'You see, since Mum was killed in the blitz he's all I've got.' She stopped to dab her eyes with a dainty lace-handkerchief, 'I don't know what I should do if he –' and she faltered – 'if anything were to happen to him.'

'Hopefully he'll be fine.' I smiled and indicated that she should follow the trolley and accompany her father to X-ray.

I made my way back to the endoscopy suite to check how the man whom I had 'scoped earlier was faring. Liston, MRCP, was sitting in the now-empty room, his long legs outstretched, a mug of tea on the desk beside him. 'Ah! Grahame. How's your asthmatic?'

'Should be okay, but I need to nip back to see his X-ray. I've also admitted a man with congestive heart failure.'

'Okay, we'll do a ward round later on. I have to go to see some referrals now. By the way,' and Liston smiled at me, 'the man you whacked with a gallon of diazepam, woke up eventually, and I sent him home. He said it was the best sleep he'd had for years!'

'Excellent. That's a relief. Thanks, David.'

'Beep – beep.' This time it was Jenny. 'Doctor Howard, you said you'd come back to look at Mr Krakowski. You haven't forgotten, have you?'

'Sorry, Sister, but it's been a bit hectic. I'll be up later.'

'Okay, but it's nearly four o'clock and I'll be going off soon, so don't forget.' Then she added breezily, 'See you tomorrow.' I put the phone down, and as I did so my pager erupted again. This time I recognised the voice of the A&E senior house officer. 'Hello, Doctor Howard? It's me again. Sorry to trouble you but I've got two more medical cases in admissions for you.'

The space called A&E actually consisted of several different areas. As well as having a receiving area for trauma patients, there was an admissions area for the assessment of those either self-referred or sent in by GPs, along with a treatment room for minor surgery; and lastly the resuscitation room for acutely-ill patients such as the one who had arrested earlier that morning.

I retraced my steps towards the admissions unit where I pulled back the curtains of the cubicle I had been directed to. There, lying on a stretcher surrounded by chattering women clad in brightly coloured saris, was a frightened-looking Asian man. He looked young, maybe in his mid-thirties, while his eyes were wide with fear and apprehension. An oxygen mask covered his nose and mouth and his face and bare chest were drenched with sweat, his jet-black hair plastered to his forehead. At the head of the couch, her arm around his shoulder and weeping uncontrollably, was his wife, while amongst the colourful ladies was a handsome, besuited, dark-skinned man.

I glanced at the long strip of paper that was the patient's cardiogram. There could be no doubt about the diagnosis: this man had sustained an extensive inferior myocardial infarction, or heart attack, as I later explained to the family. I put a drip up, drew up some drugs and began a slow infusion to reduce his blood pressure and heart rate. I turned to the nurse who was assisting me. 'Could you contact coronary care, please, and see if they have a bed. Tell them I've a patient here who should be transferred as soon as possible.' Just then the cubicle curtain was suddenly and vigorously pulled aside and a young student nurse burst in. All of us, apart from the patient, turned to see the cause of this sudden intrusion. I looked up from the injection I was administering, surprised and irritated. After the briefest of glances around the room, the clearly flustered girl turned to me. 'Doctor, please can you come next door.' The girl's eyes were wide, her pupils dilated and the words tumbled out in a frightened, staccato fashion. This was not a request, more a plea. I was annoyed by the girl's behaviour and her tone.

'I've not finished here,' I said in some irritation, while continuing the injection. I turned again to my assistant and repeated, 'Could you contact CCU for me, please, while I inject this?'

The student nurse was beginning to panic. She was hyperventilating, her fists were clenched, her knuckles were white and her voice was rising in both volume and pitch. She then virtually screamed at me, '*Please*! You need to come next door. *Quickly.*' She had now closed her eyes and was standing rigid, rooted to the spot, her whole body shaking, her face deathly white. Then, with an effort that was almost palpable, she managed to control herself and said more quietly, '*Please*, Doctor, I need you to see a patient next door.'

'Okay. One second.' I completed my injection and then followed the nurse into the next cubicle. There, on a trolley was a man: elderly, white-haired, grey-faced, unkempt and *dead*.

'Was he like this when he came in?' I asked. The student was now a little more settled.

'I don't know. I just came in to tidy the room and saw … *him*,' she hesitated, 'like this. Is he …?' She didn't want to say 'dead' in case he wasn't and was listening.

I thumped the man hard in the middle of the chest. No response at all. His pupils were fixed and dilated and I couldn't detect a pulse. I registered that his clothes and the stretcher were soaking wet. I was in two minds. Should we try to resuscitate this man who might well have been dead for some time? I remembered the conversation from earlier that morning. 'Right.' I looked at the nurse. 'Put out an arrest call, please.' Just as the nurse turned towards the telephone, the A&E doctor popped his head round the curtain.

'What are you two doing in here?' he said cheerily, 'I wouldn't try to resuscitate him. He was dead on arrival. Fished out of the river half an hour ago!'

I looked with relief at the nurse. A futile resuscitation attempt had been averted. Tears of relief rolled down her face, and she turned away to compose herself.

The senior house officer continued, 'Is your man going to CCU or not? I need the bay. I've got some multiple injuries coming in.' He looked at me despairingly, 'Would you believe it, a coachload of psycho-geriatrics has just crashed on the motorway.'

It was five o'clock before I had a moment to speak to the Indian patient's family. 'Could I speak to Mrs Patel? Mrs Patel, please.' I was standing at the doorway of the interview room where the Patel family had been asked to wait. The smartly dressed man I had noticed earlier stepped forward. He was handsome, smelled of

37

aftershave and appeared to have gold rings on most of his fingers. I looked at him, 'I need to speak to *Mrs* Patel please. On her own.'

'I am the brother. Mrs Patel doesn't speak the English, only Gujurati. I will be translator.' He beckoned to one of the colourful ladies, who came forward, trembling with anticipation, and then he smiled at me, his head tilted slightly to one side. I ushered the two of them into a small dingy side-room smelling of cigarettes and sweat, the low Formica table stained with cup rings and strewn with old magazines.

'He's had a heart attack,' I addressed this to the brother, who started to translate. After just a few words, Mrs Patel burst into tears and started to wail and stamp her feet. The brother spoke to her quietly and tenderly, trying to comfort her. Then, turning to me, he said slightly apologetically, 'She's very upset, you know. She wants to know if her husband will be all right.'

'I understand. Of course she's upset.' I hesitated. I wanted to reassure them, but the cardiograph had demonstrated a very extensive infarct. Heart failure, cardiac arrest and cardiogenic shock causing death were all distinct possibilities.

'Well, it would be wrong to deny that his condition isn't serious, but hopefully with treatment he'll recover. The first twenty-four hours or so are crucial.' The brother turned to Mrs Patel and started to translate, whereupon the wailing increased and she started to bang her fists against the side of her head. I remained silent as he tried to console and calm her. When the wailing and stamping had settled, I continued, 'He will be transferred to the Coronary Care Unit for intensive monitoring.'

Having picked up the words 'coronary care', and 'intensive', Mrs Patel promptly crumpled to the floor where her wailing became a scream as she banged her feet and arms on the floor with ever-increasing intensity. Brother Patel tried to calm her.

'Beep – beep.' I made my excuses and went to the phone.

'Where are you?' It was Liston.

'In A&E.'

'Are you ready to do a ward round?'

'Fine,' I said. Actually it wasn't fine at all. My to-do list now had twenty-three items on it, and that didn't include seeing the results of blood tests, reviewing the day's admissions and speaking to relatives.

We met on the ward and discussed the day's admissions. The man with asthma had improved, his chest X-ray was normal and he did not require admission. Mr Stewart's tests confirmed the diagnosis of heart failure and he was comfortable, having been transferred to the ward. The nurse in charge said his daughter would like to speak to me. 'I'll be back later, as soon as I can,' I assured her.

Finally, we went to coronary care to assess Mr Patel. Wires from electrodes on his chest were now connected to a heart monitor mounted on the wall behind him. Around his bed were metal stands of differing heights from which hung polythene bags and plastic tubes. Finer tubing, red with blood, was connected to a bedside machine to measure physiological parameters which were displayed as numbers and wavy lines on green screens. All this information was collated every fifteen minutes by one of the nurses who documented the readings on a large chart attached to the foot of his bed.

His blood tests had confirmed what we already knew – that he had sustained a massive heart attack – and, rather worryingly, his blood pressure was now beginning to fall. We discussed his management and amended his medication. The CCU sister asked if I would speak to the family. 'I'll be back later,' I replied.

'Right, Grahame. That's about it for now. 'Remember,' Liston continued, 'I don't want to be called at night for anything other than suspected meningitis in a child. The rest you should be able to handle by yourself.' Was there a smile on his face, or did he really mean it? I wasn't sure, but it was certainly a warning not to call him unnecessarily. 'See you tomorrow, on the ward at about ten.' I watched his shoulder blades move under his white coat as he turned and strode off towards the doctor's mess.

I headed slowly back to the men's ward, along the marble corridor, past the long array of distinguished physicians. It was now eight-thirty and the thoroughfare was once again busy with chattering, capped nurses going off duty; the crossed red ties of their capes accentuating the outline of their breasts. One briefly glanced at me and smiled as she talked excitedly of Friday evening plans: of perfume, parties and boyfriends.

'Right. Mrs ... I mean, *Miss* Stewart. I'm sorry to have kept you waiting so long.' I said this while appraising her once again. She really was the epitome of a spinster, clad in a dull, colourless woollen skirt, a white high-necked blouse buttoned right up to her chin and a dreary tweed coat. Having looked briefly at me to acknowledge my presence, she now stared down at the floor, but I could still detect the concern in her face. Her dainty handkerchief, never far away, was in her right hand and she clasped her handbag tightly with the left.

'Well, the tests confirm heart failure and the X-ray shows fluid on the lungs, which is why he's so breathless. Nonetheless, he is a bit better than when he arrived and hopefully should continue to improve.'

'Should I stay, Doctor? It's just that we've got a cat at home and she'll wonder what's happened.' I decided to make the decision for her. 'If I were you I would go home, feed your cat and come back tomorrow morning. The nurses can always get in touch if your father's condition changes.'

'Oh, thank you, Doctor. You see, we've only got each other. I've never left home. I was engaged but my fiancé was killed.' She briefly looked up and then dropped her gaze to the floor once more. 'It was during the D-Day landings, you know, and I never wanted to marry anyone else.' She then offered me an almost coquettish smile, 'Although I've had my chances, mind,' she added. A dry old spinster now, but as I looked into her eyes I thought I caught a glimpse – just a hint – of the person who some thirty years ago had been a ravishing, sensual young women deeply in love with her

41

soldier. 'I'll just nip in and say goodbye,' and so saying she bustled back into the ward to bid her farewells.

I glanced at my watch. 'Damn!' I said out loud. It was nine o'clock and I had missed the canteen yet again. I looked at my to-do list and realised that I still hadn't seen either the patient on the orthopaedic ward or the man Jenny had been concerned about. I was considering what to do first when my bleep erupted again. It was Sister on CCU to remind me that the Patels were waiting to talk to me and were becoming anxious.

Things were not looking good for Mr Patel. His blood pressure had dropped still further and his urine output had decreased. I adjusted his medication along the lines Liston and I had agreed earlier and entered the side-room where the family were waiting.

Along with Mrs Patel and the brother were the three other sari-clad ladies. One, who had that attractive pepper-and-salt hair colour and was clearly older than the other two, was now introduced as the patient's mother. The others were his sisters.

'We are very worried, Doctor. Very, *very* worried, you know. Sanjid has not spoken to us and he looks so very unwell.' Mrs Patel was staring at her brother–in-law. Like so many Indian ladies, she was small-boned and petite with a very pretty, finely sculpted face. The two brothers were the opposite – handsome, but hearty, stocky and slightly overweight. A pair of successful businessmen – both high-risk candidates for coronary artery disease and premature death.

'We know he's had a heart attack, quite a big one,' I said, 'and that's caused his blood pressure to drop. He's sedated, which has made him drowsy and that's why he's unable to talk to you.' The brother interrupted: 'But will he be all right, Doctor? That's what we really need to know, you know'

'I'm afraid it's impossible to say yet. It's too early. He may recover but there's no guaranteeing that. The first twenty-four hours are crucial.' The brother nodded his head and stared between his legs at the floor.

'Thank you, doctor. I understand. I will now have to tell his wife.' I left the room and went back to the bedside to check the observations, which had not changed. As I was leaving, a wail and the noise of stamping feet erupted from the side-room.

Back on the men's ward, I took a seat in Sister's office and started to thumb through Mr Krakowski's notes. He had been admitted a week earlier for investigation of severe anaemia. Liston had performed an endoscopy and could find no source of bleeding in his upper gastrointestinal tract and we were awaiting a barium enema to see if he was losing blood from the lower part of his bowel. It was now ten-thirty and the nursing staff had settled the patients down for the night. The main ward lights had been extinguished but hospitals are never truly dark and the desk lamps on the nurse's station, together with the dim night-lights above the beds, clothed the whole ward in a ghostly dull-yellow hue. I tiptoed down the ward and halted halfway along. 'Mr Krakowski?' He was wide awake. 'Hi! How are you?' I whispered. 'Sister said you were feeling a little unwell.'

'No. Not so good. No.' He was a labourer in his forties and his voice was guttural with an immediately recognisable Polish accent. I felt his abdomen and checked his observations. Apart from a slightly faster pulse than normal, everything appeared to be satisfactory and I felt nothing further needed to done that night. 'I'll check up on you again tomorrow. Good night.'

I glanced at my watch: eleven o'clock. I still had several things on my to-do list that needed to be completed that night, but I was in urgent need of a coffee. I walked the short distance to the doctor's quarters and to the small kitchen where I switched on the kettle and lit a cigarette. I had missed lunch and dinner but could grab a sandwich later, or if necessary wait till breakfast. I took my first sip of coffee. 'Beep – beep.' The cheery voice had gone home and a man put me through to admissions.

Back in A&E, I sat down at the nurse's station and suddenly realised how tired I'd become. The sister in charge handed me a slim folder which contained all that we knew about the patient I'd been asked to see. He had just arrived, sent in by a GP and delivered by ambulance.

'He's over there, Doctor Howard. Bay two. Chest pain. Probably a touch of angina, I should think. They're doing an ECG now. He seems to be stable. Slight tachycardia but his blood pressure's okay.'

'Thanks, Sister.' I said, opening the folder. The GP letter was short and to the point.

Previously fit fifty-two year old. On no medication.

One-hour history of central chest pain radiating down his left arm.
Probable angina.
Please see and treat.

Below was the indecipherable GP's signature.

I glanced at the man in question. He was sitting comfortably on a trolley a few yards to my right. His ankles were crossed and his shirt had been removed, ready for the ECG. He looked quite unconcerned by his situation. His neat, iron-grey hair was cut short and, even when lying on a stretcher, he displayed a distinctly military bearing. Slightly overweight, yet muscular and fit-looking, he was chatting easily to the nurse who was attaching ECG leads to his chest.

I opened my black notebook and started to update my to-do list. A moment later I felt a nudge on my shoulder. 'Doctor, I think you should see this.' The ECG strip was flashed in front of me. There could be no uncertainty about what was causing this man's chest pain. He was in the throes of having a heart attack. I glanced across at the patient and in the few seconds since I had last seen him he had changed beyond all recognition. His head now lolled forward and his body was covered with sweat. I kicked back my chair and reached him just as his heart stopped beating.

'Cardiac arrest. Arrest call please,' I shouted as I lowered the back-rest of the stretcher and started to pump up and down on his chest.

A&E is a good place to have a cardiac arrest, only CCU and ITU being better. In those settings the staff are

45

well-rehearsed in cardio-pulmonary resuscitation, whereas on the general wards it is rarely successful. Immediately I shouted, 'cardiac arrest,' I had been joined at the trolley-side by a team of doctors and nurses. One senior house officer grabbed a facemask, connected the oxygen and started to ventilate our patient while I continued cardiac massage. Liston then strode in to take charge, slightly breathless but characteristically calm. I noticed that he was no longer wearing a tie and that the top two buttons of his shirt were undone. 'Right, Grahame. What's the situation?'

'Arrested here about five minutes ago. Definite infarct. Resuscitation started immediately but he has been in ventricular fibrillation ever since.'

'Thanks.' Liston looked briefly at the ECG and then at the monitor with its irregular spiky green line. 'Defibrillate, please,' he said calmly. 'Two hundred joules.'

While I pumped, and the SHO ventilated, Liston stood back and directed, the indisputable maestro of this strange, frenetic orchestra.

For three-quarters of an hour our patient had his chest pumped, his lungs inflated, his heart bump-started and every available drug injected in every conceivable way, all without success. At regular intervals we would stop to watch the green line, which gradually became stubbornly and resolutely flat.

Eventually Liston called a halt, certified the patient dead and went to see the relatives. I sat and wondered if there was anything else I might have done.

During those proceedings I had been called several times. The Night Sister had done her rounds and wanted sedation to be prescribed for a number of patients who were restless or who, in her opinion, might become so overnight. It was two in the morning before I had completed my round of the wards. I glanced at my to-do list. 'Damn!' I had still not seen the patient on the orthopaedic ward and for the briefest of moments I thought of leaving it till the next day. I knew though that, if I did, I would just spend the night worrying, and so I made my way wearily across to the surgical wing of St Hilda's.

I walked quietly on to the ward and introduced myself to the student nurse who was in charge. Looking into the dim and somewhat ghostly interior, I could see two rows of beds, bolted to which were scaffolding-like gantries. Within these surreal structures lay patients, their grotesque white-plastered limbs held at ridiculous angles by a system of ropes, pulleys and weights, which dangled over the ends and the sides of their beds. Like so many abandoned puppets, they lay as though waiting to dance again when the sun came up the following day.

'What's the problem?' I asked.

'It's Mr Waters. The doctors are quite concerned about him. I'm not quite sure why, but he's a bit drowsy and confused.'

'What's he in for?'

'Fractured neck of femur,' came the reply. 'Fell down some steps in town!'

I looked at the case-notes of the man in question. There was a brief entry referring to his admission four days previously, but none subsequently. The investigations section was completely empty, apart from an out-of-date blood count. I quietly walked the length of the ward and viewed him from the end of the bed. His cheeks were sunken and his mouth lay open, exposing his stiff dry tongue. I didn't bother to wake him but just gently pinched the skin on the front of his neck, and when I released it the ridge of tissue remained. I went back to the nurses' station. 'He's dehydrated. He needs some blood samples taking and a drip put up. Can you contact your team to arrange that, please?'

'We don't have anyone on-call for orthopaedics. We're covered by general surgery.'

'Okay. Can you phone *them*?'

'They're in theatre. I've been trying to get them all night.' Her voice began to falter.

'For heaven's sake! I've got enough of my own work to do without …'

I glanced at this young girl who looked about seventeen. Along with another, even more junior nurse, she was responsible for the lives of fifteen patients. It wasn't her fault that this man needed attention and no one else could be found. Her forehead was furrowed and her eyes were beginning to fill with tears.

'Sorry. I didn't realise. I'll do it. Could you give me a hand, please?' Her face creased into a smile of relief as she nodded her assent. 'Thanks,' she said.

'Could you set up a trolley with some syringes and an intravenous fluid-giving set?' I asked. 'Oh! And run through a drip, please.'

By the time the bloods had been taken, the drip set up and I had convinced the on-call biochemistry technician that my requests were urgent and couldn't wait till the next day, it was nearly three-thirty in the morning and I was beginning to feel tired again. The adrenaline rush from the cardiac arrest had kept me going but that was now wearing off. My to-do list was long but I decided that there was nothing that couldn't wait until the following morning.

I headed back to the doctors' quarters where I lit a cigarette, made another coffee and unlocked the sparsely furnished room that was my home for six months. The technician would soon phone with the blood results and thus there was no point in going to bed, so I sat down on the one easy chair in the room. The single bed looked inviting and I wondered whether or not to risk undressing. While I pondered, I finished my cigarette and then lit another from the glowing stub. My eyes began to droop. 'Beep – beep.' The sound startled me. I had been on the verge of falling asleep, cigarette in hand.

'Biochemistry here.' I have the results on Mr Waters.

'Thanks. Go ahead.'

'Well you were right. The patient is both dehydrated and hypercalcaemic.'

He read out the results which I noted down. 'Thanks. That's very helpful. Goodnight.'

I walked back to the orthopaedic ward to write the results in the notes and then to adjust Mr Waters' fluid regimen. Back in my room I thought it was now worthwhile trying to get some sleep. But as I sat on the side of my bed and began to unlace my shoes, the bedside phone rang. 'Doctor Howard?'

'Yes.' I replied, glancing at my alarm clock, which registered a quarter to five in the morning.

'I have Night Sister for you.' My heart sank.

'Thanks. Put her through.' This was bad news. A call from the senior nurse at night meant work, which in turn meant no chance of getting to bed. 'Hello, Sister.'

'Hello, Doctor Howard. Sorry to wake you, but there's a patient I'm a bit concerned about whom I think you should see.'

'Is it Mr Patel?' I was worried about his condition and had been expecting a call from CCU.

'No. It's a Mr Krakowski on male medical. He's passed a melaena stool,' she said.

'Oh, well. That explains his anaemia. I'll come along. Can someone run a drip through please?'

'Certainly. I'll ask the night staff. Thanks, Doctor Howard.' And the phone went dead.

Now the marble corridor lay utterly deserted and once again it echoed to my footsteps. Through the tall Gothic windows along its length, I could detect the greyness of early dawn beginning to cast some light into the void and on to the heads of those long-dead physicians who appeared to be observing my every step. On the ward, the nurses had already moved Mr Krakowski into a side-room and as soon as I entered I could detect the overpowering, instantly recognisable, sickly smell of melaena, the unpleasant and unmistakable odour resulting from the combination of stale blood and faeces. I didn't need to look under the covers to know that there would be a pool of thick black tarry liquid originating from a haemorrhage somewhere in Mr Krakowski's upper bowel.

'Hi, Mr Krakowski.' There was no response. I sat on the side of his bed and said more loudly, 'Hello, Mr Krakowski. How are you feeling?' His eyes opened and focused on me as he lifted his head an inch or so off the pillow.

'Not so good. No, not good.' His head fell back. I took blood for cross-matching, put up a drip, ran in a plasma expander, started an anti-ulcer infusion and then went in search of a phone to contact the surgical team.

'Paraquat! What d'you mean he's drunk Paraquat?' It was now six o'clock on Saturday morning, and I was still on the ward waiting to start Mr Krakowski's blood transfusion. His condition had stabilised somewhat and his blood pressure had improved but he continued to pass black, tarry motions.

'That's what he says.' The A&E doctor sounded as surprised as I was.

'Bloody hell! How is he?'

'Absolutely fine. He only came in because after he'd drunk it he decided to read the label on the bottle.'

'God almighty! What an idiot. He's *dead*!'

'I know, but no one's told *him* yet. Anyway he needs admission. I've ordered up some Fuller's earth. I phoned the poisons unit at Guy's and they say there's nothing else to be done.' 'By the way,' The SHO continued, 'I've asked the police to see if they can retrieve the bottle.'

Once again I walked the length of the corridor back to A&E. There, I opened the door to the interview room to find a fresh-faced youth sitting quietly at the table. I said, 'Hello,' and sat down on the chair opposite him. He was subdued but quite relaxed, his T-shirt and jeans clean and neatly pressed, his hair short and combed.

'Tell me what you drank, would you?'

'Weed-killer.'

'Why did you do that?'

'It was a dare. We was 'aving a drink in the garden shed when one of me mates dared me to drink it. So I did.'

'When was that?'

'Last night, 'bout ten.'

'How much was there in the bottle?'

'About half-full, I think. Not really sure.'

'Okay. How old are you?'

'Fifteen.'

'And where are your parents.'

'I live with me Dad and he's away for the weekend.'

'Where's your Mum?

'Dunno, 'aven't seen her in years.'

My gaze dropped to the floor. If he had drunk Paraquat he was now doomed to a slow death over the next few weeks from liver failure. Fuller's earth, an unpleasant soil-like substance, was unlikely to absorb much, as the poison had been imbibed many hours earlier, but when it arrived the teenager willingly drank the foul mixture.

There was a knock on the door and a policeman entered. 'Hello, Doc. Thought you might like to see this. It was where he said it would be – in the garden shed.'

'Thanks, officer.' I said and looked at the empty weed-killer bottle. It was about six inches tall, a pale shade of green with rather elegant vertical ridges on its sides and a thin narrow neck into which a dirty cork had been inserted. Although dusty and covered in cobwebs the warning skull and crossbones sign was clearly visible on the label as were the words: BEWARE – CONTAINS PARAQUAT.

Does just what is says on the bottle: kills weeds – and people, I thought.

Surgical houseman or registrar on-call, please.' This was the third time I had attempted to contact them. The man on the switchboard said that they were still in theatre but that he would try bleeping them again. This time there was a reply. Good, I thought. 'Hello, are you one of the on-call surgical team?'

A female voice answered. 'No, this is one of the theatre nurses. All the surgeons are busy operating.'

'Could you give them a message for me please? I'm the medical house officer and I have a gastro-intestinal bleeder on the male medical ward. I really would appreciate a surgical review as soon as possible.'

'Okay. I'll tell them.' The phone went dead.

Was it worth trying to get some sleep now, I wondered? Sometimes it was better to stay awake, since an hour or so in bed could just make you feel more tired.

I decided to stay up – which was a wise decision as the second overdose of the night came in a few minutes later.

The marble corridor was now bathed in bright summer daylight and fresh-faced nurses in shiny black shoes scampered eagerly to their wards for the early shift. Capped and be-caped, they chattered of parties, pubs, boyfriends and liaisons.

This overdose was normal fare. Lying on her side, on an examination couch with the cot sides up, was a blonde teenage girl. Her clothing was dishevelled and her black tights were torn, exposing plump expanses of pale skin. Her hair was spattered with vomit and a pool of it lay on the couch near her mouth. Streaks of black make-up smeared her face and there was the predictable smell of stale alcohol and cigarettes. Sitting next to her was a sheepish-looking teenage boy, a gold chain visible around his neck above his once white T-shirt, now stained with make-up, beer and vomit.

A staff nurse entered the cubicle. 'Not a pretty sight,' she said. I turned and raised my eyebrows.

'Not quite sure what she's taken but it seems to include aspirin, some of her mum's Valium, probably a laxative or two and a whole week's supply of contraceptive pills just for good measure!'

'Okay, could you wash her out please and I'll arrange admission. We'll need to monitor her as we don't know how much Valium she's had.'

'Morning, Doctor. Just in time. I'm afraid you're too late for a cooked breakfast, but I could make you some

54

toast if you'd like.' The canteen lady looked me up and down, 'You don't look so good, Doctor. Up all night, were we, Doctor?'

'Yeah. That's right. Toast and a coffee would be great, thank you very much.' I had managed to get to the mess just before it closed.

'That's fine. You grab a seat and I'll bring it over, Doctor.'

I sat at a table and lit a cigarette. Only four left. Then I remembered that I had a spare pack in my room. The toast and coffee came. I glanced up at the clock on the wall in front of me: nine-thirty. I would have liked to have a bath and a change of clothes but Liston would want to do his ward round in a few minutes. So, after finishing my toast, I went back to my room with a view to having a quick wash – a cat's lick as my mother used to say – and to brushing my teeth, following which I felt slightly more human.

I walked to the men's ward where Liston was already waiting, sitting in Sister's office and casually flicking through some blood results from the previous day. 'Busy night I hear. Get any sleep?'

'No. None at all.' I told him about Paraquat boy.

'Wow! What an idiot! He's dead. Has anyone told him?'

'Not as such. But I think the seriousness of the situation is beginning to sink in.'

'Well, let's sort things out and then hopefully you can get off for a few hours' rest.'

'Thanks, that would be good.' The combination of coffee, toast, tobacco and toothpaste had made me feel

55

considerably better and I was reasonably alert as we started our ward round.

By one o'clock we had seen all the emergency admissions and any other patients that needed reviewing, so I thought I'd attempt to get some rest. I unlocked my room, threw off my white coat, set my alarm for five o'clock and lay on the bed.

'Beep – beep.' I woke with a start and looked at the clock. It was not quite one-fifteen. Then the bedside phone rang.

'Yes?'

'Doctor Howard,' she sang. 'Hello. Switchboard here. Can you go to CCU? Immediately please.' The cheery voice was back on duty.

From the nurses' station on CCU I could observe Mr Patel in the corner of the ward. I picked up the phone.

'David. Sorry to trouble you but I've just been called to see Mr Patel again. I'm not happy with him. His blood pressure's dropped and he's only produced ten millilitres of urine over the last hour. Is there anything else we can do?'

'I'll come along and see him. You wait there.'

'Doctor Howard, the Patels would like to see you.' Sister's eyes strayed heavenwards as she said this.

'I've got nothing more to say. You know that.' I said, exasperated.

'You know that. I know that, and I've told *them* that, but they want to hear it from a doctor.' She smiled. 'They're in the relatives' room.'

As I opened the door, all eyes converged on me expectantly. The brother jumped to his feet. 'How is he doing, doctor? We are very worried, you see.' He looked tired and worn and Mrs Patel junior now sat rigid and still, her gaze fixed on the floor.

'I'm afraid things don't look too good. He's not responded very well to treatment and his blood pressure's still low.'

The brother hesitated, then asked, 'Will he die, doctor? Please tell us. We need to know. You see our father died of a heart attack, so we are very worried.'

'Look, I really can't say. But he might. This is a critical period. If he doesn't improve in the next twelve hours or so I think the outlook is poor and he might well die.'

'Thank you, doctor. I appreciate your honesty. I need to tell the family now, you know.' He tilted his head and smiled as he shook my hand. I registered the smell of fresh aftershave and the feel of gold rings.

I left the room to find Liston sitting at the nurses' desk, replacing the phone in its cradle. 'Hello, Grahame. Just spoken to the boss. He agrees that we're running out of options but he thought it would be worth trying one of those new drugs, an inotrope. I'll prescribe it, as the dosing's a bit tricky. I'll see you back on the ward as we'll need to check out Paraquat boy.'

It was getting near visiting time on male medical, a period when it was best to avoid being on the ward if at all possible. Jenny was back on duty. 'Bad night, I hear.' She looked me at me intently then frowned. 'Why! You *do* look a wreck.'

'Thanks, Sister.'

'Well, quite a nice wreck,' she smiled. Fleetingly, her professional mask had dropped, but immediately the guard went back up. 'I see Mr Krakowski had a bleed. What's the plan?'

'Has he stabilised?' I answered her question with one of my own.

'Yes. He's quite stable now. Blood pressure satisfactory and no more melaena.'

'That's a relief. I don't suppose the surgeons have been to see him?'

'No. No sign. What's keeping them?'

'No idea, but they probably wouldn't operate if he's stable anyway. I'll try and get in touch with them again.'

Liston arrived and we wandered down the ward to Paraquat boy's bedside where he sat down.

'Did you *definitely* drink the weed-killer? It's very important that we know.' Liston was at his most sincere.

'Yeah. I was a bit pissed. You know.' He was now a frightened child trying to control himself and behave like a grown-up. A little boy who had hurt himself doing something that he knew was naughty – trying to be brave and not to cry.

'Have you any idea what that means?'

'Yeah. It's serious, innit?'

'Yes. It could prove fatal.' We need to speak to your father. The police are waiting for him to return but apparently there's been no sign of him yet.'

'Could be away for days. You never know with Dad.'

'Well, that's all we can do for now. The good news is that the blood tests we took this morning are normal, but we'll need to check them on a daily basis.' Liston smiled and rose to leave. 'D'you have any questions?'

'Yeah. Can I go home? Not much point in staying 'ere, is there?' I smiled to myself, as there could be no doubting the boy's logic. Liston, however, took a firm stance.

'No. We need to monitor your blood tests and keep you here – for the time being at any rate.'

We left the bedside. 'Amazing!' Liston muttered to himself as we walked away, and then continued more brightly, 'How's your heart failure man?'

'Doing rather well,' I responded. 'Probably could go home on Monday.'

'Good. Well done. And the bleeder?'

'Stable at the moment.'

'Have the surgeons been to see him?'

'No. I don't know how many times I've called them but they're always busy in theatre.'

'Keep trying, Grahame. You deserve a break. I'll touch base about nine o'clock to see what's going on.' I headed for the sanctuary of Sister's office as Liston walked off the ward, his white coat dangling loosely from his shoulder blades.

'Doctor Howard. Sit down. I'll get you a cup of tea.' Jenny had issued an instruction, not an invitation. Anyway, it was now four o'clock – visiting time – and I was trapped on the ward. If I left the safety of her office I would have to run the gauntlet of the visiting public. Whenever friends or relatives see a white coat they always want 'a quick word.' I had learned on my first day as a houseman some seven months earlier that there was no such thing as, 'a quick word.'

'Thanks, Sister. That would be nice.' I settled into a wooden armchair that was almost, but not quite, comfortable.

'Where's the second on call? Couldn't he give you a break? You could certainly do with one.' Jenny's face registered genuine concern as she handed me a mug of weak tea. I was about to explain to her the intricacies attendant upon the division of labour while on call when there was a timid knock on the office door. This was open just a crack but sadly that was just wide enough for Miss Stewart to have spotted me. 'Oh. There you are, doctor. Not trying to hide from me, are you?' she said with a rather cheeky smile. 'I wonder if I could have a quick word?' I looked at Jenny whose eyes narrowed to convey her sympathy, and quietly sighed.

'Of course you can. Come on in.' I was actually quite happy to see her as I was gratified with her father's progress and had grown rather fond of this middle-aged spinster.

'He seems much better, Doctor. I'm so pleased.'

'Yes, he's doing very well indeed. If this progress continues we might be able to let him out on Monday.'

'That *is* good news. Thank you, Doctor.' She was a different woman from the one I had first met yesterday. Or had that been the day before? I was losing track of time.

'I'm off to feed Rupert.'

'Rupert?'

'Yes. Rupert. Our cat. We thought *she* was a *he* to start with, you see.' Having explained this to me as though I should have known it all along, she turned and scuttled away out of the office.

'Right, Sister. I'm off to have a bath and change.'

'Not before time, I think.' She smiled and wrinkled her nose. Then suddenly she tensed and her gaze lifted to the doorway where a staff nurse had just appeared.

'Sister, can you come? One of the visitors is having a fit.' The nurse said this quickly and authoritatively, then without waiting for a response turned and started to run back to the scene of the emergency.

Jenny pushed her chair back, and after a quick glance at me to utter, 'Don't go away, we may need you,' ran off in pursuit.

'Oh, no!' I groaned out loud. 'I don't believe this. I've got enough to do with sick patients, without their relatives collapsing all over the place.' I followed Jenny and the staff nurse to the ward entrance. There, a small group of visitors were standing or kneeling beside a young woman who was squirming and jerking on the floor. Snorts and grunts emanated from her tense blue lips. Mucus bubbled from her nose and mouth, while her unseeing protruding eyes bulged and stared.

'Could you get some diazepam for injection? *Quickly*, please,' I said to the staff nurse, who immediately ran back to the ward where the drug cupboard was housed. I knelt down next to Jenny and we held on to the woman's flailing limbs in an attempt to avoid her hurting herself or us. As we impatiently awaited the injection, Jenny tried to insert a gag, as the bubbling mucus became pink from her bitten tongue.

'Diazepam for injection. Ten milligrams.' The nurse handed me a shiny, stainless steel kidney dish in which was a syringe, its needle still in a small glass phial. She attempted to show me the label as she had been trained to do. I ignored it, took the syringe and, with Jenny straining to hold her arm still, slowly injected the sedative into a vein. Within a few seconds the seizures lessened and she settled into a light slumber.

All but one of the visitors had now drifted away. I looked up and saw a familiar face. I couldn't place it at first but then realised this was the man who had arrested and died the day before – or had it been the day before that? The man with the military demeanour who had been so fit looking, that is until his heart had suddenly stopped beating. How on earth could he be here on the ward? He was dead. Liston had pronounced him so. This couldn't possibly be him, yet there was the same iron-grey hair, military bearing and moustache. Hold on; the dead man didn't have a moustache – did he?

The moustachioed ghost looked at me. 'Thanks, Doc. This is my daughter. She's an epileptic. She's usually well-controlled but I suspect the events of the last few days have upset her. Her Mum's in another ward having treatment and then her uncle, my twin brother, died unexpectedly yesterday, here in casualty.' His daughter was now sleeping quietly. The ghost tenderly wiped a smudge of blood from the corner of her mouth with his handkerchief, then grasped her hand and his eyes moistened. 'Right as rain he was. Not long retired from the army. Reached the rank of Major. Bit of chest pain and then died of a heart attack. Just like that.' He clicked his fingers to illustrate the suddenness of it all. 'Worked on him for over an hour they did, but couldn't save him. Terrible shock to us all, I can tell you.' He looked down at his daughter. 'Look, she's coming round now. She'll be fine. If we can just sit somewhere quietly for a while then I'll take her home. Lucky you were here, Doc.'

I felt better after a bath, a shave and a change of clothes, during which time my bleep had gone off a couple of times. There was no phone in the communal bathroom, so once back in my room I dialled zero. Mrs Cheery Voice was still on the switchboard. 'We *are* keeping you busy this weekend, Doctor Howard, aren't we?' she sang.

'You certainly are,' I agreed, 'What d'you want now?'

'Admissions are looking for you. They've been trying to get hold of you for some time.'

It was now five o'clock on a summery Saturday afternoon, the time when young men and women were anticipating the thrills of the weekend. The corridor was busy once again, its marble ears eavesdropping on the excited, chattering, gossiping nurses going off duty. How many secrets had unwittingly been shared with these ancients over the years, I wondered. Saturday night: an evening for fun and frolics, pubs, parties, silliness and sex. I recognised the staff nurse who had helped me manage the epileptic. She smiled at me. 'Got

any plans for tonight, Doctor? Doing anything exciting?'
I grimaced, 'On call, I'm afraid.'

'But you were on last night, weren't you?' She
looked at me, puzzled.

'Yes. And I'll be on tomorrow night; and on
Monday.'

'Oh!' she said, and then the puzzled look on her face
gave way to a bright smile, 'Well, have a nice night
anyway,' and she turned and ran to catch up with her
chattering friends.

There were two more emergencies in admissions
waiting to be seen and treated. Another overdose, and a
chronic bronchitic whose breathing had worsened over
the course of the last day or so, and whose face and
extremities had gradually become a deeper, more vivid
shade of blue. Not difficult patients to manage but still
time-consuming. Histories had to be taken, examinations
performed, notes written, blood tests done, lab
technicians phoned and X-rays ordered; beds then had to
be found and relatives seen.

Later that evening I ran through my list of
admissions with Liston. It was after eleven before we
had completed our review of those and other sick
patients. My to-do list now ran to two pages with
disappointingly few items crossed off. I retraced my
steps around the wards, completing all the tasks all that
needed to be done that night. It was now one in the
morning and I realised that, apart from some toast, I
hadn't eaten since nine a.m. on Friday.

The corridor was quiet again as I walked to the
canteen. There would be no hot food but there was a

vending machine which stocked sandwiches, with another for hot drinks. Once there, I sat down near a window and stared into the impenetrable blackness of the night. As I ate my sandwich and drank my coffee, I wished I was anywhere but where I was. I began to wonder if I could cope with what the rest of the weekend had to throw at me. This was about stamina, not medicine. Those who could stay awake longest would survive. I didn't really want to do this job. My training had not prepared me for this test of endurance. I wanted another job, another vocation, but what could I do? Five years at medical school leaves one fit for little else than being a doctor. I was stuck here with no way out. It's true that after my house jobs I could move out of patient-based medicine and become a pathologist, for example, where I could look at tiny bits of living patients, or all of them once they'd died. At that time of night, in the middle of a long on-call weekend, I wanted nothing more to do with this hospital, this profession or these people. If I had been a soldier I would have considered deserting. But I couldn't, could I? I *had* to see it through. Essentially, if *I* wasn't there, no one else would look after this interminable stream of crumbling humanity. But then again, I thought, no one is indispensable and the graveyards of the world are full of people who had thought they were. But if I left the canteen and walked out there and then – as I yearned to – there could be no doubt that the sick and the lame would suffer as a result. It was a rather like cross-country running: you were desperate to stop and rest, but you just kept on going, because that was what you did, that was what you'd been taught to do, so you did it. My thoughts wandered this way and that, looking for an escape from this imprisonment that was *being* a junior doctor – until my bleep awoke me from my reverie. The lab technician read out some results. I thanked him and looked at my watch. It was two in the morning. I scanned my list, and decided to go to bed.

The ringing of my bedside phone dragged me back from a deep sleep.

'Doctor Howard?'

'Yes.'

'It's staff nurse on male medical here. Mr Krakowski has deteriorated. Could you come and see him immediately, please?' I glanced at my wristwatch. Two thirty. A measly half-hour's sleep. I was desperate to put my head back on the pillow and my eyelids started to droop. I smacked my face with my hand and forced myself to sit on the edge of the bed. Dressed again, I once more ran the gauntlet of my distinguished predecessors as I made my along the deserted corridor. The ward was in darkness but the side-room to the left of the entrance was brightly lit and two nurses were busy changing the sheets, rolling the patient this way and that as they did so. The nauseating stench of melaena was immediately apparent and sheets, stained black, were lying on the floor.

I ordered more blood to be cross-matched and speeded up my patient's intravenous fluids. As I was leaving the room I heard a gurgling sound coming from the newly-made bed and when I peered beneath the fresh sheets I saw the lava-like flow of black, tarry blood-stained faecal fluid ooze from between Mr Krakowski's buttocks.

'Switchboard, could you bleep the surgical registrar on call for me, please.' I held the line and was pleased to hear a ringing tone and eventually a voice answered. It was the theatre nurse again. 'Could I speak to the surgical registrar please? … Yes I *do* need to speak to him now … Why? Because I need a surgical opinion on a bleeder on male medical … No. I don't think it can wait … How long do you think? … Look, I've been waiting for a surgical opinion since yesterday. This man is seriously ill and in my opinion needs a laparotomy … No. Monday's list is too late. He needs an emergency laparotomy, *now* … Sure, I *realise* they're busy … Yes, please. Put the houseman on … Hi. Thanks for coming to the phone.' I told him the story. He asked me several questions. 'Yes. I've done all of that and he's still actively bleeding. Is there anything else I can do? … I've done all of that … Blood pressure's low but stable … Okay, thanks. Soon as you can, please.' I slammed the phone down with frustration.

'Staff Nurse, have Mr Krakowski's relatives been contacted?'

'Yes. There's just a younger brother, and night sister has asked him to come in.'

'Good. I need to speak to him as soon as he arrives. Can you run those two units through as quickly as possible, please?'

For a while my bleeder stabilised. Although his pulse was fast, his blood pressure was maintained and for nearly an hour he passed no further melaena. I informed his brother of the seriousness of the situation and explained that unless the bleeding stopped he might well die, that an operation was being considered and that I was awaiting a surgical opinion. There was no point in me trying to get any sleep now. Mr Krakowski required constant attention and hopefully the surgeons might arrive soon. I lit a cigarette while one of the night nurses made me a coffee.

Just forty-five minutes later Mr Krakowski started to exsanguinate. A fit patient can compensate for the loss of a vast amount of blood until suddenly their heart fails. As his blood pressure dropped, a flood of liquid, now fresh dark-red blood, identical to that in the bag hanging by his bedside, poured out of his rectum. I used a pressure device to transfuse him more rapidly but it was proving impossible to infuse blood into Mr Krakowski as quickly as it was leaching out. Effectively, he was exsanguinating into his bed.

The door of the side-room opened and in came a tired-looking surgeon, dressed in theatre greens, over which he had thrown a grubby white coat. 'Sorry to take so long but we've been operating non-stop since Saturday morning.' He glanced at the bed, and its occupant, now white and unconscious. 'Is this your bleeder?' he asked, turning to me.

'Yes.' I knew that one look was enough and that he needed to do nothing more to make a decision, but he went through the routine of examining the charts and then palpating Mr Krakowski's abdomen. As he stood up he nodded to me to leave the room with him. 'I'm sorry, but he's not fit for surgery. He's not fit enough for a haircut, let alone a laparotomy. I really don't think there's anything more you can do. If I were you, I'd stop transfusing him and give him a shot of morphine. He's had a truly massive bleed and I doubt if an operation would have helped. Do you want me to speak to any relatives?'

'Thanks. That's kind of you, but now I've spoken to you I can deal with that. Thanks for coming over. Sounds like you're having as bad a weekend as I am?'

'I've two more awaiting surgery. An acute appendix and a large bowel obstruction. Sorry not to have been more help.' He grimaced and turned to walk away. His green theatre trousers, visible below the white coat, stopped well above his ankles, below which he wore incongruous black brogues on his otherwise bare feet.

I ushered Mr Krakowski's brother into the relatives' room. 'As you know, your brother's very ill. His only hope was an operation but the surgeon says that he's not fit for an anaesthetic. I'm afraid all we can do now is keep him comfortable.'

'He should have operation yesterday?' It was a rhetorical question. He was resigned to his brother's inevitable demise and was not taking issue with his management, but felt he had to ask. He needed to know for himself and on behalf of his dying brother.

I thought for a moment. 'It's impossible to say. Possibly yes,' I said, 'and, looking back, that might have helped, but he did appear to be stable for a while on the drugs we had started.'

'So, Doctor. Do you think earlier operation would have saved him?' In my heart of hearts I thought it might have done, but would knowing that help this man to cope with his brother's death? And in all fairness, the results of surgery for acute bleeders was not good. Few survived. This man needed clarity and closure, not confusion and uncertainty.

I looked him straight in the eye. 'In all honesty, your brother had such a massive haemorrhage that I doubt if anything would have made any difference to the outcome. If he had been taken to theatre he might well have died on the operating table.' I said this calmly and convincingly.

'I think you are right, Doctor. Well, I will go and see him now and pray for miracle.'

There was to be no miracle and at six-thirty on that Sunday morning I took his notes into sister's office and wrote, *Certified dead. RIP. Cause of death, acute gastrointestinal haemorrhage*, and then signed it, *Doctor GCW Howard*.

Suddenly I became aware of chatting in the room. I looked up from the case notes. The early shift had arrived, talking of frocks and frolics, parties and pubs, boyfriends and sex.

'Oh! Hello, Doctor Howard.' A young student nurse was looking at me excitedly. 'Did you have a good time, last night?' She smiled at me and her bright, enquiring face seemed genuinely interested. I was about to say, 'Bloody awful,' then thought it churlish to dampen her exuberance and after an initial frown I smiled back at her. 'Fine, thank you,' I said. 'And you?'

'Really good – actually.' She blushed slightly, looked at the floor for a moment and then blurted out, 'You'll never guess – *I got a proposal.*' Her eyes were bright and excited and she lifted her left hand, the fingers extended, to demonstrate the diamond ring that was the proof. Then, filled with excitement, she turned to her friends to recount in the minutest detail the elation of the previous night. All that day an excited buzz of talk concerning engagement rings and wedding bells resounded up and down the ward.

I took blood from those patients who required tests, including Paraquat boy, delivered the little bottles to the labs, and then reached the canteen just as it was opening. With bacon, eggs and fried bread on my plate, I ordered four cups of tea.

'Wot? Four cups of tea, did you say?' The canteen assistant looked at me askance, her eyebrows raised as though she must have misheard.

'Yes. Four cups of tea, please.'

'Expecting guests, are we?' she joked, while she slopped tea from a large pot into the cups. I couldn't think of a witty reply.

'No. they're all for me. I'm very thirsty,' I said lamely.

'Jenny. Any chance of doing a ward round? I feel I've lost touch with what's going on.'

'Good idea. Looks as though you've had another busy night. Shame about poor Mr Krakowski.' She turned her tidy face, framed by her neatly-pressed white cap and collar, to look at me. 'Sister,' I said, 'it was grim. Fifteen units I gave him in the end, but he just bled out. By the time the surgeons came he was just about dead.'

'D'you think an operation would have helped?'

'To be honest, I really don't know. Maybe not. We had no idea where he was bleeding from but I do think he should have had a laparotomy while he was fit enough.'

'You did everything you could.'

'Yes, I guess so, but it wasn't enough.'

We wandered down the ward and stopped alongside a bed on the right. 'Now, Mr Stewart. How are you feeling this morning?'

'Fine, Doc. Fighting fit. I have only *one* question for you,' he paused for emphasis. 'Can I go 'ome?' The elderly man, too breathless to say a word on Friday, was transformed. Freshly shaved and smelling of carbolic soap, with his thinning white hair now combed tidily back along the side of his head, he was sitting beside his bed reading *The News of the World.*

His chest was now clear, his pulse regular and a repeat X-ray had improved, although his heart was still much larger than it should have been.

'Well, I'll ask Doctor Liston later but I think we'll need to keep you till tomorrow, just to make sure you've got all your tablets.'

'That's fine by me, Doc. By the way, has that daughter of mine been pestering you?'

'She's been very concerned about you.' I answered non-committedly.

'Oh! So she *has* then?'

'No, not at all.'

'Should've got married rather than turn into an old spinster getting under my feet all the time. Had her chances too, but she still hung on to that damn fool who got himself killed in '44. Has she told you about that?'

'Well, she did say that her fiancé was killed during the D-Day landings.'

'Wish 'e 'ad been. Copped off with a French tart and deserted. That's what really 'appened. Shot for desertion. What a disgrace. She don't know that I know, mind, so I just take her version of events: that 'e died an 'ero.' He gave me a knowing glance and touched his nose. 'That's between you and me, Doc, mind. I think Violet uses that story as an excuse not to get involved and avoid getting 'urt again.'

Violet – shrinking Violet, so that was her name. How fitting, I thought. I smiled as he lifted his newspaper while Jenny and I headed along the ward towards Paraquat boy.

'What's going to happen, Doc?' he asked, putting his car magazine down.

'How do you mean, "what's going to happen?" '

'To me? After drinking that weed-killer an' all.' His juvenile, fresh-faced demeanour was genuinely enquiring. There was no point in lying to him but the police had still not traced his father or mother.

'I'd rather talk to you with your Dad present, but we've not managed to contact him.'

'He could be away for ages. Sometimes his binges last a week or more.'

That might be too late, I thought, and this boy needed to know the score. I hesitated briefly. 'Firstly, the blood tests I took this morning were normal. So there's no sign of any liver damage yet. The problem is that the Paraquat in the weed-killer that you drank causes damage to the liver which can take days or even weeks to develop, so it's a question of waiting and seeing.'

'That other doctor, the skinny one who was with you yesterday, said it could be fatal. Does that mean it could kill me?'

'Yes. That's true.'

'How many people survive then, Doc?'

If I hadn't been without sleep for forty-eight hours I might have phrased my response more delicately. 'None,' I replied.

'Just a question of waitin' and seein' then, Doc. Right?' I was thankful that he seemed not to have fully grasped the significance of what I had just said.

'Exactly so.' As I moved away he picked up his magazine and resumed reading.

The other admissions were progressing satisfactorily. Both the overdoses were grumpy and wanted to go home but the policy was to have then seen by a psychiatrist (or nerve doctor as Liston called them) prior to discharge. That would be Monday at the earliest. Jenny and I left the ward and headed for her office, 'Thanks, Sister,' I said. 'No doubt I'll be back later.'

'You need to get some rest.'

'I'd like to, believe me. The problem now is that it's probably best just to keep going. If I fall asleep you'll probably never wake me!'

On my way back to CCU I was paged to see two more admissions in A&E. and it was three in the afternoon before I finally managed to review Mr Patel. When I swung through the doors my heart sank to see the family once again gathered around his bed. As I approached they looked up expectantly, with doleful eyes, questioning yet ever hopeful. The brother rose to his feet. 'Good afternoon, Doctor. We have been awaiting you for an update, you know.' There was no way round it. I would have to speak to them again. I didn't mind talking to them – that came with the territory – but it would be the same unanswerable questions all over again.

'Fine. Would you mind waiting in the relatives' room, please, while I have a look at Mr Patel.' I smiled weakly. 'I'll be with you in a minute.'

There was now a male charge nurse on duty. 'He's doing a bit better, Doc,' he said. Sure enough, I was pleasantly surprised to see Mr Patel sitting up, conscious and alert – and I even thought I could detect a slight smile from behind his oxygen mask. We looked at the charts. His blood pressure was up, his urine output had increased and some of his blood tests had begun to improve. 'Well,' I said, as much to the Charge Nurse as to the patient, 'You're doing much better now. Good progress. Well done.' His head moved from side to side in a gesture of acknowledgement and thanks.

'How is he, Doctor? He seems better. Is that true?' The brother was as well-dressed and as courteous as ever.

'Yes. I must say I'm delighted to see how much he has improved.' I tried not to sound too surprised.

'But will he be all right, Doctor?'

'Well, I still can't guarantee that he'll recover. This is still a critical period. But there's no doubt he's made significant progress and hopefully that will continue.'

'Thank you, Doctor. I will now tell the family. Thank you.' He put his hands together, fingers extended in a gesture of prayer, and smiled at me. I had just reached my room when my pager went off again. It was Jenny.

'Grahame. Sorry to trouble you. I don't know how to say this, but I need you to see one of the visitors. It's a man who's just collapsed and has chest pain.'

'*What*! Not another? We've got enough problems with our own patients without the visitors needing treatment. It's you, Sister. It must be you, what with that girl fitting last night and now this!'

'I know, I know. I'm sorry. I'll get an ECG arranged. See you shortly.'

I headed back to the main corridor. My feet hurt and my toes felt sticky in my socks. I knew that if I took my shoes off there would be an unpleasant odour. How many times had I walked this corridor so far during the course of the weekend? Twenty: thirty or forty? Maybe a hundred times, I had no idea. My mind was now drifting and unfocussed; suddenly I found myself back at the ward without realising where I was. I was now functioning like an automaton, both mind and limbs functioning at a reflex level. If the instruction was, 'Come to the ward,' I would somehow find myself there.

If it was, 'Treat this patient,' it would be done without thought or rationality. I was startled back to reality by Jenny. 'God, Grahame! You look all-in.' I didn't have the energy to respond. 'Where's our visitor, Sister?'

'I put him in a side room in case you need to admit him.' Jenny offered me the cardiogram. 'Here, take a look at this.'

I went into the room, not registering anything about the visitor except that it was a male.

'Hello, sir. How're you feeling now?' I said this as I looked at the cardiogram which showed the changes of acute angina.

'Much better now, thanks, since I put a tablet under my tongue.'

'Do you often have attacks of angina?'

'Every now and again. This was just a bit more uncomfortable than usual.'

'Your ECG shows angina, nothing more. I think we should just keep an eye on you for an hour or two and hopefully get you home later. I will need to check some blood tests though, just to make sure you haven't had a small heart attack.'

Back in her office I smiled at Jenny. 'Sister, for God's sake, we're going to have to ask visitors to have a medical check before they're allowed on the ward!' She smiled back and remarked, 'Quite a weekend!'

The afternoon shift were readying themselves to go off duty. 'Bye-bye, Doctor Howard. What are you doing tonight? Anything exciting?' asked the newly-betrothed student. I couldn't be bothered to explain that I was just starting my third consecutive night on call and so far had

had about half an hour's sleep in total. 'No, nothing in particular,' I replied, attempting a smile. Then she and the others straggled untidily off the ward in the direction of the corridor, talking of early nights, engagement rings and days off.

Jenny was last to leave. 'I'm going off now. I hope you manage to get some sleep tonight.' She gave me another bright smile, shouldered her bag and strode off her ward.

I took a seat and glanced at my to-do list. Shit! I thought. The orthopaedic patient. I haven't seen him since ... well, I can't remember. I walked to the surgical wing and to the ward where plaster of Paris limbs were strung up from a Meccano-like scaffold. It was growing dark and the night staff were doing the evening drug round as I arrived. I recognised the third-year student who turned and gave me a welcoming nod as I approached.

'How's our man? Sorry I haven't been able to get back earlier.'

'Oh, he's fine. Much better, thank you. The surgical team came to review him during the day. His drip's now down and he's drinking well.'

A sense of relief flowed over me. 'Good. I'll leave you in peace then.'

'Thanks for your help the other night. Much appreciated.' The nurse's smile was broad and genuine.

'A pleasure,' I said, and meant it. That smile was thanks enough. Leaving the ward, I headed down the corridor, now once again dark and deserted. Suddenly I stopped: disorientated, unsure of where I was. The corridor was unfamiliar and I couldn't remember where I was supposed to be going. There was something different about my surroundings: the marble busts had all disappeared, as had the windows and the columns. I felt dizzy and sat down on a long thin bench, reminiscent of a church pew, which was at the side of the corridor. I wracked my brain and came to the conclusion that I must have fallen asleep. I wondered if it was possible to do so while walking. I stared at the floor, and felt physically sick and disorientated.

The arrest call came just in time, as the adrenaline rush instantly brought me back to reality.

'BEEP – BEEP. Cardiac arrest, male medical. Cardiac arrest, male medical.' I looked around and realised that I was actually in the underground passageway below the main hospital corridor: that was why it had seemed so unfamiliar. I must have descended one too many flights of stairs on the way out of the surgical wing. I ran to the stairwell, up one flight and then along to male medical. Slamming open the doors I could see Liston just ahead of me running to a bed half way down the right hand side of the ward. Beside the bed, on which lay a discarded copy of *The News of The World*, lay Mr Stewart, a nurse bending over him and rhythmically pressing his chest, while an anaesthetist was lifting his chin and attempting to intubate him.

'What's happened? He was fine earlier on,' I asked the nurse as I took over the cardiac massage from her.

'He was fine all day then called out for a bedpan, attempted to get out of bed, and suddenly collapsed on the floor.'

As she said this, night sister ran on to the ward just ahead of a porter pushing the arrest trolley. Then, all the paraphernalia – the wires and tubes, the bits and pieces – were attached and connected.

Liston once again took up the baton and started to conduct. 'He really is very good at this,' I thought as he calmly assessed the situation and, looking at the green line on the screen, pronounced, 'Looks like a massive pulmonary embolus. It fits with the history as well.'

Poor Mr Stewart, I thought. So lively this morning. How will Violet cope with this sudden change of circumstance? Now his head nodded and bobbed with each chest compression, but the eyes were lifeless and unseeing, the pupils widely dilated.

Thirty-five minutes later it was clear his heart would never start pumping again and Liston called a halt.

'Time of death – let's say, ten p.m. Thank you, everyone. Grahame, d'you mind seeing the relatives? I've still got some outlying patients to assess.'

'That's fine, David. I know his daughter, Violet, quite well.' Night sister had already telephoned her and told of the sudden deterioration in her father's condition. She was sitting, neatly waiting in the relatives' room and silently staring at her shoes. I thought she was wearing the same clothes as when I'd first met her in A&E, but that now seemed a million years ago. She looked directly at me. 'Has he died, doctor?' This forthright question made it easier for me; there was now no need for any preliminaries to try to soften the blow.

'Yes, I'm afraid he has.' Both her hands grasped her bag and, sure enough, in the palm of one of them was her dainty lace handkerchief yet, to my surprise she remained calm. I continued quietly. 'He was well during the day, as you know, but suddenly deteriorated this evening. It's likely that that he had a blood clot which affected his lungs. We did everything we could.'

'I know you did, Doctor. To be honest, I thought he was going to die the day I found him like that at home. But he did so well, I began to think that maybe, just maybe, he would recover – but that was not to be.' She looked up at me. 'What has to be done now, Doctor,' she said in a surprisingly business-like fashion.

'I suggest you go home now and perhaps you could come back tomorrow afternoon, about three o'clock, to pick up his belongings and the death certificate,' I said and stood in preparation to leave.

'Thank you, Doctor. At least he had those two extra days when he was well, and died suddenly, as he would have wanted. A bit like my fiancé.' I remembered Mr Stewart's revelation earlier that day. Violet continued, 'Two good men gone. Of course my George died in his prime.' She paused for a moment, smiled slightly and then suddenly appeared to make a decision. She looked straight towards me. 'It's funny really, you don't need to know this, Doctor, but I'll tell you anyway. My father always thought that George died during the D-Day landings. The truth is that he got involved with a French girl and was executed. I let Dad think he'd died on the beaches because I know he would have been mortified if he'd discovered the truth. To be honest, George was quite a philanderer even before he went off to war. The story's been helpful to me, as I've used it over the years to avoid the attention of men. You see after mum died in the blitz, although he would never dream of admitting it, Dad has always relied on me to look after him.'

Well, I never, I thought. How complex can relationships become when there are secrets and subterfuge. I wondered if Violet felt a sense of relief now that the lies and untruths were no longer necessary. Certainly she left without a tear, and I'm sure I detected a new spring in her step as she passed through the doors of the ward and into the corridor.

Back in sister's office I set about writing up the deceased man's notes. I was appalled to find that I hadn't written an annotation since his admission. I summarised his progress up to and including his sudden collapse and was signing the final entry when my pager once again erupted. I lifted the phone. It was Liston. 'Grahame. The king is dead!'

'Hey?'

'The *king*. He died this afternoon. I've just heard it on the television.'

'Sorry David, I must be overtired. I've no idea what you're talking about.'

'The king! *Elvis* has died.'

'What. Oh no! How? Why?'

'Probably drugs I should think. Anyway, I didn't bleep you just to tell you *that*. I've admitted a couple of patients who you need to sort out, please.'

It was one in the morning before I reached my room. I took off my white coat and my shoes then lay on the bed. The next thing I knew I was being startled into wakefulness by the cardiac arrest pager.

'BEEP – BEEP. Cardiac arrest, male medical. Cardiac arrest, male medical.' It was cheery voice again. That's odd; I thought, she's normally on during the day. God, who is it this time? The ward was full of crumble and it could be any one of them.' My hands shook as I tied my shoelaces and grabbed my coat. The corridor was dim and quiet and my running footsteps echoed around the marble-clad walls and pillars. I glanced at my watch: two-fifteen, I'd been asleep for three-quarters of an hour. Seemingly random thoughts jostled for attention in my mind. No wonder it was quiet. It wasn't a shift change or meal break and it was too early for the cleaners to go about their endless mopping. I wonder who's arrested this time? The bronchitic? Hope it's not Paraquat boy – that would be a disaster. I threw open the doors to Jenny's ward. It was strangely calm and dark. No rattle of the arrest trolley, no shouts of instruction or sound of running feet. In the centre of the ward sat the two night nurses, heads bent, writing at their desk in a dim pool of light. They looked up at me in surprise.

'Where's the arrest?' I panted.

'What arrest?'

'Cardiac arrest, here, a call just went out.'

'Not here, Doctor. We didn't put out a call. It must be somewhere else.'

'*Shit*! Wrong ward.' I began to panic. I was wasting crucial time. I'm felt sure cheery voice had said male medical. Maybe she'd meant *female* medical. I dashed across the corridor. There, the tranquil scene was repeated. The ward was blissfully settled and quiet, the night nurses writing up their notes. 'No arrest here,

Doctor. Have you tried male medical?' the senior nurse suggested helpfully. I reached for the phone. 'Switchboard, it's Doctor Howard. Where's the cardiac arrest?' It was the man who answered, not cheery voice. 'I haven't put out a call, Doc. When was it?'

'Just five minutes ago.'

'You must be mistaken, Doc. Hasn't been an arrest call since the afternoon. Goodnight, Doc.'

I slumped into the nearly comfy chair in sister's office and took the arrest bleep from my coat pocket. I peered at it, then shook it as though somehow it must have malfunctioned. Could I have dreamt the whole episode? I was now totally confused and disorientated, but at the same time wide awake. I looked unseeingly at my to-do list and wondered what I should do next. I hadn't long to ponder as my pager went off at that moment. This time I was put through to A&E.

'Sorry to wake you, but I'm afraid we have another medical emergency. She's a sixty-year-old asthmatic, who's not very well. Probably got a superadded infection. Can you come and sort her out please?'

Indeed, she wasn't very well and it was seven in the morning before I left A&E and headed back to my room.

Finally it was Monday morning and my stint of being first on-call was nearly over, but I still had to get through the post-take day *and* I was second on call that night. In addition, Tuesday was a normal working day which I had to survive before actually going off duty. The many similarities of terminology with that of the armed forces suddenly struck me. I was a house *officer*, I took *leave*, not holidays, and I was either on or off *duty*, not at work like everyone else. This weekend had been a tour of duty, days and nights to be conquered, an offensive to be survived.

The elation of seeing the light at the end of this seemingly interminable weekend tunnel, combined with a bath, shave and a change of clothes, quite rejuvenated me and I almost had a spring in my step as I headed for the doctors' mess.

'Morning, Penny. Morning, Neil.' I sat down opposite them. 'Penny, this belongs to you, I think,' I said as I passed the arrest bleep across to her.

'Busy weekend, I gather,' she said, reluctantly accepting the pager.

'Bloody awful. Hardly been in my room since Friday,' I said as I tucked into my fried breakfast with gusto. 'By the way,' I looked up at Neil. 'I haven't forgotten that you owe me half a breakfast.'

Male medical was now buzzing with gossip. Weekend stories were being exchanged as fast as word of mouth permitted. Proposals, parties; engagements, entanglements; bleeders and seizures, vomit and Valium; arrests – real and imagined – 'the king is dead,' 'long live jailhouse rock.'

'Yes, a visitor, would you believe it, right *there* in the entrance, an epileptic apparently.'

'Then another had acute angina.'

'No, *acute angina,* idiot, not a cute vagina!'

All this and more passed the lips of the nurses on the early shift that Monday morning.

'Apparently he collapsed at home.' David and I were having coffee with Jenny in her office before our post-take ward round.

'Who? The asthmatic?'

'No, you idiot, *the king.*'

'Oh!'

'I think Doctor Howard probably has other things on his mind rather than Elvis Presley just now, Doctor Liston, such as *bed.*' I looked at Jenny and grinned broadly, 'Nice idea,' I said. She blushed, realising how her words might well be misconstrued and changed the subject, 'And what's all this about an imaginary cardiac arrest in the night? Weren't you busy enough with real work?'

'Don't!' I said. 'I know I must have imagined it but I was convinced there was a call.'

'Right! To business.' Liston put an end to our chatting. It took us an hour to see the patients on male medical and then, bidding farewell to Jenny, we repeated the process across the corridor. Liston told two young women that they needed to see the 'nerve doctors' before they could go home and thence we moved on to CCU. Had the Patel clan left the ward at all since Friday, I wondered. There they were, looking fresh and chatting excitedly with their relative.

Liston looked at the charts and then examined the patient. 'You're making good progress, I think we can transfer you to the ward.' After a pause he continued, 'Sister, could you liaise with Jenny and transfer Mr Patel when she has a bed available.'

'Yes. Thank you, Doctor Liston. We could do with freeing up some space here in CCU.' She then turned to me. 'Doctor Howard, the Patels would like to see you.' I smiled to myself and thought of Violet Stewart. Her father had also been doing well; right up to the moment he died.

It was now mid-afternoon and most of the items on my to-do list were now done. 'Beep – beep.' Cheery voice put me through to Jenny. 'Doctor Howard, You are *not* dreaming. It is I, sister on male medical,' she giggled. 'Seriously, Paraquat boy's father has just arrived. I think you should come and speak to him.'

'Good. Thanks, Sister, could you put him in the waiting room and I'll come along immediately.'

This would be a difficult interview, but there could be no backing down. I walked along the corridor. Now the sunlight flooded in and the marbled hall was cheerful, the busts relaxed and refreshed after their weekend off and the space was now filled with weekday noise and bustle. Those on the early shift were going off duty and swapping weekend stories. The faces had changed but the music was the same: boyfriends, parties and 'you'll never guess what!' The watchful busts listened and remembered but were utterly discrete and never divulged their secrets.

'What's all this about, Doctor?' Paraquat boy's father was looking somewhat dishevelled. He had on an ill-fitting suit and wore a tie loosely round the unbuttoned collar of his shirt. Broad and burly, he had tattoos on both hands and had not shaved for days.

'Have you seen your son today?' I asked.

'No. The nurse asked me to come in here to speak to you first. The police were waiting at my house. I'm scared stiff, Doc. What's this all about?'

How was I going to tell this man that his son had drunk poison for a dare, and would die slowly in the next week or two of irreversible and untreatable liver failure? I thought I should run through the events of the past few days.

'Your son came into A&E of his own accord in the early hours of Saturday.' I searched my memory. 'Yes, Saturday, and said that he had drunk some weed-killer for a dare.' I looked at the man who was visibly shaking with anxiety. 'The weed-killer contains Paraquat which as you may know is poisonous. Unfortunately I'm afraid that it's likely to prove fatal.'

'Where did he get the stuff? Tell me where?' I wasn't expecting that response. Surely it didn't matter *where* he got it from; the important thing was that he *had* got it, somehow or other.

'Apparently from the garden shed. The police brought the bottle in. There is no doubt it contained the poison.'

'What? My garden shed? A little green bottle, was it?'

'Yes.'

'Do you have it?'

'Yes. I think it's in the office.'

'I have to see it. *Please.*' I was puzzled, but retrieved the bottle, giving Jenny a quizzical look as I did so. I handed the bottle to Paraquat boy's dad. His response was not as I had predicted. His whole body appeared to relax, his shaking stopped and his face broke into a smile.

'Thank God for that!' he said as he looked down and wiped his eyes with relief. 'There was no weed-killer in there. Just water. I used it to water the seedlings. It's a kind of joke that I use a Paraquat bottle to water my plants.'

My legs felt wobbly and I took a seat. 'I think you and I need to go and speak to your son,' I said, and led the way down the ward.

As Paraquat boy left the ward, his father's arm around his shoulder, I saw the ghost figure again, the man who had died in A&E. Then I remembered that this was his twin. He was telling another visitor about how his brother, the Major, had suffered a heart attack and how the doctors had worked on him for two hours, all to no avail.

It was seven o'clock when I finally left the ward and headed for my room. I was second on-call but decided that I'd had quite enough and would do no more that day. Now the corridor was bustling once again. How many times since I had started my on-call, all those hours ago, had the wall of marble turned full cycle – from dark and sinister to sunlit and welcoming? How many times had the statues slept peacefully while I remained awake? Now, once again it was filled with chattering nurses, striding doctors, relatives – some weeping, some laughing – and patients: walking, wheeling, or just sitting between the physicians of old in the marbled coolness of the corridor.

The door to my room was unlocked. I usually locked it but wasn't surprised that I'd forgotten – and frankly I couldn't care. I took off my white coat and began to undress then realised that someone was in my bed. Lying on her side, smiling and looking up at me was Jenny. She pulled back the covers, exposing her warm nakedness. I finished undressing, climbed in beside her and immediately fell into a deep sleep.

A bell jangled. I automatically lifted the phone expecting cheery voice but all that emanated from the earpiece was a dialling tone. The ringing continued and then I realised that it was my alarm clock. It was eight in the morning, I had slept through the whole night and mercifully there had been no calls. As I struggled awake I recalled that vision of Jenny. There remained no trace of her. Could I detect just a subtle hint of her perfume? Had I dreamt it all or had she really been here, in my bed?

'Morning, Sister.'

'Good morning, Doctor Howard. Did you manage to get some sleep last night?' Jenny – as tidy and neat as ever – looked at me cryptically. Had she been in my bed? She offered me no clue. Her manner was friendly and affectionate, but there was no hint of intimacy.

'Yes, I feel much better, thank you.' Had she really been in my bed and left while I was sleeping or had it all been a hallucination. The sleep deprivation of the weekend had undoubtedly made me somewhat disorientated, and I *had* imagined a cardiac arrest. If I *had* slept with her, clearly I should acknowledge the fact; but if it was all in my imagination, a sleep-deprived delusion, then it would be embarrassing to behave as though we were now as good as lovers. She gave me no clue. Had she been there, lying in my bed?

'Jenny, I had a strange dream last night. I thought that you were in my room. I suppose it *was* a dream?'

'*Doctor* Howard, what *are* you suggesting?' Jenny looked at me with a hint of a smile but, before I could pursue the matter further, Liston arrived and the moment was gone.

We spent the morning reviewing the emergency admissions from our long weekend on take. Against all the odds, Mr Patel continued to improve and his family wanted 'a quick word.' Across the corridor, the young women who had taken overdoses had seen a 'nerve doctor', and had been discharged. Then there were those admissions, like the chronic bronchitic, who would stubbornly refuse either to get better or to die. Those were the 'crumble': patients who would block beds until they finally succumbed to their disease or else rallied sufficiently to be discharged, only to be readmitted at some later date.

As the afternoon drew to its close, I wearily climbed the steps to my room where I exchanged my soiled white coat for a tweed sports jacket, stained with the detritus of five years as a medical student. I then locked my room and strolled slowly down the marble corridor. The busts were welcoming and appeared sympathetic as they recalled their own long hours of duty, while the thoroughfare once more echoed to the clatter and squeals of cleaners, nurses and all the rest.

I heard a familiar voice. 'Ooh! Hello, Doctor Howard. Doing anything nice tonight?'

'Well yes, actually, I am,' I said, smiling, 'I'm going outside.'

'Oh, that's nice,' and she started down the corridor, displaying her diamond to the long-dead greats. I covered the remaining yards to the imposing entrance and pushed open the heavy wooden doors. Outside, I stood for a moment on the top step to light a cigarette, and then walked out into the warm, early evening sunlight.

PART 2

BEYOND THE MARBLE CORRIDOR

GRIM HARVESTING

'Are you the new SHO?' The voice was deep and gravelly.

'Yes, sir.' I nodded my confirmation. The Professor of Surgery had paused briefly as he headed in the direction of the ward.

'It's a difficult job,' he added sternly before continuing down the corridor to begin his evening ward round.

That had been my introduction to the high-octane world of transplant surgery. Now, barely two weeks later, I was about to enter the intensive care unit to take over the management of a man who had been officially declared dead. Well, to be precise, half-dead. His brain was dead, but the rest of him, more or less, was in good working order. His heart pumped, blood circulated and urine flowed; it was just that he needed a ventilator to do his breathing for him and, so far as anyone could tell, all higher cerebral function had ceased. This man had been declared brain-dead, kept alive courtesy of the bellows wheezing beside his bed.

My role was to maintain this man's blood pressure while a selection of his organs were removed for transplantation. Earlier that morning it had occurred to me that an embalmer might be better placed to perform those macabre duties or, if a doctor was required, surely an anaesthetist would be better qualified. As I timidly entered the intensive care unit, I was blissfully unaware that at least two other doctors had refused to take part in this procedure on conscientious and religious grounds. True, I had been asked at my interview whether I had any ethical qualms about organ transplantation, however since this medical rotation involved the care of just such patients, to be appointed, the answer clearly had to be 'no'.

The donor was a thirty-two year old builder who had been in a car accident five days previously and had suffered appalling head injuries. After a few days of active treatment, he had been certified brain-dead but had subsequently remained ventilated while his relatives came to terms with his condition. His wife, devastated by the situation she found herself in, had eventually agreed that his ventilator should be switched off. With that most painful of decisions made she subsequently gave consent for his kidneys and any other suitable organs to be used for transplantation. This generous act, at a time of overwhelming grief, would release two other human beings from the purgatory that was renal dialysis. Two lucky recipients had been identified, contacted and rushed into hospital. The first of those was Robert Scott, an elderly newsagent with end-stage renal failure, who had been on dialysis for over five years while awaiting a transplant. He still attempted to run his business, but struggled to work even four hours a day. In his own words, dialysis was 'a rubbish existence,' and he had confided to his family that if he failed to receive a transplant soon he was going to sell his shop and go away somewhere warm and pleasant to die. The second was a pretty, young woman who had developed kidney failure as a result of being a diabetic since infancy. She was to be the recipient of a combined kidney and pancreatic transplant in an attempt to cure both these ailments. Handicapped by those two illnesses, Annette had fared badly at school but now, at twenty-three years old, she had succeeded in gaining a place at her local Domestic Science College. She desperately wanted to become a chef but, although a naturally vivacious and intelligent woman, the combined exigencies of dialysis and poorly controlled diabetes had held her back. So far as she was concerned her whole future, indeed her life, depended on the success of this operation.

Wednesday was the day chosen for the transplants. The first act in this drama was finally to extinguish the non-sentient existence of the man whose chest was rising rhythmically in harmony with the bellows beside his bed. Only then could the numbing sadness of the donor's family be ameliorated in the knowledge that the lives of two others would be transformed for the better.

When I arrived at the agreed time to take charge of the donor the atmosphere in the ICU was tense and unsettling. I could see that the donor's bed was still surrounded by his family delivering their heart-rending, tearful, final farewells. I kept a respectful distance and peered at my shoes as, their final goodbyes completed, the family were assisted, stumbling and weeping, out of the ward. As the stern unsmiling nurses went through their final checking procedures, I felt like some harbinger of death. I was a scavenger, hovering in wait for my prey to die and about to feed upon the newly-dead carcass. I was not at peace – far from it – nor was anyone else.

The procedure was complex and the timing crucial. Two floors down, both recipients were already anaesthetised, awaiting their new organs. Now the patient, the donor, the body (whatever was the correct term) had to be kept 'alive', with the relevant organs perfused to ensure that they were in the best possible condition for transplantation.

'Okay! Now everyone knows what to do, I trust.' The consultant anaesthetist in charge of the ICU looked sternly at those of us who had gathered around the donor's bed. No words were spoken but some grunts and a few nodding heads satisfied him, and so without further ado he disconnected the ventilator and immediately walked away to dissociate himself from what was to follow. No one spoke as I began to ventilate the patient manually and, with the help of two porters, carefully steered the bed out of the ICU, along the corridor to a waiting lift, and having descended two storeys we then made our way rapidly to the operating theatre. The surgeons harvesting the organs were scrubbed ready and wasted no time in opening the donor's abdomen to retrieve his pancreas and both kidneys.

As soon as the main vessels to the organs being harvested were severed, uncontrolled haemorrhaging began. I increased the flow rate of the intravenous drip, and continued to squeeze the rubber bag until the donor's kidneys and pancreas were removed. Then his heart stopped beating and, with no more than a slight shudder, the physical remains of this already torpid man passed from life to death.

'Right, Grahame, you can stop now.' I felt sick and light-headed, barely hearing the surgeon as he carefully took the organs into the adjacent theatres where the two recipients were ready, abdomens gaping, awaiting their salvation.

***

I glanced at my watch; it was 5.30, the designated time for the daily evening ward round. Garry, the surgical SHO, and I waited at the nurses' station in front of the large white-board on which were documented the blood results of all the transplant patients. The pair of us covered the renal unit and, for the next eight months, shared a one-in-two rota. One of our many duties, as the most junior members of the team, was to update the results of that morning's blood tests before the evening round.

I heard the Professor before I saw him, his gravelly voice having the sound of stones being stirred in a cement mixer. As always, he was followed at a respectful distance, by an entourage of attendants. The most senior of the group was another consultant: a tall, slim man with an aquiline face who, I considered, would have made an excellent Sherlock Holmes. In fact he was actually known as 'the bishop', not because of any religious persuasion but on account of his pious demeanour. Straggling behind were four registrars of varying seniority.

The Professor took up his accustomed position in the centre of a semicircle of doctors, nurses and other hangers-on, where he peered at the day's results on the white board in front of him. Good results – where a renal transplant seemed to be working well – were noted, while deteriorating kidney function was discussed and anti-rejection drugs changed.

As was their custom, the renal physicians arrived late. The senior of the two, Doctor Hay, looked as though he had just come off the fell after a hearty invigorating walk. Ruddy-faced, with a tweed sports jacket and cavalry twill trousers, he was wearing brown brogues and a green V-neck jumper, underneath which was a crumpled checked shirt. A green wool tie adorned his neck and a smouldering briar pipe was clasped firmly in his jaw.

The Professor turned to the new arrival. 'Ah, Allan! What do you make of these results?' and pointed to a line of blood tests on the board which had initially showed improving transplant function but which, over the last two days, had deteriorated.

'How many days post-transplant is she?' asked Doctor Hay.

Garry rapidly counted and replied, 'Seven.' This was another part of our job – to know everything about every patient, all of the time.

'Mm.' Allan Hay scrutinised the blood tests. 'I think we should biopsy the kidney. She *might* be rejecting.'

The Professor looked at his feet and sighed. 'But, Allan, surely we're going to change her immuno-suppression anyway. Why bother? Why not just do it?' The Prof. was a surgeon through and through; his customary tool the scalpel.

Doctor Allan Hay took the pipe out of his mouth and placed it in his jacket pocket where it continued to smoke. 'It might just be a poorly functioning kidney. I think we should make a formal diagnosis before changing her treatment. If there isn't any evidence of rejection we could probably afford to watch things for a while longer.' Doctor Hay was a physician through and through – thoughtful, careful and unhurried. His interactions with the Professor could at times be confrontational and acrimonious, sometimes leaving us junior staff caught in the middle.

The Professor looked up from the floor at Doctor Hay. 'Okay, Allan, if you insist, but I want her treatment changed as soon as possible tomorrow.' His dark eyes were threatening but Doctor Hay was not one to be bullied.

'I'll do it after the round if you want and we could review the pathology tomorrow.'

The Professor turned his gaze towards Garry and myself. 'Who's on call tonight?' he asked.

'I am, sir,' I volunteered.

'Well, make sure you get those results and change her treatment tomorrow.' The Professor looked briefly but meaningfully at me. The biopsy was irrelevant to him. As far as he was concerned he had made his decision and it ought to be implemented immediately, not deferred to satisfy, what he considered to be, the mere curiosity of a colleague. Disgruntled, he turned his back to the board and the human semicircle parted to let him through to the ward.

After speaking to three patients on whom he had operated he encountered a patient he didn't recognise. '*Who* is this?' he demanded. As far as the Professor was concerned, this was *his* ward and only *his* patients should be there. In reality it was a ward for all patients with kidney disease, not just for transplant patients, but if they weren't either awaiting an operation or recovering from one, the Professor was simply not interested. 'Who is *this*?' he repeated, looking around at the surrounding ensemble accusingly, as though he had found a cuckoo in one of his beds.

'Oh! That's my patient, Prof.,' came the cheery response from the back of the assembled group where Doctor Harrison had been chatting with one of the registrars. He was the junior consultant renal physician whose main base was at a nearby district general hospital. He made his way through the melée to the front of the group where he joined the Professor. 'Yes, he's my patient, Prof.,' he said brightly.

The Professor stared at the floor and the cement mixer rotated. 'What's he doing here then?'

'I admitted him yesterday for dialysis. He came into my hospital with acute renal failure on Monday. I treated him conservatively at first but he didn't respond.'

In fact, I had managed this man the previous afternoon when he had been admitted acutely ill, having seizures and requiring emergency dialysis. It appeared that the severity of his condition had not initially been fully appreciated by the team at the DGH.

The Professor was not impressed. '*You'd* better see him then,' and he stood back to allow Doctor Harrison to move to the bedside.

What followed took us all by surprise when, on recognising his consultant, the patient suddenly sat bolt upright in his bed and shouted, 'You're full of shit, you are.' Then to make sure that he had made himself quite clear he waggled his right index finger in Harrison's direction and repeated, 'You're just full of *shit.*'

Not surprisingly, Doctor Harrison was somewhat taken aback. When last seen, this patient: a muscular, strong labourer in his forties, had been semi-conscious and delirious. Now, restored by the magic of dialysis, he was fully alert and clearly felt aggrieved by the way he had been managed. Doctor Harrison literally took a step backwards, fearing physical violence might follow this verbal abuse.

'I told you I was ill but you ignored me.' The patient's voice rose as he continued his diatribe. 'I nearly died. I nearly died thanks to you! Full of shit, that's what you are! Full of shit.' It was clear to all in the vicinity that this man, who had been nearly dead the day before, was making a good recovery.

One by one we all stood back to distance ourselves from Doctor Harrison whose discomfiture was palpable. Garry and I secretly agreed with the patient's own assessment of his management, while the Professor chuckled quietly to himself as he moved on to the next bed, leaving the flustered physician to explain himself.

The ward round finished at about six-thirty and we then retired to the seminar room at the entrance to the ward. Here, Garry and I served up bottles of beer to the team, another of our duties. Personally, I would have preferred to complete the remaining tasks of the day rather than sit around drinking beer, but the Professor expected his entourage to share beers with him on the completion of his round, so we did. It was only later on that evening that I realised Doctor Hay had left without performing the biopsy. I called him at home and he reassured me that he would do it first thing the following day.

It was midday before Doctor Hay performed the biopsy. I then carried the specimen to the pathology department and explained that I needed a result as soon as possible so that I could change the patient's immuno-suppression if rejection was confirmed.

'I'll process it straight away and should be able to give you a preliminary result this afternoon. I'll give you a call.' Reassured by the pathologist, I was heading back towards the ward when my pager went off. I phoned the extension displayed on its tiny screen.

'Are you the transplant SHO?'

'Yes. How can I help?'

'I'm the casualty officer. An ambulance has just brought in a young man who's drowned. Are you interested in his organs?'

'How long has he been dead?' I asked.

'We're not sure. Can you come and take a look at him, please?'

'Certainly.'

This was always a difficult situation. I was acutely aware that immediately an individual dies, the kidneys begin to deteriorate rapidly and become less likely to function adequately if used for transplantation. For the recipient, an old, poorly-functioning kidney might result in the worst possible outcome: a continued requirement for dialysis and an increased risk of a subsequent transplant being rejected. The other side of the coin was that, every now and again, one would work surprisingly well and there were undoubtedly some happy patients walking around with kidneys that had been 'scraped off the road,' as Garry put it. It was also difficult to convince well-intentioned relatives that their loved one's organs were not good enough to be used. I walked briskly to the A&E department and sought out the casualty Dtor.

'In the ambulance,' he said, nodding towards the bay outside the main entrance where the vehicle was parked, its rear doors open.

As I approached the large doorway, the huge panes of glass slid open automatically. I walked through, towards the ambulance man standing guard at the rear of his vehicle.

'Hi, I'm Doctor Howard,' I said shaking his hand.

'Are you the transplant Doctor?'

'Yes.'

'We fished him out of the river about an hour ago. A dog-walker spotted him floating mid-stream; then he drifted to the river bank.'

'Any idea how long he's been dead?' I asked, peering into the interior of the ambulance.

'Couldn't be sure, Doc. No witnesses to him falling in, I'm afraid.'

'D'you think it's less than two hours?'

'No idea, Doc. It's over an hour since we were called and I've no idea how long he'd been in the river.'

'Any family?'

'None found as yet, Doc. But the police are trying to trace them now. The reason we brought him along is that he's carrying a donor card.'

The ambulance man opened a sodden wallet from which he withdrew a soggy but recognisable organ donor card. He offered it to me but I just nodded and climbed into the ambulance. On my left, lying on the stretcher was a young man, possibly in his early twenties with his mouth slightly open, as were his unseeing eyes. His wet, dark brown, bedraggled hair was plastered over his forehead and he had the cold, clammy, pasty paleness of a corpse. He was fully clothed in green fishing gear. Over his rubberised dungarees was a weather-proof fishing jacket with its myriad pockets of all sizes, while green wellington boots covered his feet. He was soaking and smelled of the river. Scraps of mud and riverside debris covered his face and were visible on his teeth and within his open mouth. His hands were grimy, his nails black. I looked down at him for some time, before picking up his hand. It was stone-cold yet moved quite easily: rigor mortis had not yet set in. I hesitated, thinking more about the fisherman than the possibility of transplantation. How had this happened? What had caused him to fall into the river and to be dragged under? Had he been aware of drowning? Certainly his waterlogged gear would have made it difficult to swim. Maybe he was a non-swimmer. 'What d'you think, doc?' The ambulance man jerked me back to reality.

'D'you think it *could* be less than two hours since he died?'

'Look, I'm sorry, Doc.' The ambulance man sounded slightly exasperated by my repeated question. 'I really can't say. As I said, we've no witnesses to say when he fell in.'

Here, lying beside me, lay the potential salvation for two patients on dialysis but it was quite possible that his kidneys were already so damaged as to be beyond use. I made a decision. 'I'm sorry, but I don't think he's suitable. Too many uncertainties about the time of death. I suspect he's probably been dead for a while, maybe many hours. Thanks very much for bringing him in anyway.'

'Fine, Doc. Just thought we should give you guys the opportunity. We'll take him round to the mortuary. Obviously he'll be a coroner's case.'

Slowly and sadly I climbed out of the ambulance and walked disconsolately back into the hospital. I looked at my watch and was alarmed to find that it was approaching five-thirty.

I reached the ward just behind the professorial procession. The semi-circle had already formed around the whiteboard and the well-rehearsed daily performance was being played out. The results for Robert the newsagent were improving nicely, demonstrating that his transplanted kidney was working well, while Annette's were also encouraging, suggesting that both her transplanted organs were beginning to function. Then we reached the patient who had been biopsied earlier that day. The results of that morning's blood tests showed that her kidney function had deteriorated further.

'You've changed her immuno-suppression I presume, Doctor Howard?' The Professor asked while continuing to stare at the board.

'I'm still awaiting the biopsy result, Professor,' I stammered.

Not a muscle in his face moved but his demeanour changed from benign to malignant in an instant. Immediately the previously relaxed atmosphere in the assembled group became charged as though an electric switch had been thrown. The background chatter ceased, all eyes were turned on me, and some actually took a step back to distance themselves physically from me. The Professor's gravelly voice did not change in volume but somehow the tone had become both aggressive and violent, every syllable a poisoned dart spat out and aimed at me.

'Doctor Howard,' he said, pausing long enough to look directly at me, 'I told you to change her immuno-suppression this morning. Why didn't you do that?'

'I'm sorry, Professor, but I was waiting for the biopsy result and I was expecting a call this afternoon.'

'I instructed you to change it as soon as the biopsy had been performed.' His eyes were now as hard as diamonds, his gaze piercing. There was no one to come to my rescue; no point in saying the biopsy had only been performed late that morning, that I'd believed it was necessary to wait for the result, that I'd been busy with a dead fisherman and that the promised telephone call from pathology had never come. I sensed that prolonging the conversation could only make things worse.

'I'm sorry, Professor,' was all I could say.

His eyes dropped from mine and he sighed.

'Well, do it *now*!' he said with one final glower as he turned and stalked off to the ward in order to check that nothing else idiotic was being perpetrated on his patients by the imbeciles that surrounded him.

It was some weeks later when, first thing in the morning, the bishop summoned me to his office. Like the man himself, the office was extremely tidy and exuded an aura of organisation and efficiency. A meerschaum pipe sat neatly on his desk in its polished wooden stand, next to a framed picture of his family, and decorating the walls were photographs of him with well-known surgeons from around the globe. He was sitting at his desk in a swivel chair and as I entered he waved me graciously toward the vacant seat opposite him. I sat down.

'Grahame, the reason I asked you along here today is to let you know that we – that is, the Professor and myself – do not hold you responsible for Annette's death.'

I was puzzled and bemused. Annette had died unexpectedly the night before. Certainly, I had been on call but had never considered myself *personally* responsible for this tragic event. Now here was the bishop saying as much, which of course implied that exactly the opposite was true and that somehow I *was* personally responsible.

There was no doubt that her management had been extremely complicated. Combined renal and pancreatic transplants were a relatively new procedure. Her initial post-operative recovery had been promising, with evidence that both transplanted organs were functioning. In addition to the complex regimen to manage her blood-glucose levels there were the usual post-renal transplant problems of fluid management and immuno-suppression. As it transpired, her diabetic management had been the easier of the two, but her biochemistry had begun to go awry about two days before she died. Her diabetes had become less well controlled and the sodium level in her blood had decreased alarmingly. Gary and I had been adjusting her dose of insulin and intravenous fluid regimen accordingly.

The previous evening, the night staff had asked me to review her as her urine output had dropped. She had an intravenous line inserted into one of the veins in her neck, the tip of which lay in the right atrium of her heart. This device meant that her central venous pressure could be monitored, essential to the safe management of a patient with poor renal function where careful fluid balance was crucial. Too much would lead to fluid overload, while too little might irreparably damage the precious transplanted organ. This line made fluid replacement and management much safer.

It had been about eleven-thirty when I'd entered the darkened room to assess her. 'Hello, Annette,' I'd said. There was no response. 'Hello, Annette,' I repeated. She appeared drowsy, her urine output had been minimal for the last few hours and the central line indicated that she was dehydrated. I increased her intravenous fluids in an attempt to get a positive venous pressure reading. It didn't budge, nor did her urine output increase. After about half an hour, with no evidence that my management was working, I left her room and went to the nurses' station to phone the registrar on call for advice.

From where I was sitting I could see into Annette's side-room and as I lifted the receiver I saw her collapse. Her head suddenly lolled forward and her right arm drooped over the side of the bed. Slamming the phone down, I dashed across to the side-room accompanied by one of the nurses. Annette was unconscious, her eyes wide and the pupils dilated. She had suffered a cardiac arrest.

'Put out an arrest call, please,' I said as I hit Annette hard in the centre of her chest. There was no response and after lowering the head of the bed I started chest compressions. The senior night nurse now rushed in and took over the cardiac massage while I put a mask on Annette's face and started to squeeze the green bag in an attempt to get some oxygen into her lungs. The cardiac arrest team arrived promptly and took control of the situation. An anaesthetist intubated her and started to ventilate, cardiac massage was continued, monitors attached and electric shocks administered. I stood back and returned to the nurses' station to phone the Professor. There was no reply so all I could do was watch until all attempts at resuscitation were finally abandoned about an hour later.

So there I was the following morning, bemused by the bishop's comments.

'The whole purpose of the evening ward round is to pick up problems like this and manage them appropriately.' The bishop paused and looked at me for a moment before continuing. 'On this occasion none of us spotted the problem with Annette. We must *all* learn from this.' I was becoming more and more confused by the way events were unfolding.

'We *did* notice the low sodium and mentioned it on the round two days ago.' I said. 'Garry and I were actively managing it.'

The bishop seemed surprised. 'I wasn't aware of that.' He looked at me and I continued.

'The other problem was the central line, which in retrospect, I think must have been blocked.'

'Ah!' he said, leaning back in his seat and staring up at the ceiling, his fingertips together in prayer-like fashion. 'Well, I just thought it was important you didn't feel that you should shoulder all the responsibility for this tragedy yourself.' He smiled to indicate that the interview was over.

'Well, thank you. I appreciate that,' I said, still puzzled, and stood up to leave.

'See you later on the round when no doubt we will discuss this further.' The bishop then turned his attention to some papers on the desk in front of him.

After this interview I felt deeply concerned. Ostensibly the aim of the meeting had been to reassure me and not to apportion blame, but of course exactly the opposite was the case and I now felt personally responsible for the events of the previous night. I sought out my immediate senior, the medical registrar, to discuss my management of the situation the previous night. I had a real concern that I had placed too much reliance on the readings of the central line, which I now was increasingly sure had malfunctioned. I spent the day seeking vindication and, although none of my colleagues had anything critical to say, I found none.

There was a sombre mood that evening on the ward. As the Professor arrived, he stopped alongside the nurses' station from where I had tried to call him the previous evening. 'I'm upset about Annette,' he said to the gathered company. 'Very upset about the whole series of events.' His voice was at its most gravelly. What exactly did he mean? We were all upset, but he implied some sort of culpability and I felt this was aimed at me.

Doctor Hay placed his still-smoking pipe in his pocket, 'Absolutely. Very sad. But of course we don't know *why* she died.' The Professor looked up with surprise, 'Oh, I think we do!' My whole body froze and my muscles tensed; he might just as well have said, 'Yes we do. Doctor Howard killed her!'

Doctor Hay continued, 'No, we don't. We still don't know the cause of death. Why was her sodium level so low? She might have thrombosed her graft, either the kidney or the pancreas, or indeed both?' But the Professor was not to be persuaded. 'I think we do,' was all he said, and without further delay walked to the whiteboard where that evening every result was scrutinised with extra vigilance.

***

'Is it illegal to transfuse a Jehovah's Witness?' The door of the doctors' mess had been flung open to reveal an agitated, rather pretty but slightly bedraggled young female doctor. Her white coat hung lopsidedly from her shoulders due to the weight of *The British National Formulary* in her left-hand pocket. She stood beside the door for some seconds looking first at me and then at the only other occupant, a surgical registrar who was deeply ensconced in a two-year-old, dog-eared Christmas edition of *Good Housekeeping*. After a moment she blurted out, 'I think I've just transfused a Jehovah's Witness!'

This was a week after Annette had died and I was seated in the doctors' mess reading a newspaper in a rare moment of calm. This was a rather uncomfortable, shabby place. It's true that newspapers were replenished every day and there was a kettle, where one could make tea or coffee and drink it out of one of those heavily-stained mugs that are a feature of every communal kitchen; but it was an empty, soulless space.

'I think I've just transfused a Jehovah's Witness!' she repeated, addressing neither of us in particular.

'Oh?' I said, looking up. My colleague continued to read his magazine.

'Is it *illegal* to transfuse a Jehovah's Witness?' she asked again, glancing at us both in turn, her voice trembling.

As the surgeon, who was my senior, didn't respond but continued to concentrate on his copy of *Good Housekeeping*, I felt obliged to reply, 'It's not an offence as long as you've obtained their consent.'

'That's the problem, I didn't know she *was* a Jehovah's Witness at the time.'

'Well, surely she would have mentioned it when you started the blood transfusion?'

'That's the thing. She was under a general anaesthetic. It was during an operation.'

'Was it documented in the notes?' I asked.

'Well, yes, but I didn't know that at the time. I was assisting in theatre. She was having an emergency lap for a perf, and had lost a fair amount of blood. Mr Bottomley, who was operating, said to give her a couple of units. And so I *did*!'

'Oh!' I wasn't sure what to advise as, strictly speaking, this was an assault. 'I don't think it's illegal, but my understanding is that she should have given her consent.'

'Oh help! I wonder what I should do?' She bit her lip and laughed nervously. 'I wonder if I should go and own up? What do you think?'

There was a rustle of paper and for the first time the surgeon looked up from his magazine. 'Does she know?' he asked quietly.

'No, I haven't told her.'

'Then, if I were you,' he continued calmly and deliberately, 'I would just keep quiet about the whole thing.' His advice delivered, he lifted his magazine and resumed his reading.

'What do *you* think?' she asked, looking at me.

I smiled, wishing that I had demonstrated such sound common sense, 'That sounds like good advice to me.'

She heaved a sigh of relief, slumped down in one of the armchairs and promptly fell fast asleep.

***

The television crew had swelled the professorial entourage considerably. As we waited at the entrance to the ward, the small crowd of doctors swept on to the ward accompanied by a cameraman, a sound engineer and the director of what was to be a television documentary about the transplant unit. The cameraman stood in front of the group, stepping backwards in order to film the Professor entering his ward. Unfortunately he couldn't walk backwards as fast as the Professor was walking forwards so the Prof. had to slow down and even stop intermittently to avoid bumping into him. Meanwhile, a technician trotted alongside, holding his boom so that the furry microphone was somewhere near professor's head to record every gravelly sound bite. Our destination was to be a side-room in which lay Robert Scott, newsagent and transplant recipient. He had given his consent to be filmed and also, as luck would have it, was progressing rather well. As soon as the Professor entered there was something of a scrum to follow him. There wasn't space in the room for all of the hangers-on but Garry and I found ourselves pushed to the fore. With the camera rolling, the Professor began his questioning. His voice was at its deepest and most sincere.

'Hello, Mr Scott. I hope you don't mind me bringing these gentlemen with me this evening?' The Professor smiled and glanced over his shoulder as though he had only just noticed there was a television crew in attendance. Our patient had been rehearsing for this moment all afternoon. He was freshly washed and shaved and his thinning hair, which seemed to have become a degree or two darker since I had taken his blood that morning, was neatly combed. With an exaggerated gesture of simulated surprise at seeing his visitor he put his newspaper down very deliberately and in his most refined accent responded. 'Good afternoon, Professor. How very nice to see you. And, very 'appy to welcome the gen'l'men of the press, being a newsagent meself, as it were.'

'And how are you feeling this evening, Mr Scott?'

'Thanks to your good offices, in the pink, I'm pleased to say. Never felt better.'

'Good! I'm delighted. Perhaps you can tell us how long you were on dialysis, Mr Scott, and how that affected your life?'

'It was awful. I was on that there machine three times a week for about eight hours for five and a 'alf years, give or take. Couldn't eat nor drink what I wanted. Just felt lousy, completely washed out. Could barely run me business, didn't 'ave the energy. But *now,* thanks to you and your team, my life's been transformed.' Our patient was behaving impeccably and beginning to play to the camera. 'You've a wonderful team, Professor. Everyone, all the nurses and everyone, are wonderful, absolutely won'erful. Them nurses is angels, that's what they are.' The Professor tried to get the interview back on track and turned towards Garry and me, 'What's his renal function doing?'

'Urea and creatinine coming down nicely, Prof., just above normal now,' answered Garry.

'That's very good. And the immuno-suppression?' This time I answered. 'Cyclosporin alone, Prof.'

The Professor looked at the patient. 'Well, things are going very well and maybe in a few more days we can start thinking of getting you home.'

'Thanks. That's great. Just great.'

'Right then. See you tomorrow.' The Professor made a move toward the door but Mr Scott was now in his element, growing confident in his role and wanting to stay in the limelight for a while longer.

'I did have a bit of a cough this morning, Professor. Is that normal?' He coughed twice, politely into his right hand, to illustrate the problem.

The Professor halted, turned to Garry and myself and, with one eyebrow slightly raised, asked, 'Has he a temperature?' Without any hesitation I said, 'No,' at exactly the same instant that Garry said, 'Yes.' The Prof. sighed, looked at the chart and said with a smile, 'Well, on this occasion you're both right. It was slightly raised this morning but is now normal. Do keep an eye on it, won't you?' So saying, he pushed his way back though the scrimmage to the door of Mr Scott's room.

A one-in-two on-call rota leaves little time for anything other than work. Although I now had a wife and a house in a small village a few miles away, I saw little of either. In order to get the bleeding round (that is, the morning blood-taking round, not the one with the Professor in the evening) finished at a reasonable time, I would start soon after eight in the morning. The evening Professorial ward round rarely finished before six-thirty, and so, even if not on call, I was never home before seven. Then of course on alternate nights and weekends I lived in, and not uncommonly would be up most, if not all of the night. Like my house job at St Hilda's, this was more about survival than education and during my eight months I learned very little about kidney diseases but a great deal about getting things done to suit my seniors. In this role we were variously administrators, clerks, porters, databases, licensed victuallers, gofors and whipping boys. Why did we put up with it? It looked good on the CV: that's why. It was a prestigious post and in the competitive world of hospital medicine it constituted an extremely useful rung on the long ladder to becoming a consultant.

PRIMUM NON NOCERE

'That's going to be depressing,' my mother had said when I informed her that I was going to work on a cancer ward. 'All those patients with cancer, losing their hair and then dying.' Indeed Oncology had been the least attractive element of this medical rotation, but was the price to be paid for two other jobs – the prestigious posts on the transplant unit and chest medicine at the renowned Papworth Hospital. In fact, like most young doctors at that time, I had never been exposed to Oncology as such. Of course, cancer patients were a significant part of both surgery and medicine but essentially, once the diagnosis was made, the patients were passed on to Oncology to die – or at least that was what I and most of my colleagues had been led to believe.

It was noticeable, however, from the very first moment that I stepped on to the cancer ward that this was a happy place. It is hard to explain the concept of a *happy* or a *sad* ward, but in my experience some general medical wards were sad. Those wards were mostly full of patients, usually elderly, with diseases that were incurable, but hadn't yet killed. There, often for months on end, were the breathless and the bed-bound, the droopy, dribbling stroke patients, and the wheezing blue bronchitics with zimmers and walking sticks scattered about like so much jetsam. Confused and disorientated, away from home and loved ones, those elderly and infirm casualties of life adapted poorly to the hospital environment, often becoming disinhibited and aggressive.

Gynaecology wards also seemed to me to be full of tears. Women who were pregnant but didn't want to be; women who wanted to be pregnant, but couldn't be and the womb-less who'd, 'had it all taken away.'

Not so Oncology. On my first day there were cheerful greetings from the sister and staff. It was noticeable that many of the patients were relatively young. The senior registrar, Chris, helpful and supportive, had said, 'Cancer patients tend either to either get better, or die.' Then those who couldn't be cured often had their symptoms ameliorated by the judicious use of powerful drugs and radiotherapy.

This was a whole new world where the word 'cancer' was spoken out loud, where the concepts of palliation and care of the dying were actively and openly discussed and pursued.

'One of the nice things about Oncology,' said Chris, 'is that you tend to take over the total care of the patient, almost like becoming their personal GP.' Far from being depressing, the care of those patients was uplifting and rewarding, with the results of one's interventions seen rapidly.

The professorial unit, as in so many academic centres, specialised in the difficult and the rare. Thus I cared for patients with lung cancer, brain tumours, and bone cancer in children and adolescents, this last group representing some of the most tragic and distressing cases seen in any cancer centre. I was also introduced to the world of 'evidence-based' medicine. It wasn't called that at the time: that phrase wouldn't be introduced for another twenty years, but that's what it was. If there wasn't evidence for any tangible benefit from an intervention, be it a drug or radiotherapy, the rule was – either don't do it, or do it within a trial setting. This was consistent with the concept of *primum non nocere,* which (roughly translated) means, 'Whatever you do, don't actually harm your patient.' It was a simple philosophy but amazingly still at odds with the way many clinicians practised at that time.

I was in my third week on the unit when Paul was admitted as an emergency. Chris had seen this young farmer in the chest ward at Papworth Hospital that very morning, wheezing and gasping for breath, and had transferred him immediately. When I entered his side-room he attempted a greeting but was too weak to smile and barely managed to move his hand in recognition of my presence. An oxygen mask obscured his features but I could see that his face had a blue tinge, particularly noticeable around his lips.

'How are you feeling?' I asked, immediately realising what a banal question that was. Too breathless to talk, Paul just raised his hand again and moved his head slowly from side to side.

'Okay. Don't worry, I'm going to get on and start your treatment.'

Paul had an unusual type of lung cancer, but one which often responded well to chemotherapy. His chest X-ray was grossly abnormal. Where there should have been black areas demonstrating the presence of air there was the patchy whiteness of cancer – lots of it. I went to the small side-room, to prepare the prescribed cocktail of three cytotoxic drugs.

After injecting the requisite amount of sterile water into a small glass bottle which bore the label Cyclophosphamide, I started shaking it vigorously to dissolve the white powder. I knew from experience that this would take a long time and so ran hot water from the tap over the bottle to speed up the process. For about fifteen minutes tiny particles continued to swirl around in the bottle, like a snow scene, until gradually the fluid cleared and was ready to be drawn up into a large syringe. The second drug, Adriamycin, came ready-dissolved and was a brilliant red liquid, almost crimson. The trick to drawing up those liquids was to inject the correct amount of air into the sealed bottle first. Too little, and it was impossible to withdraw the fluid because of the vacuum created; too much, and when the syringe was withdrawn, the drug would spurt out in a fine spray through the rubber bung. Vincristine, the final drug, was simple to prepare as the requisite amount was always two milligrams, for an adult anyway, and came ready prepared in a small glass phial. Here, the only problem was breaking the top off the phial without cutting your finger. With all three drugs prepared, I returned to the side-room, inserted a butterfly needle into a vein in Paul's arm and then slowly injected them. This done I gave Paul a brief smile of reassurance and then left the room.

'Doctor Howard.' Judith, one of the staff nurses, was waiting for me outside the room. 'Paul's father would like a word with you if that's possible. He's in the seminar room.' Then, with a slight smile, she turned and walked back to the nurses' station. I opened the door to the large room which was used for teaching, and interviews.

'Mr Critchley?' I offered my hand to the man standing in the sunlit room.

'Yes. I'm Paul's father.' As I guided him to one of the spindly moulded plastic seats of which about twenty were scattered about the room, I looked at this man. On his head was a flat cap of the type so beloved of farmers and country folk. His face was weather beaten, with red jowly cheeks on which were split veins. Obviously a farmer, and dressed appropriately in green corduroy trousers, checked shirt and tweed jacket, he was the picture of ruddy good health. He looked at me expectantly.

'How much have you been told about your son's condition?' I asked.

'Very little, apart from the fact he's got lung cancer and it's incurable.' That probably says it all, I thought to myself.

'Well, essentially that's right, but we do hope that he will respond to chemotherapy.'

'What will that do, Doc?'

'Well hopefully, *if* he responds, his breathing will improve and he'll be more comfortable as a result.'

'But it won't cure him?'

'Sadly, no. But sometimes we do see good, durable responses.' I was waiting to be asked how often 'sometimes' was and how long a, 'good, durable response,' might be, but either Mr Critchley didn't want to know or he forgot to ask, so no further questions were forthcoming.

'I've just given him his first shot of chemotherapy, and we'll now just need to wait to see how he responds over the next few days.'

'Thanks, Doc. I know you'll look after him. This has come as such a shock, you see. He was working on the farm till two weeks ago, then he developed a slight cough and before we knew it he became breathless. We thought it was a cold, you know, but when it didn't get better, thought we should take him to the doctor who sent him straight to Papworth. It's all been so sudden.' I nodded but said nothing.

'Can I go and see him now, Doc?'

'Yes of course. I'll see you again tomorrow. Just let the nurses know if you have any questions.'

I walked out of the room with him and, as I turned to leave, he grabbed my hand in both of his. 'Look after him, Doc, won't you? He's all I've got. I don't know what I'd do if I lost him?' He looked directly at me, his eyes moist and his lips trembling with emotion. A strong man, down to earth and of the earth, but now unexpectedly in uncharted emotional territory.

'Of course. We'll do our best,' I said, and made my excuses to leave. Outside, Judith was once more waiting to speak to me. 'Grahame, that American – John. You know, the one in the Air Force. He would like to see you sometime too – when you've got a moment.'

It was the following day before I managed to see John. He was sitting beside his bed in an armchair. 'Morning,' I said. 'I gather you wanted a word. Sorry I didn't get along yesterday.'

'Hi, Doc. Yeah, thanks for comin' by,' he drawled then stopped to wipe some foamy spit from his mouth. Hanging from a drip-stand beside him was a bag of white milky fluid connected to the naso-gastric tube which could be seen entering his left nostril, pulling it slightly out of shape. His neck looked red and sore and the left side was concave. There, a long, livid, thickened line of skin marked the surgical incision beneath which most of the muscles had been removed. His face was gaunt, his hair thin and, although only in his early forties, he looked at least a decade older. He had a mid-American accent, and came straight to the point.

'How long d'you think I've got, Doc?' he asked, once again applying the sodden handkerchief to his mouth. 'The Professor said a few weeks. D'you think that's right?'

This man had a cancer of his throat so that he couldn't even swallow his own saliva, let alone any food. In time this cancer would grow and block his airway. Death was inevitable.

'What exactly did the Prof. say?' I enquired as I sat down next to him.

127

'A few weeks; mebbe a month or two.'

'Well, I'm sorry, but I think that's as accurate as anyone can be, and of course it depends on how much the radiotherapy helps,' I replied referring to the course of X ray treatment which he had just completed.

'But look, Doc. I know I'm not goin' to get better. I can't swallow. I'm in constant pain. This ain't much of a life.' He turned his head to look directly at me and then came the request: 'Look, Doc. What I'm asking is …' and he hesitated briefly, '… will you help me to end it? I know I ain't gonna get better, I'm goin' to die soon. This is a lousy existence and I'd rather just die right now.' He paused for a moment. 'If I had the means, I'd do it myself, but I don't. Can you give me something, Doc. Please!' He was still looking directly at me, his eyes pleading.

I dropped my gaze for a moment before replying. 'I think you know that I can't deliberately give you something that will kill you.' I looked around, uncomfortable that others might overhear this conversation. 'There may be more treatments that we can offer you and certainly we will give you whatever is necessary to control your symptoms.' I said this with as much enthusiasm as I could muster. He looked at me knowingly and dabbed his mouth.

'The treatment's not working. *You* know that, and *I* know that. Look at me.' He made a gesture to highlight his emaciated body. 'I'm completely fucked. I'm used to being fit, a sportsman. A fighter pilot, for god's sake.' He paused to wipe more spittle from the corner of his mouth, 'I was flying jets only two years ago. Shit, Doc, this is awful. There ain't no point in going on. *I* know you can't do anything. *You* know you can't do anything, so let's just finish it.' Throughout this speech, at every third word or so, he paused to wipe the saliva from his mouth where it had pooled between his lower lip and his teeth.

He continued, 'Sorry, Doc, I know this ain't easy for you, and you can't go around just killing people willy-nilly, but if you could just slip something into my drip to finish it I'd be eternally grateful.'

I was confident of my own moral stance. To me, it was unthinkable deliberately to end someone's life, whatever the situation. 'I can't do that, John. You know that.' He sighed audibly. I felt that somehow I had let him down, so I repeated, 'You know I can't deliberately give you something that will…' I hesitated '… end your life.' I still felt this was inadequate so I added, 'But I will adjust your medication to better control your pain.'

'Okay. Thanks, Doc. But do think about what I've said, won't you. No need to say anything. Just tip me the wink when you're going to do it and I'll know.'

I got up from my chair and walked slowly off the ward. Mike was sitting in the seminar room, drinking a mug of coffee and eating a lunchtime sandwich. He was the other consultant on the firm, a quirky lateral thinker, and probably not the best person to share my thoughts with, but he was there, and he was approachable.

'Mike, one of our patients has just asked me to help him commit suicide. Well actually, he's asked me to *kill* him. What should I do?'

129

'Is your insurance paid up?' Mike answered with a smile. Then, seeing my concern, he continued more seriously. 'Well, there's potassium in the drip, that's probably the best way: a sudden cardiac dysrhythmia.' He clicked his fingers to illustrate the suddenness of the process. He was then silent, thoughtful for a while, realising that I was genuinely looking for guidance. 'It's difficult, Grahame. It's happened to us all at one time or another and everyone responds differently. I've done it.' He paused for a moment and decided not to pursue that point. 'Morphine is probably the best option, escalating doses until he stops breathing.'

'No, Mike. I don't mean *how*. I mean *should* we do it. It's that American. He's dying slowly and wants to end it all. Surely you can't just keep piling in more and more morphine until he's dead. That's nothing short of murder.'

'The party line, of course, is that we don't deliberately end life, but it is entirely reasonable to administer large doses of drugs for a clinical indication, such as pain, which may, as a side-effect, result in death.'

'So, it's okay if there is a clinical indication, you just deliberately give a bit too much! That's a complete fudge, Mike, isn't it?'

'Life's a fudge, Grahame.' Mike took a sip of coffee. 'Good symptom-control is of paramount importance, and that often requires doses of drugs which may lead to side-effects such as respiratory depression. What you're asking, Grahame, is, should we be allowed to administer drugs with the sole aim of ending life, and that's a different and much more controversial question. Personally, in exceptional circumstances, I think we should, in the same way vets that put their patients down when there are no other options available.'

'What would you do?'

'Difficult. Is he in pain?'

'Yes, appears to be.'

'Then morphine's the best option, I would say. Anyhow I've got to get to the clinic now,' and finishing his coffee, he got up and left. I increased John's dose of morphine and made a mental note to speak to him again the next day.

As soon as I entered his side-room I could tell that Paul's condition had improved. Four days after his chemotherapy, he was beginning to breathe more easily. Although still reliant on oxygen, he was sitting up in bed and reading a newspaper. He pushed his mask up on to his forehead, 'Hi, Doctor Howard.' The blue tinge had gone and his now pink face bore a broad smile.

'There's no need to ask if *you're* feeling better,' I said. His father was sitting at his bedside, beaming. He looked up at me and didn't say a word. He didn't need to – the eyes said it all.

'Well, I just need to take some blood off you, then I'll send you for an X-ray. The Prof. will be along to see you this afternoon.'

'How long will I need to stay in, Doc?'

'His dog's missing him,' explained his father with a grin.

'And I'm missing my dog!' added Paul.

'Ask the Prof. this afternoon,' I said placing a small plaster over the puncture site where I had taken the blood.

I then went to see the rest of my patients in preparation for the professorial round that afternoon. Last of all was John. He was asleep, but he woke as I drew the curtains around his bed.

'Hi, Doc.'

'How are you feeling today?'

'You know, much the same.'

'Isn't the pain any better?'

'Nah. Still there, Doc.' He looked me directly in the eyes as he gathered some saliva into his handkerchief. 'Quite a lot of pain actually, Doc.'

'Okay, well the Professor will be along this afternoon. We'll ask his advice then.' 'Any more thoughts about our chat yesterday?' he asked.

'No, nothing, I'm afraid.'

'Okay, I understand. See you this afternoon.'

The professorial ward round was not as grand as the one on the transplant unit but it was still attended by all the doctors on the team. Along with Mike, there were two senior registrars, two middle-grade registrars and of course myself, the senior house officer – at the bottom of the food chain.

The Professor never examined a patient: he said that he had excellent junior staff to do all that for him, so he was happy to be led from patient to patient, where he would have as brief a conversation as he could without appearing to be rude.

Chris explained the background to Paul's admission and the treatment that had been instigated. We all filed into the side-room where the Professor took up his customary position standing at the side of the bed. He shook Paul's hand, 'You're doing very well,' he said with a hint of a smile. 'How's the breathing?'

'Much better, thanks, Professor.'

'Good. Good,' the Prof muttered absent-mindedly as he turned to leave the room. Sensing that this brief interview was drawing to a close, Paul almost blurted out, 'When can I go home?'

'He's missing his dog,' his father explained from near the window where he was standing.

'We'll see how you are at the end of the week. Maybe then.'

'Thanks, Professor.'

We filed out of the side-room and halted in the corridor just outside the door. Here I presented the assembled group with an update of John's progress – or rather, the lack of it.

'Prof. He can't swallow, his breathing's getting worse and he's uncomfortable.' I stopped short of saying that he had asked me to help him end his life. 'Is there anything else we can do for him,' I asked somewhat naïvely.

We reviewed all his previous treatment going back nearly two years, which had involved long intensive courses of both radiotherapy and chemotherapy.

'Could we give him some more chemo, Prof?' I asked hopefully.

The Professor smiled at me. 'Grahame, I know you would like to give him some further treatment, but there comes a time when you have to accept that there is no more that you can do for a patient. Although it's tempting to keep trying more and more therapy, you must consider whether it is in the *patient's* best interest or whether you are really just treating yourself. Sadly, that's the stage we have reached with John. Keep him comfortable, please.'

I then realised why the Prof. did a ward round. He was right: he didn't need to examine patients and only rarely needed to decide what treatment was required, for that was usually straightforward. *His* role was the most difficult one – to decide when *not* to treat. He was there to stop his enthusiastic junior staff from over-treating his patients.

By the end of the week Paul was fit enough to go home, with instructions to return for a second course of treatment three weeks later. John's condition had changed little. No better but essentially no worse, he was not dying quickly. 'Still in pain?' I asked him.

'Yeah, Doc. It's no better.'

I was confused as to why his pain wasn't responding to escalating doses of morphine. I sought help and advice from the nursing staff. Judith was sitting at the nurses' station writing up patients' notes. 'Judith, John says he's still in pain. It doesn't seem to be responding to increasing doses of opiates? How do *you* think his pain-control is?'

'I wasn't aware it was a problem,' she said and continued writing. I returned to John's bedside.

'John,' I asked, 'when you get an injection of morphine does the pain go away for a while?'

'Nah, Doc. Still there.' He dabbed his face with a paper tissue, where a flow of saliva had reached his chin.

'When I increased the dose yesterday, did that help at all?'

'Not really, Doc. Ah reckon the dose ain't high enough.' He looked up at me, his eyes penetrating, his mouth drooling. Suddenly it all became clear to me and I understood what was happening. Pain wasn't a problem at *all*. He just wanted me to give him increasing doses of morphine until he stopped breathing. I thought for a moment. 'You're quite sure you're in pain?' I asked.

'Yeah, Doc. It's terrible. Please do something.'

'Okay. I'll increase your morphine.'

'Thanks Doc.' As I got up to leave I turned and glanced at him. His whole demeanour had changed. The facial intensity and piercing gaze had resolved and relaxed into an expression of overwhelming relief.

'Thanks, Doc,' he repeated quietly, with full understanding.

'Judith, John's in a lot of pain. I'm going to increase his morphine.'

'Fine. I'll give him a stat dose if you want to write it up.'

Next day I went to see him again. He was in bed, propped up, slightly drowsy and again dabbing at his chin. 'Still in pain, John?' I asked.

'Yeah, very painful, Doc.' His head slumped forward slightly.

'Okay.' And so, day-by-day, John's morphine was increased until he was unconscious, and he remained that way until he died peacefully, six days later.

I informed the Professor of his death on the ward round. 'Comfortable, I hope?' he said.

'Yes, Prof. Seemed to be.'

'Good.'

'Difficult cases these,' Mike added. 'Escalating morphine?' he asked, his eyebrows raised.

'Yes. Until his pain was controlled.' I replied, then added, 'I'm confident he died pain-free.'

'Good,' said Mike, then repeated, 'Good,' before nodding solemnly as our entourage moved on to the next patient.

'You should come down to the clinic some time, Grahame.' Chris and I had just finished reviewing several ward patients.

'The problem with the wards is that you just see the patients who are on active treatment, and also those who are dying. The clinic's the place to see patients who've recovered from their treatment and those that have been cured.'

'Thanks, Chris. Yes, I would like that.'

'Come along on Wednesday morning then, at about ten.'

So at ten o'clock precisely I arrived in Oncology Outpatients, and rather nervously entered a large room with several desks where the medical staff read the notes, looked at X-rays, dictated annotations and, where necessary, discussed difficult issues around the management of patients.

Mike was seated at one of the desks, a set of case notes lying open in front of him, while holding a telephone in his left hand. He looked up and acknowledged me, waving towards a pile of case-notes and then, holding the phone away from his mouth for a second, whispered, 'Help yourself, Grahame. Have a look at some notes, go and see the patient, then discuss any problems with one of us.' He put the mouthpiece back in position. 'Ah, good morning. Is that the Member of Parliament for Bedford?' There was a pause. 'No, tomorrow will *not* do, I have a patient who needs to be seen and the ambulance service say they cannot bring him up. He needs to be seen today.' There was another pause. 'Thank you. I would be most grateful if you would try to locate him … No, I'll hold the line, even if it may be some time, thank you.' Mike sighed, raised his eyebrows, then sank back in his chair with a resigned look on his face. Chris entered the room and smiled. 'Any luck, Mike?'

'No one knows where he is, apparently.'

Chris smiled at me with an expression that said as clearly as words that he thought Mike was barking mad trying to speak to the local MP simply because a patient's transport hadn't turned up. But Mike was not like the rest of us. To him this was a matter of principle and if he had to spend the whole morning on the telephone, then so be it.

Chris and I saw a patient together and then returned to the communal room. Mike was still on the phone and

137

becoming increasingly agitated. 'I don't care if he *is* in the House of Commons. I want to speak to him *now*, as a matter of urgency.' There was a brief pause before the conversation appeared to come to a halt. Mike slammed the phone down, only to pick it up again and dial zero. There was a moment's silence, 'Switchboard? Good. It's Doctor Connor here. Get me the House of Commons please. *Urgently*.' Chris smiled broadly. 'Having trouble, Mike?'

'Bloody MPs!' he scowled, 'you can never find one when you need to. The only time they're in evidence is when there's an election, when they come knocking on your door and stuffing leaflets into your hand as though they're suddenly your new best friend. When you need them they're nowhere to be found.'

An hour later, with Mike still on the phone, the ward staff informed me that Paul had been admitted for his second course of chemotherapy. I thanked Chris for his help, nodded to Mike and made a move to leave. As I turned, I saw a poster sellotaped to the wall. It bore the picture of an owl along with the caption: MOST OF BEING CLEVER IS KNOWING WHAT YOU DON'T KNOW. How apposite, I thought.

Back on the ward Paul and his father were waiting for me. Paul's hair had fallen out but apart from that he looked much better. He was able to walk slowly on the flat and could manage one flight of stairs without oxygen – a huge improvement. I sent him for an X-ray while I prepared his chemotherapy. With the tray of syringes ready, I went to his room where his father was seated awaiting his return.

'How's he doing, Doctor?'

'Very well,' I replied. 'Obviously we'll need to see his X-ray, but the fact he's breathing better means that he's responding to the treatment.'

'That's excellent. So he's definitely responding then?'

'Yes,' I replied, but I knew he wanted more. He wanted more than reassurance that his son was responding to treatment; he was desperate to be told that he might be cured. Mr Critchley was silent for a while and appeared to be studying his shoes, then quite suddenly he looked up. 'Is there *any* chance he might be cured, Doctor?'

I wanted to say, 'Yes.' I desperately wanted to say – 'Yes. Of course there is'. I wanted to say that there was a good chance this kind young man who loved his dog would be cured. But in reality I knew that wasn't the case. I also didn't want to remove all hope from his father who was struggling to cope with his son's prognosis. 'Be honest and optimistic but realistic,' I had been advised by Chris when discussing prognosis with patients and relatives.

'Well, I'm afraid this isn't a curative treatment, but clearly Paul has responded well and sometimes patients have durable responses which can last for many months or even years.'

'And science is moving on all the time, isn't it, doctor? By then there may well be other, better treatments?' He looked at me expectantly. In all honesty the chance of a new treatment becoming available during

Paul's lifetime was zero, but I couldn't bring myself to say that.

'That's true,' I said with a reassuring smile, just as Paul was wheeled back into the room. His chest X-ray had improved dramatically and I demonstrated the findings to both father and son.

On the ward round later that week the Professor affirmed what I'd said, 'He's doing very well, a definite response. I'm very pleased with his progress.' But Mr Critchley still yearned for more. He wanted a cure for his son – longevity, a normal lifetime of ups and downs, pleasure and pain, farming seasons – three-score years and ten.

A few weeks into the job, Chris had introduced me to the arcane world of radiotherapy. Unlike many such departments, which were hidden away underground, this one, which had opened only a few years previously, was spacious and airy. There, within thick-walled rooms with green porthole windows, stood massive rotating gantries supporting bulbous chunks of lead within which a small cube of cobalt 60, the source of high-energy gamma rays, was housed. There was no 'off' switch: this beast emitted constantly and the radiation could only be tamed by moving the source to a safe area within its leaden head. Used correctly, this ionizing radiation, these photons of energy, could be harnessed to cure cancer. Used incorrectly, it could just as easily kill or maim. Essentially, of course, this was no different to other medicines I routinely prescribed which in appropriate doses were therapeutic and beneficial, but useless or potentially lethal in the wrong dosage. Even everyday substances such as water and salt *can* kill, yet without them we cannot survive.

Then Chris showed me the new high-energy X-ray apparatus, the linear accelerators – massive machines which could treat deep-seated cancers and did not contain a radioactive source. As we walked across the open spaces and along wide sunlit corridors of the radiotherapy department, physicists, radiographers and nurses bustled about, directing, helping, encouraging and cajoling the hundred or so patients that were treated each day. Chris explained the basic principles of radiotherapy to me and I was enthralled. I could do this, I thought. As he turned to go, Chris said, 'Come along to the seminar on Wednesday if you're not too busy. There's a speaker from the Marsden. It's in the Medical Research Council building just across the road – you know, where all the Nobel prize-winners work.'

It was unfortunate that the night before the seminar I was on call and had been up most of the night. Nonetheless, as the designated time for the talk approached, I made my way to the venue and entered the room where the seminar was to be held. In front of me were several comfortable-looking settees, behind which stood the inevitable collection of red moulded-plastic stackable chairs. The Professor and Mike had already taken up their positions in the front row and the visiting lecturer was loading his slides into a projector carriage. This was not of the more usual carousel type, which is set on top of the projector and rotates, but one of the straight variety which moves forward and back in a track at the side. The projector itself stood on a table just in front of the settees, its power cable taped to the carpet where it crossed to the plug socket on the wall behind the screen which hung from a flimsy metal tripod.

I walked in front of the screen and sat down on one of the comfy settees, which, as it turned out, was to prove a grave error. At the allotted time, Mike introduced the speaker as, 'Someone who needs no introduction' – a sure sign that he'd forgotten his name – and then promptly sat down. After thanking Mike for the invitation and making a polite joke, our guest launched into his lecture which concerned a certain enzyme process and reminded me of the interminable biochemistry lectures to which I had been subjected as a medical student.

It didn't take long for my eyes to start to droop. I fought valiantly for ten minutes or so but then dozed off. I must have fallen asleep, because I vividly remember waking up. I might well have slept right through the lecture unnoticed if my pager hadn't gone off – but it did. This initiated the inevitable startle response. As it bleeped, I sat bolt upright and let out a loud yell. That was enough to draw everyone's attention to me, but worse was to follow. Realising that I must leave the room to locate a phone, in a moment of post-somnolent disorientation, I opened a door, thinking it was the exit, only to walk into a large cupboard. I was now in a difficult situation and not sure quite what to do for the best, since a number of people in the audience were already looking at me in bemusement. The options available seemed either to pretend that I had meant to go into the cupboard all along and come out with the Hoover that I had identified inside, or to disappear completely into the cupboard and close the door behind me to give the impression that this really was an exit. I quickly realised that if I did that I'd have to spend the next hour or so in the cupboard until the seminar had finished and everyone had gone home. In the end I decided to bluff it out and just to head for the proper exit.

After closing the cupboard door in a deliberate fashion that was meant to imply that I was carefully checking what was in there before leaving the room (as any sensible person would) I started to walk towards the exit. The only route to the door necessitated crossing between the screen and the projector and so, with exaggerated casualness, I passed in front of the screen but, in doing so, somehow my shoe snagged one of the cables. This destabilised the screen which started to fall forward. Luckily I was in the ideal position to catch it, and just as it was tipping forward I grabbed it and gingerly set it back upright while apologising to the lecturer. With the screen back in place I then set off on the final stage of my journey. It could have been because of my eagerness to reach the exit without further event that I nudged the table on which sat the projector but, whatever the reason, at that very moment, the slide carrying carriage suddenly shot backwards in its groove and landed on to the floor, distributing sixty or so slides in a random fashion just in front of the Professor's feet. This is any lecturer's nightmare, and I was the cause. I left the room as quickly as I could before I could cause further mayhem.

Next day, Mike said that the lecturer never fully regained his composure after I'd left, adding that it had been the most entertaining seminar he'd attended for a long time.

***

Initially Paul continued to improve and his chest X-ray, although never normal, showed an excellent response to the chemotherapy but when he arrived for his fifth course of treatment he had become more breathless and was looking less well. Worryingly, he had also become reliant on oxygen once more.

'I'll be back when I've got your blood results and seen your X-ray,' I said as I left his room where, as always, his father was in attendance. Mr Critchley senior had not altered at all over the three months I had known him. I suppose he must have changed his shirt on occasion but his appearance seemed identical every time we met, looking as if he had just stepped off a tractor or out of a cowshed. Paul, however, having made rapid gains early on, was now looking frail and had developed the appearance – bald with waxy grey skin – of patients who had taken about as much chemotherapy as they could tolerate. When I said I needed to see his X-ray, I was lying. I had already looked at it and there could be no doubt but that it had deteriorated markedly, yet I needed time to think before sharing this devastating news with father and son.

I went to the clinic to get advice and was pleased to find Chris there reading some case notes between seeing patients.

'Chris, you remember Paul?' I said, putting his X-rays up on the illuminated box, 'Well he's due his fifth course of chemo today but his count is too low and his X-ray has got worse.' Chris scrutinised the films for some time. Eventually he murmured, 'Shame. Sometimes happens though: quick response, then quick relapse.' He paused briefly. 'No point in continuing with his current treatment as he's clearly no longer responding. What's his blood count?' he asked, looking at me. I showed him the results of the morning's blood tests. After a brief look, Chris continued: 'And it looks from his count that we are running out of marrow reserve for further treatment. That is if there was any – which there isn't.' Chris handed back the blood results, 'I'm afraid we've run out of options. I'll come up to see them after the clinic but in the meantime it would be helpful if you could break the news so they are aware of the situation.' Chris turned back to his case-notes.

'We thought as much, Doc.' Mr Critchley senior was speaking for both himself and his son. I was amazed by how well they took the news. Having told them the results of the tests and explained the absence of further treatment options, their response was resigned and stoical. Paul was now too breathless to say much, but I could just detect a weak smile from behind his oxygen mask.

'Well, we've had a good three months which we wouldn't have had if not for you, and for that we're grateful, Doc.' He paused. 'I suppose we can go home now?'

'Well, my senior registrar is going to come and have a word with you both later on.'

'No need, Doc, unless he has something else to add. What you've said is good enough for us. I think we'll just head off. We've got oxygen at home and I know I can phone if we need any advice. Thanks for all you've done, doc, it's much appreciated.' The father then rose from his chair, grabbed my hand and forearm and began to shake it vigorously. I was having trouble controlling my own emotions and knew that I would lose control if I tried to speak so I just smiled weakly, looked into his eyes and continued to shake his hand. I turned to Paul, put my hand on his shoulder and patted it a few times – not confident that I could say anything without breaking down. From behind the oxygen mask I heard a weak whisper, 'Thanks, Doc,' he said.

'Would it be possible to get a wheelchair please, doc?' asked the father, 'we're keen to get off as soon as possible.' He glanced towards Paul, who nodded ever so slightly. Both silently acknowledging that now, every moment and every second was important – a bonus, time to be savoured and appreciated.

'Of course.' I replied as I turned to leave the room, my eyes moist. Once outside I walked to the end of the ward and retrieved a wheelchair which had been left there. I trundled it back to Paul's room where his Dad and I helped him settle into it. Once seated and with all his belongings gathered I wheeled him back along the corridor towards the entrance. Here, farmer Critchley found his voice again, 'I'll take it from here, thanks.' As he grasped the handles and began to push, he turned to me and said, 'Thanks again, doc.' I watched as Paul left the ward for the last time, his head lolling forward, the tube from his oxygen cylinder curling across his shoulder to the mask which was held in place by green elastic.

It was the end of the following week at about two in the morning when I received the call. I was not 'on call' and therefore annoyed at being wakened.

'It's switchboard here, Doctor Howard. Sorry to trouble you. I know you're not on call but I've got a Mr Critchley on the line who was insistent that he wanted to speak to you. Can I put him through?' I sensed the worst.

'Yes of course,' I said.

A moment later I heard the familiar voice of Mr Critchley senior. 'Is that Doctor Howard?'

'Yes. Hello, Mr Critchley.'

'Gerald Critchley here.' There was the briefest of pauses before he continued, 'I thought you would like to know that Paul has just died.'

For a moment I couldn't speak as the tears ran freely down my cheeks.

'I'm so sorry,' was all I could manage.

'Just thought you'd like to know, Doc. Paul thought a lot of you.'

'Thank you so much for letting me know. It was a pleasure...' my voice began to falter but I recovered enough to add, '... and a privilege to look after him. I'm truly grateful you phoned.' My voice cracked and I could say no more.

147

'It was all very peaceful in the end. Goodnight and thanks again for all you did, Doc.' The phone went dead, leaving me with my tears.

A RURAL IDYLL

There are two villages called Papworth – Papworth St Agnes and Papworth Everard – the hospital is in the latter. This secondment was a rural idyll compared with the previous sixteen months where I had been on a one-in-two rota. Now I was on call only one in every four nights and weekends, while my patients, although ill, tended to get worse or better slowly and quite predictably.

Entering the campus of Papworth Hospital was like stepping back in time. Because a campus it was: not a single building but a small village set around its own village green complete with pond and ducks. Driving from Cambridge, this journey back in time began after one turned right at a junction called the Caxton Gibbet. Sure enough, clearly visible at the side of the road, alongside a pub of the same name, there stood a gibbet. Placed at the junction of two major routes, it had been intended as a deterrent to highwaymen and others who were considering rising up against the authorities of the time. It had been some considerable time since the metal cage, which still hung there, had contained any human remains and it was now inhabited by a solitary bird's nest. Here was the gateway to a veritable time-warp, where the years were rolled back to pre-war, rural, middle England, to an age before two ugly wars had shattered and scarred our society forever.

Papworth Hospital had originally been a sanatorium. Built on a gentle slope, at a safe distance from the unpleasant effluvia of the industrial revolution, it was situated in the healthy country air of rural Cambridgeshire. Its accommodation resembled a collection of Swiss holiday chalets rather than a complex of hospital wards. A pair of two-storey crescent-shaped wooden buildings carried a series of single rooms on the outward side, each having an external door opening directly on to a wooden veranda which ran the full length of the building. Internally, the rooms were connected by a corridor and within the concavity of the crescent were the clinical and administrative facilities. The veranda faced on to a large patch of undulating grass in the centre of which lay a pond. This village green was carefully set out with mature trees and bushes, while the pond itself was home to a variety of animals and wildfowl. Patients could sit and inhale the fresh country air while gazing out over a landscape that had been untouched for centuries.

This was an environment for gentle recuperation rather than intervention, and the hospital was struggling to embrace the era of modern medicine with its paraphernalia of X-rays and antibiotics. It belonged in a more peaceful time when tuberculosis was the 'romantic' disease. This was the illness which playwrights and poets invoked to dispatch their unwanted characters. Gracefully and elegantly, they would cough into their red handkerchiefs as they grew ever more pale and interesting, only to succumb tragically at a time to suit their creator. This had been the disease of Keats, the Brontës, Beardsley, Stevenson and Wilde.

Adjacent to the hospital was Papworth Village Settlement, where in the past those who had recovered were taught a trade and sold their wares. This colony of artisans still thrived by producing leather goods and wooden utensils which were marketed locally. It wouldn't have surprised me if there had still been a wheelwright's shop there, for this remained the rural England of Edwardian times. It should be said that there had been some attempts to embrace the twentieth century. The old round-pin electric sockets had been replaced when it was discovered that much emergency equipment, including defibrillators, had square-pin plugs. In the cardiology ward, monitors had been mounted above the doorway of the rooms so that patients might be assessed without the need to enter every cubicle; and a tractor and trailer, rather like those used at fêtes for children's rides, were used to transport patients around the hospital. Modern additions to the hospital, such as the X-ray and cardiothoracic surgical unit, were housed in somewhat incongruous new brick-built buildings at the top of the hill.

The whole scene was highly picturesque and quite delightful. In clement weather I would conduct my ward round out of doors, moving from room to room along the balcony. I could then step down on to the village green, stroll across the undulating sward, past the pond, and so on to the next ward.

I also suspect that the doctors' mess had changed little over the past sixty years. True, the dray delivering beer was no longer horse-drawn, nor was the white-coated flunkey in evidence, but there *was* a full size snooker table and alongside it a small bar with its ever-empty honesty box. The bar was subsidised by some long deceased benefactor who felt that the hard-working doctors should have a cheap beer or two at the end of their day's labours. Not only was the environment anachronistic, but so were two of the three consultants. Those venerable physicians, both about to retire, had witnessed the discovery of antibiotics and the introduction of triple therapy for tuberculosis, the only previous treatment being a 'nourishing diet and plentiful supplies of fresh air'. Patients who had previously been placed in a bed or seated on the balcony until they either recovered or died could now be treated and in most cases cured.

The successful treatment of tuberculosis was an exemplar of the seismic changes occurring in medicine during the middle part of the twentieth century. Doctors who previously had little in the way of therapeutic tools apart from leeches (a jar of which, interestingly, was still kept in the pharmacy at Papworth) now suddenly found themselves aided by therapeutic interventions which could dramatically alter the entire course of a disease. Physicians could now administer drugs which *worked*. Along with those treatments, however, came the responsibility for their accurate delivery and a gradual awareness of their associated side effects. Toxicity became a highly relevant issue, as did the need for rapid intervention when it was realised that patients, previously unsalvageable, could now be cured.

This sea change in the management of our patients had a devastating effect on medical staff, particularly those more junior. Intensive rotas such as being on-call one in every two days had previously not been too arduous. Inconvenient – yes – but with few interventions available and none urgent, an emergency admission could normally be put to bed and assessed the following day, allowing the doctors to finish their game of snooker while drinking subsidised beer. Now, patients needed to be managed urgently and intensively. Blood samples had to be taken, intravenous drips set up, drugs prescribed and administered, X-rays performed and examined and, on occasion, patients mechanically ventilated. Doctors were now actively treating the sick out of normal working hours and previously sustainable rotas became unworkable.

Nonetheless, the world of chest medicine evolved slowly and my days at Papworth were still relatively gentle and relaxed. Gradually the crocuses pushed through the snow, the ice melted on the pond and winter burst into early spring with an explosion of perfumed colour. Then, as the cherry blossom turned the grass confetti pink, and the anachronism that was Papworth Hospital geared up for yet another summer, my sojourn drew to an end and once again I had to find another job.

After due consideration I decided to apply for a training post in Oncology and was duly appointed registrar at a north London teaching hospital.

PART 3
AN IVORY TOWER

'Doesn't take much to be a senior registrar these days, does it?' Edward took a sip of coffee. He was a short, thin man with what could only be described as a weasel-like face. His nose protruded in a way that his chin didn't, resulting in a pinched, rat-like appearance while his thinning fine-brown hair was cut short. Edward's most notable feature, however, was his voice. This was rather high-pitched and nasal so that whatever he said sounded like a whinge. Even the most mundane of comments such as, 'Good morning,' would somehow come across as: 'Mm. Well, it might be a good morning for you, but you don't realise what I've had to put up with already today.' His glass wasn't just half-empty; there had never been anything in it.

'When I was appointed as S.R. here,' he said, 'I'd done four years at Bart's *and* passed the final fellowship.' Edward carefully replaced his cup on its saucer and then continued, 'and there *you* are with just over one year's experience and having only passed the first part of the exam!'

After spending just over a year in London, I was now back at the Ivory Tower, this time as a research fellow and senior registrar in Oncology. Edward had been correct in observing that I had been appointed an S.R. early, but mine was a research post, funded by a charity.

By contrast, he was the NHS senior registrar, fully trained and largely autonomous, responsible for many more patients and clinically much busier than any of us in the academic team. When this criticism was levelled at the professor he would quite rightly explain that his staff were there to perform clinical research and not to prop up the NHS.

I was a little taken aback by Edward's remarks. 'Really?' was all I could think of in response.

'Mm. Well, I've got to go. I've a huge clinic to do and then a theatre list.' He gave me a meaningful look as though I ought to be doing the same and that somehow I was a bit of a malingerer in being part of the academic team. Edward stood up and, with a final 'Enjoy your coffee, lads,' marched to the door and slammed it shut behind him. Lionel, the only other occupant of the room, looked over the top of his copy of *The Times*, 'Miserable bastard,' he said. 'The reason it's taken him so long to be an S.R. is that he couldn't pass the exams *and* he's such a pain in the arse.'

'Oh! So it's not just *me* he's at odds with?'

'No, no, Grahame. He's at odds with the whole world. Didn't you notice his shoulder?'

'No,' I said, somewhat puzzled.

'Well, take a close look next time you meet him. You'll find there's a rather large chip there.' Lionel chuckled, lifted his newspaper and resumed his reading.

Lionel was the lecturer in Oncology and revelled in his role. He loved academic life, ensconced, as he saw it, at the very pinnacle of an ivory tower. He yearned to be the epitome of an academic: the Cambridge don, sharing journal-strewn, smoked-filled rooms with fine thoughts and glasses of port. He had thick, coarse sandy hair and a full beard; he wore horn-rimmed spectacles and was comfortably living out his academic dream. The only problem was that academically he wasn't very productive. His propensity for drinking large quantities of beer, enjoying erudite discussions while keeping up with the news, left him little time for research. He had his own office at the lower end of the department adjacent to the high-energy accelerator and there, in his journal-stacked room with its views of the countryside, he conducted tutorials, smoked his pipe and exercised his intellect.

'More coffee?' he asked.

'Thanks.' I held out my cup to be refilled.

'What research will you be doing?'

'Well, I don't know yet, but I'm seeing the Prof. later on this week to discuss that.' After a sip of coffee, I continued, 'Things have changed a bit since I was last here as an SHO. Is Chris still the S.R.?' I asked.

'No. He's been appointed to the Ipswich post. Mike's still here though.' Lionel smiled. 'And as mad as ever.'

'Ah! Yes, I remember Mike well. Who else is on the team?'

'Well, there's the Pink Panther and the Pope. You'll soon meet them both.'

'A Pink Panther *and* a Pope? Interesting mix.' I smiled and finished my coffee.

'Here, I'll show you where you can park your bum,' said Lionel as he laid down his newspaper.

We walked a short way down the wide linoleum-floored corridor to an internal room which contained three desks and a row of grey filing cabinets. There were no windows but a small, round cupola let in some daylight and on the wall hung a whiteboard on which figured some graffiti, a diagram of the cell cycle and a caricature of Einstein. Seated at one of the desks, facing the wall and with its back to me, was a pink panther: not a real one obviously but a large child's soft toy the size of a skinny ten year-old. Lionel indicated a vacant desk to the right. 'Well, I'll let you settle in. I have a tutorial to give. 'Bye for now.'

Next day I met the Professor. 'Welcome, Grahame,' he said, indicating a chair. 'We enjoyed having you on the team last time and it's good to have you back.' This was praise indeed from a Prof. who had a reputation for being grumpy. 'You'll be taking over the management of the wards from Stephen so that he can spend more time on his research. Have you thought what *you* want to do?'

'I'm looking for advice, Prof?'

'Well, the options essentially are either joining the laboratory programme developing monoclonal antibodies, or running the proposed hyperthermia project. We're going to set up a clinical facility here. D'you want to give it some thought?' I didn't need to think about it: the clinical option was the only one for me. All I ever did in laboratories was spill things and fall asleep.

'I would much prefer the clinical hyperthermia project if that were possible, Prof.'

'That's fine. I'll introduce you to the rest of the team later.' And so my research for the next four years was decided.

I made my way back to the registrars' room. The pink panther had been moved and was now lolling in the corner of the room, its spindly legs stretched out in front of it, while in the vacated chair sat Peter. As I entered, he turned and rose to shake my hand. He had straight, wiry, very ginger hair, and his chin was embellished with a neatly-trimmed beard of the same colour. He was thin, slightly stooped and appeared to walk on his toes. As he offered his hand I could see why Lionel had given him the epithet, Pink Panther. He had a slight stammer – more the hesitation of a polite and mild-mannered man than an actual stutter.

'H-hello! You must be Grahame. I'm Peter.' He smiled and his head nodded gently as he hesitated, not sure what to say next.

'Hi. I'm Grahame Howard. Nice to meet you. I was told to sit there.' I indicated the empty desk, 'is that okay?'

'Absolutely. Stephen sits there,' he said, gesturing towards the remaining desk.

'Stephen?'

'Y-yes. Lionel probably called him the P-Pope. He's got a brain the size of a planet and he keeps telling us to stop blaspheming.'

'Ah. It begins to make some sort of sense. I think I'm taking over from him on the wards.'

'Yes, that'll be right. He's up from the H-Hammersmith and Prof. wants him to take over the monoclonal antibody project.'

The wards hadn't changed greatly since my time as a senior house officer and there were many familiar faces who seemed happy to welcome me back. At the end of my first week I met up with Lionel for a beer and a chat. We walked the short distance from the hospital to the social club where there were excellent facilities including a swimming pool and a bar.

'Well, Grahame, how are you settling in?'

'Fine, thanks, Lionel. Not much has changed.'

With a pint each, we adjourned to a free table where Lionel started to fill his large hooked briar. After several attempts and half a box of matches he eventually got it going to his satisfaction and settled back luxuriously in his seat while blowing thick clouds of smoke towards the ceiling. Satisfied that this conflagration was under control, he raised his glass. 'Well, cheers!' he said then sank half his pint in one gulp, I followed suit. We chatted and drank several more beers and, as the evening wore on, I noticed Lionel was becoming more garrulous and beginning to drink his beer from the left hand side of his mouth.

'You see, Grahame, the Prof. always likes to think he arrives first in the morning and is last to leave at night. You've got to fool him into thinking that you're here before him and leave after.' He took a long swig of beer. 'Once I discovered this, I used to wait until I saw him drive off in the evening before I left. Then, seeing my car was still there, he started leaving later and later. So rather than sit in my office I started to come here for a few beers and only returned when I was sure he would have gone home.'

'That's fine,' I said, 'but what about the mornings?'

'Exactly!' Lionel steered his pint glass unsteadily towards the corner of his mouth.

'Exactly. That's the really clever bit.' He looked at me triumphantly. 'You leave your car here *all night*!' Lionel smiled broadly as he placed his pint mug carefully on the table. 'I'll never forget the first morning when Prof. saw my car already outside the department as he drove in. Of course it had been there all night.'

'But doesn't that rather defeat the purpose? Essentially you're saying you can't ever use your car or go home?'

'Yes. It's *brilliant*, isn't it?' I was puzzled, as even after numerous beers the inherent flaws in this scheme were all too apparent. 'But where do you sleep on these occasions?'

'Oh, that's simple.' He looked at me as though he had just solved a highly complicated problem and I was an imbecilic pupil unable to follow his logic. 'I sleep in one of the beds of the outpatient chemotherapy ward.' He glanced at me to make sure I was keeping up with him. 'Of course, you have to make sure you get up early, otherwise you're liable to wake up with an intravenous drip in your arm and some chemotherapy going in.'

By about nine o'clock we had drunk eight pints apiece and agreed it was time to go home. I took my leave and set off on the mile and a half walk home across the fields to Trumpington where I was living, leaving Lionel to bed down for the night in the chemotherapy suite.

'The coffee room's clear, chaps.' Stephen had poked his head round the door of our office, 'Prof.'s left.' This was our cue to go for an extended coffee break. Being there at the same time as the Prof. not only looked as though we were underemployed, but often resulted in being landed with some additional chore such as giving a presentation. We considered the Prof. to be like a radioactive source – the inverse square law applied. Essentially this fundamental law of physics states that the further away you are from a radioactive source the better. We felt that the same principle could apply equally well to any noxious body, such as the Prof. The maxim was to keep as far away as possible and, if exposed, to keep the duration down to a minimum. This meant that the Prof. usually found himself alone in the coffee room – that is, unless our early warning system failed. In a similar vein, Lionel reckoned that a holiday taken when Prof. was away was a holiday wasted.

We filed out of our office and walked briskly to the coffee room. Edward was sitting there, a coffee by his side, reading a magazine. As we entered he looked up. 'Mm. Oh look! It's the professorial academic team. Found time to break off from *thinking* for a coffee, have we?' His pinched features took on a smirk, the nearest he ever came to a smile. Lionel took up the challenge, 'Yes, we need some cerebral sustenance. More coffee for you, Edward, or perhaps you don't have the time?'

'Well actually, *no*, I don't. Mm. I've got a huge clinic to do in Huntingdon this afternoon all on my own.'

'Shame.'

'Seriously, it's outrageous that the three of you look after fewer than half the number of patients that I do.'

'You've missed the point,' said Stephen. 'We are researchers, pushing the scientific boundaries forward, day by day, inch by inch.'

'N-nanometre by n-nanometre,' added the Panther.

Lionel went over and peered intently at Edward's right shoulder and then, after a moment, gently brushed it. 'What on earth are you doing?' Edward demanded angrily as he moved away, a look of disgust on his face.

'Just thought I saw something on your shoulder?' Lionel smiled at me as he moved to sit down.

'Well, I'm off to do some *real* work.' The door slammed.

Poor Edward: he really didn't have the necessary talents to be an oncologist. Any interpersonal skills he might have once possessed seemed to have been surgically excised at birth, along with his sense of humour. His first major gaffe, for which he'd never been forgiven, was perpetrated soon after taking up his current post. He had referred a patient to his old *alma mater,* St Bartholomew's Hospital, clearly implying that the treatment there would be better. Needless to say, that hardly went down well with the local consultants. It was, however, true that his current job did not allow him time to carry out sufficient research to further his career. So he continued to be busy and to irritate everyone with his whining. He was unmarried and I wondered if he was gay, but apparently he was just so miserable that any girlfriends lost the will to live after a few weeks at the most.

Lionel, on the other hand, had a simple, seemingly foolproof plan. He would carry out some groundbreaking research and be awarded a Nobel Prize. But before all of that he wanted to seduce Shona, a rather attractive staff nurse from the ward.

'Not free for a beer tonight, Grahame. I'm going out with the lovely Shona,' he said one afternoon as we were finishing a clinic.

I hadn't actually asked him if he wanted a beer that evening but he was clearly keen to tell me of his conquest.

'Oh! So Nurse Shona has succumbed to your charms?'

'Well, not yet. But she's agreed to come out for dinner with me tonight and that should be it, I reckon. Booked a table for two, ordered flowers, chosen the wine – the lot.' He paused, savouring with anticipation the evening ahead. 'In the bag, I reckon.'

'Will you be taking her back to the chemotherapy suite for a bit of therapy?' I asked.

'Ha, ha!'

'Well, good luck.'

Next morning Lionel looked a little under the weather. After the all-clear, I asked him, over a coffee, how things had gone. He smiled bleakly. 'Well, it was a bit of a cock-up really' – then, realising the pun, he added, 'but not in the desired way. The problem was that

166

I was a trifle over-anxious and thought a couple of beers in the club would relax me. I met Mike there and one thing led to another so that by the time I picked Shona up after her late shift I was half-cut.' Lionel took a sip of his coffee. 'As you know, after a few, I get a little garrulous and so I started to tell her all about myself. I can't remember much about the dinner except that I bought two bottles of wine, most of which seemed to be all over my shirt this morning.' Lionel paused and grimaced at the memory. 'I do remember inviting her to come to bed with me and I'm pretty sure she said "No!" or words to that effect. Quite vehemently actually, as I recall.'

'Sorry to hear that, Lionel. Could happen to anyone.'

'I'll give her a call later and try to find out what really happened. That's the whole problem with me. I seem to see a girl only twice, the first time to take her out and the second time to apologise!'

The door opened and Panther popped his head round, 'P-Prof.'s coming!' So we drank up and left just as our boss turned the corner.

***

'Well, Doctor Keen, *I* think marrow ablative therapy and a transplant is her only chance.'

'But there's no evidence to support its effectiveness, and the outcome is still appalling.'

'But it's her only chance.'

'It's not really a chance at all. I'm worried that all we're doing is using a new technology simply because it's available.'

'The haematologists have done thirty or so now with good results, we know it's relatively safe.'

'A thirty percent mortality is hardly safe.'

'But that's from the disease, not the treatment.'

'Bit of both, I would say.'

And so they slugged it out, the senior registrar in Medical Oncology: young, confident, risk-taking Doctor Hamilton; and the rather diffident middle-aged, conservative consultant, Mrs Keen. This regular weekly difference of opinion was being played out in the corridor of the oncology ward next to a side-room within which, reading a paperback love story, lay Helen. She was only twenty-five years old and some six months ago had attended her doctor with abdominal pain. After a myriad of investigations and numerous opinions, no one was any the wiser as to what was truly wrong with her. Then a surgeon decided to do what surgeons do – open her up and have a look. He had found a large mass in her pancreas adherent to her bowel, and after several hours of trying to remove it – and in the process unintentionally making holes in various organs where holes shouldn't be – he decided that it was inoperable; so he took a biopsy, stitched her up and referred her to oncology where she had remained ever since.

The sample taken suggested that the underlying problem was cancer of the pancreas but this is a notoriously difficult diagnosis to make on biopsy material alone and was unusual in someone so young.

Thus, every week, at this stage of the ward round, there had been the same heated discussion about Helen's management. Each week the decision was deferred for some reason or another. To start with, she needed time to recover from her operation; then all manner of further tests were performed and expert opinions sought, but soon a decision would have to be made. Bone marrow had been harvested from a matched donor and stored, and subsequently all the preparations made for her to receive high-dose marrow ablative chemotherapy.

The theory behind this novel treatment was that if a high enough dose of chemotherapy could be given, then all the cancer cells would be killed. The inevitable side effect, however, was that her bone marrow, where all the constituents of her blood were produced, would also be destroyed. The innovation was that she could then be rescued from certain death by a bone marrow transplant. Leukaemia patients had already been treated in this way with some success, but to date it hadn't proved successful for solid tumours such as Helen's.

Doctor Hamilton, with all the confidence of youth, felt strongly that every moment's delay lessened the chance of a successful outcome, while Doctor Keen with the reserve of experience and age, remained unpersuaded.

'We're not even one hundred percent sure of the diagnosis,' she murmured, as she did every week. 'It could still be chronic pancreatitis.'

'Well, the pathologists are as sure as they can be, Doctor Keen,' countered Hamilton, 'and her condition will soon start to deteriorate.' He paused for emphasis.

'She's beginning to lose weight. She'll die if we don't do anything.'

'But that *could* all be due to pancreatitis.'

'I think that's unlikely. We should give her the benefit of the doubt and treat her aggressively while we still can.' I was reminded of the words of the Professor, 'Grahame, you must learn when *not* to treat. Treating is easy but may not be in the patient's best interest. Beware of giving medication simply in order to be seen to be doing something.'

'Well, let's talk it over with her,' and Doctor Keen headed for the door to the side-room. I had not seen Helen before and was surprised how well – indeed how normal – she looked. She was about my own age, attractive and vivacious, even a touch flirtatious sitting up in bed with her ever-so-slightly revealing nightie. She had thick blonde hair which fell heavily to her shoulders and she was wearing bright, colourful make-up, with shades of red and blue decorating her pretty face.

As we entered, she gave us all a wide smile. ''Ello, doctors. So! What's the verdict then?' she said brightly. Doctor Keen smiled weakly.

'Well, Helen, as you know, things aren't black and white and it's not clear what the best course of action is. We could wait for the time being to see how you progress, but as you know you've lost a considerable amount of weight.' Doctor Keen paused for a moment, inviting a response. Helen said nothing, but continued to look inquiringly at her consultant. Slightly unnerved, Doctor Keen continued. 'We feel that the likely diagnosis is a malignancy,' (Doctor Keen had still not come to terms with using the term 'cancer' in front of patients) 'and treatment outcomes are not all that good.' Neither, I thought to myself, had Doctor Keen come to terms with being entirely honest about prognosis.

'One option is this high dose chemotherapy but there is no guarantee that it will work.'

I looked at the patient who was gazing intently at Doctor Keen, uncomprehending. *I'm* getting confused now, I thought to myself. Lord knows what Helen will make of this.

Our patient then interrupted, 'But it might work, mightn't it?'

'Well, yes. Of course. It *might* work,' Doctor Keen conceded rather grudgingly.

'Well, why don't we get on with it then?'

'The problem is there are also potentially serious side effects to take into consideration. You'll be in hospital for a minimum of six weeks before your blood count recovers and of course there is the possibility that the transplant won't engraft.' Doctor Keen was measured and at her most sincere. She was genuinely trying to inform and educate Helen about the uncertainties surrounding her management, but all she'd succeeded in doing with this obfuscation was to confuse the poor girl. Helen wanted to be told what the best treatment was and what decision should be made – not to take part in an academic debate. Her puzzled expression turned to one of frustration.

'Look! I'm an 'airdresser not a bleedin' doctor. Just tell me what's best. I don't understand any of this grafting stuff.' Doctor Keen looked uncomfortable; she knew she wasn't handling the interview well.

'I don't think we should rush into a decision.' She looked at Helen who just sighed, exasperated: As well she might be, I thought.

'What d'you think?' Helen turned her enquiring gaze to Doctor Hamilton.

'Well, Helen. Doctor Keen knows my view, I think we should give you the treatment as soon as we can. However, the final decision must be made by yourself and Doctor Keen.'

Helen hesitated for the briefest of moments, 'Well, let's get on with it then. What are we waiting for?'

Doctor Keen stood silent at the bedside, unsure. She was clearly uneasy about the decision and ultimately, as the consultant in charge, she was responsible for Helen's treatment and its outcome. But Hamilton was persuasive and the patient had been convinced. Eventually, after some further discussion, the die was cast. Helen would start the high-dose treatment the very next day.

***

Prof. walked on to the ward flanked by three Japanese doctors. 'Grahame, this is Professor Takasaki. He and his team are visiting us for a few days.' The oriental professor turned towards me, stood to attention with his heels together and hands at his sides, then formally bowed his head. He did this this at exactly the same moment as I proffered my hand to shake. Realising my mistake, I withdrew my hand and started to bow at the identical time that he straightened up and extended *his* hand. This happened several times before we agreed mutually that the introductions had been satisfactorily completed. But the whole farce was inevitably re-enacted with the two other visitors.

'Grahame, I'm just going to show our visitors around the department. Would you care to come along and demonstrate our hyperthermia equipment?'

'Yes, of course, Prof. I'd be delighted to,' I replied as we all set off down the main corridor.

'We'll go to the simulator first: that's where we plan our radiotherapy treatments. It's the most up-to-date technology.' With this, Prof. flung open a door, only to find that it was a clinic room in which there was a rather surprised semi-naked patient stretched out on a couch. 'Hmm! Sorry. Wrong room,' he muttered but as he turned to leave, our enthusiastic visitors tried to squeeze past him in order to view the interior. The Prof. blocked the door and then gently but firmly herded them out of the room. 'Nice woom,' said Professor Takasaki as the door was closed behind him.

'Wrong room. Sorry,' said the Prof. with an attempt at a smile.

'Wong woom? Oh.' Then the senior visitor explained to his colleagues that they had just been in the wong woom.

'A wong woom? Ah.' The others nodded sagely to one another. Our visitors obviously thought that this was some sort of new experimental treatment room and proceeded to chatter excitedly amongst themselves.

'Must be where the wong tweetment is given,' explained one.

The Prof. was becoming flustered. 'This is hopeless, Grahame. Where on earth have they put the simulator?'

I led the way to the next corridor, muttering something about all the corridors looking identical and how easy it was to get confused and forget where things were. The fact was that the Prof. hadn't carried out any radiotherapy planning for years and had probably never been in the new simulator, let alone used it to plan a patient's treatment, since he left this process entirely to his junior staff.

'Right, Grahame. You can go now while I take our visitors down to the high-energy accelerator.' So I was dismissed, leaving the Prof. and his three guests to finish their tour.

'God, Grahame! That was a close thing last night.' I was having coffee with Lionel the following day.

'What d'you mean?'

'Prof. and his visitors. They nearly caught me out.'

'Why, what happened?'

'Well, I was in my office at about six o'clock. I thought it was nice and quiet and that everyone had gone home. So I settled down to do some reading and have a smoke. I had just got my pipe going nicely when I heard Prof.'s voice.' Lionel paused for a moment – clearly the memory was still painful. 'Prof. normally never goes anywhere *near* that end of the department. I've always considered it to be completely safe down there, but it was definitely his voice. Anyway, I didn't know what to do, the voices were getting louder and they were definitely coming in my direction and I panicked. You know how Prof. hates smoking and I couldn't possibly let him find me with my pipe going like a volcano, so I opened the window and threw my pipe and the ashtray out. However, there was still quite a fug in the room and I thought the best way to avoid discovery was to throw myself out of the window as well. So I clambered out, with some difficulty I can tell you, and fell into that small ditch just below the window. The problem was that Prof. obviously detected the smell of smoke and entered my room – luckily I don't think he's any idea whose it was – and seeing that nothing was on fire he closed and locked the window, so that I couldn't get back in.'

'What a nightmare!' I said. 'What did you do then?'

'Well, by now I was covered in mud and obviously didn't want to bump into Prof. and his guests. I could hear someone talking in Japanese saying something about "another wong woom," so I thought it best to stay there, underneath the window in the ditch, until the coast was clear. I waited for about an hour, by which time I was getting pretty cold so I carefully crept round the building to the main entrance, keeping under cover of that low hedge. I arrived just as the Prof. was leaving, and – guess what – he locked the front door of the department after him!'

'Gosh, that's harsh. How on earth did you get back in?'

'Well, I remained hidden until I was sure the Prof. had gone then climbed in though another window, which

fortunately had been left open. God, that was close!'
Lionel looked distinctly pale at the recollection.

'You *do* lead a complicated life,' I said.

'It's not my fault. Things just happen to me!'

'By the way,' I asked, 'have you spoken to the lovely Shona?'

'Oh. Please don't ask.'

'Why? What happened?'

'Well, I suppose I might as well tell you. You know I said I was going to phone her subtly to see if I could discover what had gone on the other night because I was far too pissed to remember?'

'Yes.'

'Well, eventually, after a lot of persuasion she agreed to speak to me. I thought I'd try to get her to talk about the evening so I could begin to piece the events together myself. So I said quite nonchalantly, "Thanks for coming out the other night. I enjoyed it, I hope you did?"'

'Clever. *Very* clever,' I said.

'Yes, I thought so, too, but her response wasn't quite what I anticipated. She said, "You don't remember anything about it, do you?" So I decided to come clean and said, "Well, to be absolutely honest, no, I'm afraid I *was* a bit pissed." She then said, "Well, you invited me to go back to the chemotherapy suite for some *therapy*." She was growing a bit hysterical by this time. So I just looked at the floor and squirmed, hoping she had finished; but she continued, "And when I said, what do you mean? You said: you know, for sex." '

'Oh my hat! That's not good,' I said.

'I know, I know, *and* it got worse. I obviously wasn't in full control of my faculties because apparently I then said, "Well, we could go to your place if the chemotherapy suite isn't good enough." That was when she left, which in retrospect was a good thing because it was then that I threw up.'

'Oh my hat!' was all I could say.

'All in all, not one of my best performances.'

'Well, I suspect it fell a trifle short of expectations for both of you.'

Panther and the Pope then entered and each poured themselves a coffee. 'Lionel, d-did you have a nice evening with Shona?' Panther asked politely.

Lionel groaned, 'Oh god, not you as well.'

'You shouldn't blaspheme,' said the Pope.

'Sorry. But it was a complete washout, as I was just telling Grahame. I think the Shona chapter is probably closed for good.'

'I don't know, Lionel,' I said, 'you really shouldn't let a small setback like that put you off, for heaven's sake.' I turned to Stephen, 'Sorry,' I apologised, before he could chastise me, 'but faint heart never won fair maid, and all that. Give her a call. Might be wise to drink a bit less next time though.'

'More a case of piss-head never won fair Shona.' Lionel sighed.

'At least there can be no misconstruing your intentions now. She knows exactly what you're about. She's seen you at your very worst, so it can only get better.' I was quite impressed with my sales pitch and almost believed it myself.

'Well, maybe. I'll probably let the dust settle for a week or so and then see.' Just then Edward entered.

'Mm. Hello, professorial team. Gosh, the coffee room's getting too small for all you academics.' He took the last remaining empty seat. 'Lionel, how did your night out with Shona go?'

'Bugger off, Edward!' we all yelled in unison.

***

The following week we once again congregated outside Helen's room. Doctor Hamilton was enthusiastic and upbeat. 'The chemotherapy was administered two days ago, Doctor Keen.'

'How's she getting on?' Doctor Keen asked quietly.

'Well, nausea and vomiting have been a real problem, as expected.'

'Have you started parenteral nutrition?'

'No. But I think we should, so we're getting a central line put in tomorrow.'

'And the transplant?'

'I've spoken to the haematologists and they think tomorrow would be a good time to start infusing the donor marrow.'

'That'll give us a few weeks to support her with blood products, antibiotics etc. until her count recovers. That is, *if* it does.' Doctor Keen said this pensively and, with a small grimace, she headed towards the door of the side-room. Clearly she was still not entirely happy with the decision that had been taken.

As members of the academic team, our remit, our *raison d'être*, was to perform clinical research and publish the results. The Pope had performed in an exemplary fashion and published numerous papers. He was a very tidy person, with a very tidy mind and a very tidy life. Having completed all his projects, he had been awarded a doctorate. His oncology training was now finished and he was busily applying for consultant posts. As far as I was concerned, he was the fount of all knowledge and his intellect was truly awe-inspiring. The Panther was at a similar stage of training to myself. He was running a trial to assess how some drugs, called radiosensitisers, might improve the effectiveness of radiotherapy.

To date none of these drugs had proved to be of any significant benefit, but the Panther remained optimistic. Over coffee one day, he was waxing lyrical about the prospects of a new drug he was testing. 'You see, G-Grahame, this latest sensitiser is t-ten times as active as the previous ones.' I thought for a moment.

'But surely, Peter, ten times bugger all, is – well – still bugger all?' From behind the *Times* there came a chuckle and, as the Panther got up to leave and tiptoed to the door in his characteristic way, I could hear Lionel quietly humming Henry Mancini's theme, 'Dum – de-dum – de-dum, de-dum, d-dum.'

As Panther closed the door behind him, Lionel continued: 'There goes chief experimenter, Herr Doctor Panther. You're right, Grahame. I don't think sensitisers are going anywhere.' He put his paper down. 'By the way, you may be interested to know that you were right about the lovely Shona.'

'Oh, why?'

'Well, partially right to be precise. She has accepted my offer of another date, but there are conditions.'

'Let me guess' I pretended to think for a moment. 'Could it be something about being sober, at least at the start of the evening?'

'Well that's part of it.'

'What other conditions are there for this re-match?'

'No mention of therapy in the chemo suite.'

'Sounds reasonable to me.' I said, 'and when is Round Two?'

'Well, tonight actually.'

'Okay. Well, good luck!' I paused, then mischievously added, 'Fancy an early beer to get you in the mood?'

'Well, just a quick one – or two. See you shortly.'

Lionel and I wandered across to the bar at about six o'clock. There, sitting at a table, was Mike. In front of him sat a thick sheaf of computer printouts on a clipboard next to a half empty pint of beer. On his face were two pairs of spectacles, one pair balanced rather precariously in front of the other. I wandered over, 'Hi, Mike. Ready for another beer?' He looked up. 'Ah, Grahame, perfect timing. Yes, please.' With beers bought, Lionel and I joined him. I should have known not to ask the obvious question, but I did.

'Mike, why are you wearing *two* pairs of glasses?'

'Why aren't you?' he replied, looking at my rather more standard, single pair.

'I didn't realise it was a two pairs of spectacles evening.'

'Okay, if it makes you feel more comfortable, I'll take one pair off.' He removed one of the pairs of glasses and sat back in his chair. Lionel gestured towards the computer printouts. 'Mike, when *are* you actually going to get your Nobel Prize?'

'Well, *never,* if Grahame is going to limit me to a single pair of spectacles.' He put the second pair back on and lifted up the sheaf of papers that lay on the table in front of him. 'This ...' and he peered over the top of both his pairs of spectacles at Lionel and me to emphasise his point '... *this,* is the genetic code of the gene which protects us from cancer.' Our conversation drifted from Mike's research to more mundane topics until an hour later when, as good as his word, Lionel left after just two pints, announcing that it was time for Act Two of the Shona saga.

'So, lads. Made a breakthrough this morning yet?'

'Piss off, Edward.' Lionel didn't even look up from his paper.

'Mm. Oh look, there's a patient. You guys probably don't remember what one looks like.'

'Look, Edward, do you remember you were wondering why there were three academic senior registrars?'

'Yes, I never understood why there needed to be so many. Are you going to tell me?' Edward sounded genuinely interested.

'Well,' Lionel peered over the top of his newspaper, 'it's so that one of us can hold you down while the other two kick the holy *shit* out of you.'

Before Edward could respond I thought I would try to defuse the situation. 'By the way, Edward, how did the interview go?'

'Fine, but I didn't get the job.'

Lionel looked up, 'Sorry to hear that, Edward, genuinely sorry, because quite frankly we'd love to see the back of you.'

'Seriously, what went wrong?' I asked.

'Well, nothing went wrong it's just that there are ten candidates for every job at present. You guys would do well to remember that, because you'll be in the same position in due course.'

'What's next then, Edward?' I asked.

'Well, to be honest, Grahame, I'm seriously thinking of joining a pharmaceutical company.'

'Taking the pharma shilling, eh?' said Lionel from behind his paper.

'Yes. Excellent pay, lots of travel and no dickheads like you to contend with.' Panther entered the coffee room, and from behind the *Times* came, 'Dum – de-dum – de-dum, de-dum, de-dum.' Panther ignored his theme. 'How did the interview g-go, Edward?'

'Oh god, not you as well?' Panther looked surprised and Stephen said, 'Don't blaspheme.'

Now that Helen's white count was low she was susceptible to infection and was being reversed barrier nursed for her own protection. Doctor Keen donned the white paper gown, face-mask and gloves that were required and having followed suit we all entered the cubicle. Helen's appearance had changed dramatically in the two weeks since her treatment. She looked pale and wan, most of her hair had fallen out and thick wads of it lay on her pillow. On her bedside locker, the ever-close vomit bowl stood half full, next to the pile of soggy tissues. Gone was the make-up and vivacity, but she managed a weak smile as we entered. 'Hi, doctors. Welcome.' She then grabbed the vomit bowl and started to retch. Little vomit was produced as there was nothing in her stomach to bring up. She spat and then wiped her mouth with an already saturated tissue. A fine plastic tube now entered the left side of her neck where the milky fluid that was feeding her entered her bloodstream along with the drugs she was receiving.

Doctor Keen stood rather awkwardly at the end of the bed. 'How are you feeling?' she asked unnecessarily.

'Fine!' came Helen's response. Bless her, I thought. She was fine a few weeks ago, before we made her ill.

'Well, not *that* good – to be honest. But I'll manage. Worth it as long as it works.' She attempted a smile which immediately faded on her lips as she made a grab for the vomit bowl and retched once more.

Back outside, Doctor Keen looked at the charts, then moved on to her next patient without further comment.

***

My own research, using locally applied heat to treat patients with cancerous lumps, involved collaborating with the local veterinary college where animal researchers had been doing the same for some time. Before trying this treatment on human patients, I was keen to glean as much information as possible about how it had worked with animals. My initial introduction to the vet conducting this research had been a trifle disconcerting. He was a nice, mild-mannered man but had an obvious squint so it was always difficult to know which eye to look at when speaking to him. One moment his left eye would appear to focus on me and, while I concentrated on that, his right eye peered into the middle distance over my left shoulder. Then suddenly, without warning, the right eye would come into play while the left drifted out laterally. As a result of this, when he was speaking I found myself dodging to right and left in an effort to maintain eye contact, occasionally finding myself some yards away to one side or the other. He enthusiastically told me how he had treated a dog called Albert, which had a large tumour on its haunch. We discussed the details of the treatment and the temperatures achieved, and then came the all-important question – did it work?

'Did the cancer respond?' I asked.

'Well, that's the sad thing,' he said. 'Unfortunately we never found out because Albert was run over by a bus before we could evaluate the response.' It occurred

184

to me that vets had even more variables to contend with than we doctors had.

'How do you treat patients with sarcomas?' he once asked me. These are aggressive, nasty tumours which are often incurable and so very complicated combinations of treatments were being tried. I took a deep breath and launched into what was at the time being offered to our human patients.

'Usually we'd begin by administering six courses of anthracycline-based chemotherapy, after which we'd give a course of high-dose radiotherapy, maybe lasting seven weeks or so starting with a large field and then gradually reducing it in size. *Then,* if there has been a good response we would ask an orthopaedic surgeon to excise the site of the primary tumour and insert an adjustable prosthesis. Depending on the pathology we might then give some further chemotherapy.' I paused for a moment. 'The treatment is highly toxic and very complicated – it can last six months or more.' I stopped, satisfied with my exposition of the most up to date management of those patients. 'And you – how do you treat sarcomas in animals?' I asked.

'Oh!' he said absentmindedly. 'We shoot them.'

***

The following week Helen looked even worse. The normal constituents of her blood were no longer being produced by her bone marrow and she was being kept alive by blood and platelet transfusions. She would remain that way until her transplant engrafted: that is, *if* it engrafted. She now had those extensive bruises all over her body so characteristic of patients with bone marrow failure and, worryingly, she had a temperature.

We pondered over her charts. Doctor Keen was the first to speak. 'D'you you think it's infection or graft versus host disease? Or even a transfusion reaction?' She looked at Hamilton.

'Impossible to say, but we are treating all possible causes. She's on broad-spectrum antibiotics and high-dose steroids.'

'Any sign of her count recovering?'

'No. Not yet. But it's a bit too soon to expect that.' Hamilton smiled, perhaps just a little less confidently than on the previous week. Doctor Keen sighed, and moved on to the next patient.

***

'Dum – de-dum – de-dum, de-dum, de-dum. Here comes Chief Experimenter Obergruppenführer Doctor Herr Panther.' Lionel had spotted him at the end of the corridor coming towards us. Panther man stopped. 'Oh! Hi, ch-chaps, how're things?'

'Excellent, thank you,' said Lionel. 'The lovely Shona has agreed to be mine.'

'Oh, r-really. That *is* excellent news.'

'Yes, good news indeed and I'll buy you and Grahame a beer tonight to celebrate, if you care to come along to the bar at about five-thirty?'

'That's fine,' I said. 'Panther and I will be there but we have a tutorial at six with Mike.'

186

For the Pink Panther and myself it was exam time yet again. Tutorials with Mike were held in the bar. The deal was that he gave the tutorial and we bought him beer. This worked well for a time but inevitably some of the received wisdom was leached out into a urinal. I began to question the educational value of those sessions when I noticed that, of the three of us, one was invariably at the bar and one in the toilet, often leaving Mike delivering a tutorial to himself.

Panther and I had a number of excellent ideas on how to improve our intellects and thereby enhance our chances of passing this exam. We took to drinking in the same pub that Nobel Laureates Watson and Crick used to frequent, and Panther thought it might well prove beneficial to inhale the rarefied atmosphere of the Medical Research Council building. This was where several other Nobel Prize winners had performed their research, two of whom were still working there. We wandered the corridors, seeking inspiration and trying to identify what marked out a Nobel Laureate from the rest of us mere mortals. Panther thought that it could be something in the food and that it might help if we had lunch in the same canteen as those super-beings. Sitting quietly in a corner, where we could watch without looking out of place, we examined the other diners, trying to observe any behavioural differences that distinguished the super-intelligent from the rest of us: any little clue that might help us pass our exam, the final hurdle for us as trainee cancer doctors.

Panther had been monitoring the entrance to the canteen for some time when suddenly he stopped eating and froze, his macaroni-laden fork poised between plate and mouth. After a brief pause, without taking his eyes off the man who had just entered, he whispered urgently, 'There he is! That's Milstein.'

'What? The piano maker?'

'No, you idiot! That's Bechstein. Milstein's the most recent prize-winner. The man who discovered monoclonal antibodies!'

'Oh!'

'Look, he's getting his lunch.'

'What's he ordered?' I asked quietly.

Panther squinted at the Nobel Laureate's red plastic tray. 'Looks like porridge, but very pale.'

'No. I think it's macaroni.'

'That's exactly what we've got! So that's no help.'

'No, Peter. That's fine. It demonstrates that nutritionally we are at one with a Nobel Prize winner.'

'What's he ordering now?'

'Just a coffee.'

Then came the Pentecostal moment, the instant of enlightenment. Panther could barely contain his excitement. '*Look!* That's it. *That's it*. He's put his saucer on top of the cup.' Panther repeated his observation slowly, 'The – saucer – is – on – *top* – of – the – cup. Not underneath it like everyone else. That's it. *That's* the difference between a Nobel prize winner and us.'

The Pink one immediately moved his saucer from underneath his cup and surreptitiously placed it on top, while I followed suit.

***

'Grahame, I'm away this weekend, I think you're on call?' Hamilton looked at me over the top of his mug from which he was taking noisy sips of coffee. We were in the doctors' office on one of the two cancer wards, having completed a Friday afternoon pre-weekend ward round. 'Yes, that's right. Anything you want me to do particularly?'

'Well, as you know I'm concerned about Helen. Her transplant doesn't seem to have taken and her general condition is not good.'

'Yes I know, and her temperature's still unexplained.'

'I think we should change her antibiotics today, and if her temperature's not down tomorrow add anti-fungals, and then, on Sunday, if there's no improvement, start antivirals. I don't think there's anything to lose at this stage. It's still only a month since the transplant and hopefully she may still engraft.'

'Okay, that's fine. I'll keep a close eye on her.'

'If you're concerned, you'd better call Doctor Keen.' He looked up at me, finished his coffee and with a cheery, 'Have a nice weekend,' left the room.

That weekend I adjusted Helen's therapy as we had agreed, but her condition did not improve. At some stage over the weekend a series of visitors started to appear. I asked her why she hadn't had visitors before. 'I didn't want to tell anyone,' she explained. 'You know, I thought I'd just get the treatment then get back to work, you know. But now that things aren't looking so good I thought I'd better let someone know what's goin' on. You know.' She tried to smile but the corners of her mouth were cracked and sore and she winced with the pain. 'Any sign of the transplant working yet?' she asked.

'Not yet,' I said, 'but it's early days and we'll check again on Monday.' I tried to sound optimistic, but knew I hadn't fooled her for a moment.

'Oh!' she said and turned her attention back to the magazine she was reading.

The inevitable happened and after a slow but inexorable decline she died three weeks later. I never discovered what killed her – the cancer or the treatment.

***

Panther and I were both delighted to pass the final fellowship examination. Prof. even popped his head round the door of our office, after trying several other rooms before finding the correct one. I was sitting there alone and jumped to my feet at this unexpected visitation. 'Well done, Grahame,' he said with a change in facial expression that was his attempt at a smile. 'I don't like any of *my* team to fail the exam.' His gaze then fell on the large soft toy that was a pink panther, sitting in one of the chairs. 'What's that panther doing there?' he asked. Prof. very rarely entered our territory and, like Lionel some weeks before, I was caught off-guard so, unsure how to respond, I decided to pretend ignorance. 'What panther would that be, Prof?'

'That pink one. The one over there,' he replied pointing at the chair which Peter normally occupied.

'Oh, *that* pink panther – No idea, Prof.'

He shook his head grumpily. 'Hmm, it's no wonder we never get any decent work done,' he muttered as he left.

***

'It's not fair. It's just not fair! Why should I have to be on-call over Easter weekend? Why can't one of you two do it?' Ruth's piercing gaze darted from the Panther to me and then back again. I looked down, pretending to concentrate on the papers which lay strewn untidily on the desk in front of me. The problem was that the Pope had left us, having been appointed to a consultant post, and his replacement was a woman.

There had never been a female on the academic team before and we were all horrified. A girl in the chaps' room? It was unthinkable. The Pope might have had his idiosyncrasies about blaspheming and standards of dress, but he didn't complain when Lionel had a hangover, needed to go for a smoke, broke wind or waxed lyrical about the bodily charms of the lovely Shona. Neither did he consider it strange that the Panther, a confirmed bachelor, regularly brought his dirty washing in and used the sluice as a launderette. Now, that would all have to change. Not only did we have a girl on the team, but Ruth was a feisty female. Although short in stature, at only just over five foot, she punched well above her weight. She had short, dark bobbed hair, piercing green eyes that none of us liked to maintain eye contact with for too long in case we were turned to stone, and she didn't suffer fools gladly, a collective noun she reserved exclusively for men.

'It's because I'm a woman, isn't it? And that I'm new. Well, I'm not having it.' Her gaze fell on the Panther and I could almost see two holes beginning to burn in his forehead, like paper beginning to char when you focus sunlight on it with a magnifying glass. '*Well*? What are you going to do about it?' Ruth momentarily ceased her polemic, placed her hands on her hips and waited for an answer.

The Panther – a mild-mannered man – was visibly shaken by this assault. It was his job to organise the on-call rota. He started his defence hesitantly. 'R-Ruth, that's j-just the way it fell. It was arranged before you had arrived. Is there a problem?'

'Well, yes actually, there is. It's not fair that you've put me on call when I still live in London and had plans for Easter.' Ruth was standing in the doorway, her hands still on her hips, effectively blocking the only exit from our room. Panther briefly glanced up at the skylight but quickly realised that escape by that route was quite impossible. Sensing that resistance was futile, the Panther capitulated, 'Well I suppose *I* could do it? Grahame! Could you do the Friday?' And so it was agreed. Round one to Ruth.

Life was growing ever more complicated. Not only did we have to avoid the coffee room when the Professor

192

was there, but now we had to avoid Ruth as well. Life was becoming hard for the chaps on the academic team. Lionel, with his room at the far end of the department, had not yet been exposed to the Ruth effect and initially thought we were exaggerating the power of this feisty female: that is, until *he* got into the ring with her.

A few days later I found Lionel in the coffee room nursing his wounds – well, his head to be precise. 'Lionel, my dear chap, you look absolutely awful,' I said.

'It's even worse than it looks, Grahame. You were quite right about the diminutive feisty one.'

'Would it help if you talked about it?'

'Yes, thank you, Grahame, but to be honest I think I need more than counselling. A one-way ticket to Timbuctoo might be more appropriate. I suspect I'll be doing Ruth's on call for the next fifty years.'

'My dear chap! What on earth has happened to make you consider such a thing?'

'I think I might quite possibly have had sex with the diminutive one.'

'Oh my hat. That's not good, Lionel. You'd better tell me all.'

'Top up my coffee, would you.'

It transpired that the previous night Lionel had fallen out with the lovely Shona, and spent the rest of the evening drowning his sorrows in traditional fashion at the social club. At the end of the evening, finding himself unable to navigate his way home, he did the only sensible thing and decided to bed down in the chemotherapy suite. Because of the lateness of the hour and his degree of inebriation he had neglected to set the alarm clock that he habitually kept hidden at the back of the room for just such exigencies as this. Thus at eight-thirty next morning, when Ruth arrived to prepare the day's chemotherapy, Lionel was to be discovered sound asleep in one of the beds, snoring loudly, still wearing his shirt, tie and sports jacket, with the lower part of his body beneath a blanket.

Outraged, Ruth stormed over to where he lay. 'Lionel! What on *earth* are you doing here?' There was no response. 'Lionel!' she shouted, but there was still no reaction, just some gentle snoring, so she decided to give him a nudge. Because of her diminutive stature, she had to come quite close to him and was startled when Lionel's unconscious response was to put one arm around her shoulder.

'Lionel! For heaven's sake, wake up.' Still fast asleep, Lionel then made an attempt to roll over and in doing so his arm slipped from her shoulder to form an arm-lock around her neck and the more Ruth struggled, the tighter became his embrace. Ruth now only had one foot on the floor and her upper body was on the bed. She did the only thing she could: she punched him hard in the genitals. Still effectively anaesthetised by the large quantities of beer consumed the previous night, Lionel's initial response was to smile as he blearily opened his eyes and looked around. Gradually he registered his surroundings and noted that he was in the chemotherapy suite. Yes, he thought, I've been here before. Then he recalled bedding down there after being helped to leave the social club at closing time. But who was this in bed beside him? Shona had stormed off mid-evening; he was fairly sure of that, so who could this be? With a slight leer and a small belch he turned and to his surprise saw Ruth's head firmly trapped in his right armpit. After a moment of disbelief the dreadfulness of the situation suddenly registered and he screamed. '*Aaaarh*!' He took a second look but the situation hadn't changed: it definitely was Ruth who was lying half-off and half-on the bed right beside him. He was now wide-awake and yelled again, this time more loudly, '*Aaaaaarh*!'

'Lionel, stop it! Wake up. You stink of stale beer and tobacco.'

'Ruth, what on earth are *you* doing here?' He let his grip loosen and Ruth took the opportunity to wriggle her head from under his armpit and immediately stepped back several feet in order to be well out of reach.

'Lionel, this is outrageous. Why are you sleeping in the chemotherapy suite?' Lionel was still somewhat disorientated and endeavouring to grasp the gravity of the situation.

'Ruth, what on earth's happened? Did I sleep with you?'

'You *must be joking.* I wouldn't sleep with you if you were the last man on earth. For god's sake, get up and get out of here at once. I'm expecting my first patient for chemotherapy soon.' Lionel needed no second invitation and swung his legs out from under the blanket to reveal a complete absence of clothing from the waist down.

'Oh no! Where are my trousers?' He gazed with disbelief at his groin and legs before adding, 'And my underpants! Oh no!'

On registering the unwelcome picture of Lionel's genitalia gently swinging from the side of the bed Ruth immediately looked in the opposite direction. 'My god! What a sight. For heaven's sake, put your clothes on.'

Lionel tucked his shirt-tail between his legs to retain some remnant of modesty and looked around for some sign of his garments.

'I think you'll find your clothes under the bed.' Ruth had seen evidence of the missing items of apparel when she had been in the arm-lock.

'Thanks, Ruth.' Lionel dragged his clothes on as rapidly as he could but was hampered considerably by having less than perfect balance.

That had been two hours ago. Now, Lionel was on his second pot of coffee and when I entered he had been trying, without success, to concentrate on the newspaper which he was holding in front of his face to mask its greenish tinge.

I commiserated with him. 'Gosh, Lionel! That must have been awful – to wake up and think you'd seduced the feisty one.'

'God, it doesn't bear thinking about. I got a mouthful, I can tell you.' Lionel glanced at his watch. 'Well, I think I'd better get out of here before she arrives.' But it was too late. Just as he said this, the door opened and in walked Ruth. Lionel quickly raised his newspaper in a vain attempt to hide, but to no avail.

'I know that's you, Lionel. There's no point in trying to hide.' Lionel put the paper down. 'What on earth were you doing sleeping in the chemotherapy suite? You must have been totally inebriated.'

Any attempt at mentation precipitated a sharp pain behind Lionel's eyes, and he was far from being at his intellectual best, but throughout this tirade Lionel had been considering his options and had come to the conclusion that his best defence lay in attack. He was also acutely aware how harshly he had criticised the rest of us for not standing up to the feisty one. So he started his defence confidently and, with an almost nonchalant look in Ruth's direction, said, 'Oh, I don't know, Ruth. I probably had one or two beers while working late last night. We often sleep in the chemotherapy room when we've been working late, don't we, Grahame?'

I didn't want to get involved in this altercation as I knew there could be only one winner, and that wasn't going to be Lionel. So, after ascertaining that Ruth wasn't looking at me I just nodded silently. 'And, Ruth. *I say.* You're a one, trying to get into bed with me?' Lionel attempted a charming smile which, upon observing Ruth's face, changed into a leer and then to an expression of sheer and utter terror.

'Working late? Don't make me laugh. You were totally plastered. You complete idiot, you nearly throttled me. There you were, like some tramp, reeking of beer and stale tobacco, snoring like a constipated pig. I can tell you that if I ever find you there again, you'll have a drip put up and a lethal dose of chemotherapy given before I bother to wake you. That'll serve you right.' She glanced in my direction, 'Don't you agree, Grahame?'

I was now in a delicate position as I wanted to support Lionel but didn't want a tongue-lashing from Ruth. I decided to opt for diplomacy. 'Well, I think that might be a trifle harsh, Ruth.'

She appeared not to hear my response since she simply repeated the question, yet more emphatically. '*Don't you agree, Grahame*?'

'Absolutely right, Ruth. With you on that one. Couldn't agree more,' I concurred.

'You see? Grahame agrees. Don't you, Grahame?' There was silence. '*Well*?' She looked at me and I could feel her gaze penetrating to my very soul.

'Absolutely. Spot on, as always, Ruth.' I said.

'I'm fed up with you guys just abusing me because I'm the only female in the team.' Now Lionel and I were completely lost. We looked at each other totally bemused. Lionel made an attempt to raise his paper again.

'Don't you try to read that paper. I haven't finished.'

Lionel had had enough. His genitals were starting to ache by now from the blow delivered by Ruth earlier that morning, so he threw in the towel and capitulated.

'Sorry, Ruth,' he said, and for some unknown reason I echoed him.

'Sorry, Ruth.'

'Well I think it's appalling the way you all behave. Of you all, Peter's the only one with some semblance of normality. Where is he anyway?'

'Peter?' said Lionel, quite at a loss.

'Yes, Peter. You know? Peter! *Your colleague*.' It suddenly dawned on Lionel to whom she was referring.

'Oh, you mean the *Panther*? – No idea.'

'That's another thing. These stupid names have got to stop. And you'd better not have a name for me.'

'Wouldn't dream of it.' said Lionel, staring intently at his shoes.

'This is getting serious,' said Lionel over a beer the following night. 'The diminutive feisty one is taking over. Even the Prof. is scared of her.'

'You haven't heard the w-worst,' said Panther. 'Apparently she is going on an *assertiveness* course.'

'*What*? Ruth needing to be more assertive? I don't believe it.' I said.

'A-apparently, and the Prof. has agreed. She claimed she needed it to stand up to the domineering male members of the team.'

'What *we* need is a self-defence course.' I added.

'I agree with that: her right hook is a killer. My bollocks are still aching,' said Lionel with a grimace.

'What we really n-need, chaps,' said the Panther, 'is to escape. What *we* need are consultant posts.'

Panther was right. We had all now been in the department for some years, had passed our exams and urgently needed to start looking for consultant jobs. These were highly competitive, as Edward had discovered.

Lionel took up the challenge. 'I know. We'll start an Escape Committee. First thing tomorrow morning, we'll start tunnelling our way out to freedom.' After several pints, this seemed a truly excellent idea and we went home content that we had solved our mutual problem.

'Morning, Edward,' I said.

'Morning, chaps.' Edward poured himself a coffee, then sat down and picked up a magazine. Lionel and I lowered our papers and looked at one another, somewhat puzzled. 'Haven't you forgotten something, Edward?' asked Lionel.

'What do you mean?'

'Well, you've been in the room nearly a minute and you haven't made any gratuitously derogatory remarks about us yet. My dear chap, are you feeling unwell?'

'No. Actually, I've never felt better. The die is cast. I have accepted a job in the pharmaceutical industry. I no longer need to annoy you guys, as my future is safe. No more fruitless interviews for *me*.' He lifted his cup, a smile rapidly spreading across his face. Lionel was quite taken aback.

'Gosh, Edward, I suppose we should congratulate you, but who will we be able to wind up when you've left?'

'Ah, you see, you *will* miss me. And quite possibly you'll have to do a bit more work as well.'

'No time for that. We're thinkers. Boundaries to push forward, papers to publish and glittering prizes to win,' I said.

'By the way,' interposed Edward, changing the subject, 'I gather that all of you guys are scared stiff of the new girl, Ruth?'

'Nonsense,' came Lionel's voice from behind the *Times.*

Just then the door opened and Ruth entered along with the Panther.

'Ah, Ruth, we were just talking about you.' Edward looked across at Lionel and me and positively simpered. 'I was saying how very much more *civilised* the academic team have become since you've arrived.'

'A hard job, I can tell you.' Ruth poured herself a coffee and took a seat. 'Congratulations by the way. Hear you've got a job in Pharma.'

'Thanks, Ruth. Yes, I'll be out of here soon, unlike some others in this room.' Edward was enjoying having the upper hand for once.

Ruth continued. 'By the way, Lionel, I spoke to Prof. and he's happy to change the rota as I suggested, so you're doing this weekend. Okay?' Lionel began to bristle and his eyes sparked but just as quickly the flame died out as he recalled the unpleasant memory of being found trouserless in the chemotherapy suite.

'That's fine,' he murmured.

'Now,' Ruth went on, 'I'm away on my course next week so one of you, I don't mind who, will have to look after the wards.'

She glanced sideways at the Panther, who in a moment of sheer madness responded by saying, 'Yes, M-miss.' Lionel and I could hardly believe that he had said this. This was a reckless and decidedly unwise attempt at humour.

Ruth spun round to look at the Panther directly, 'I *beg* your pardon?'

'F-fine, I'll do it.' Panther looked at the floor, both hands carefully placed over his genitalia, like a footballer defending a free kick.

Later, back in our room, we held the first meeting of the Escape Committee. The Panther wrote along the top of the white board in bold letters, 'Escape Committee'. Underneath there were three columns, one headed 'Tunnels', the next had a tick or cross in it, indicating if the tunnel was open or had been closed, and the third had the names of the escapees in a particular tunnel at any one time.

Every week we scoured the jobs section of the BMJ and listed all posts advertised, crossing them off as they were filled.

The following week, sitting in the Escape Committee room, as we had renamed our office, the Panther announced secretively, 'I've put two jobs on the list, chaps. Both tunnels open. May be worth investigating. One tunnel leads to Coventry, the other Sheffield.'

'Where *are* they?' asked Lionel, aghast.

'Somewhere in the Midlands, I think.' I said.

'Where are the Midlands?'

'Well, you go along the corridor to the main entrance, turn left and head north-west for about a hundred miles,' I explained. 'Now, I think it's coffee time. Please check the corridor, Panther, would you?' After ascertaining that neither the Prof. nor the feisty diminutive one was in the vicinity of the coffee room, Panther and I entered, just ahead of Edward, who said with a smile, 'I've come to have a final cup of coffee with you chaps.' He looked different now that he was wearing a suit, but the most noticeable feature was the fact that on his head was a hat, a fedora to be precise. It was deep blue and he had pulled it down over his left eye in an attempt to make himself look a bit like Warren Beatty. 'What on *earth* is that?' I asked.

'Well, Grahame, it's called a hat. It's my new image. Now that I have a job, unlike any of *you lot*, I might add, I thought I'd sharpen up my appearance a bit. You chaps would benefit from doing the same. Don't you chaps agree that I look a bit like Warren Beatty?'

'M-more like Shirley Bassey,' said Panther. 'Anyway, Edward,' he continued, 'we're academics. We don't need to be smart, not like you salesmen.' Ascerbic, I thought, even for the Panther.

'You know, for a moment I thought I might miss you, but now I know I won't. Edward removed his hat and placed it on a vacant seat while he poured himself a coffee. Just then Lionel flung the door open, 'Edward, heard it was your last day. Thought I'd come to make peace and say what a nice caring person you really are. Pour me a coffee, would you?' So saying, he sat down heavily on the chair where Edward had just put his hat. Edward looked aghast, for a moment totally unable to articulate before crying out: 'Hey! You've just sat on my hat! Get up.' Lionel looked genuinely surprised. 'What hat?'

'Mine, you idiot, you've just sat on my new hat.' Lionel gradually raised his considerable bulk from the seat and looked down at the blue pancake that just a moment ago had been a stylish fedora. He was genuinely surprised.

'Oh no. I didn't realise. Gosh, Edward, I'm so sorry.' Lionel then picked up the flattened headgear and, after briefly orientating it, punched it hard several times in an attempt to restore it to its original shape. It then took on the appearance of a ten-gallon cowboy hat. You might imagine that it would be impossible to make this situation worse but somehow Lionel did. Not satisfied with the result thus far, he hit the blue felt several more times in an effort to recreate its original form until ultimately it resembled a dead cat. Then, like a superior milliner, Lionel brushed it with the back of his hand, and offered it with a final flourish, to Edward who by this time was beside himself.

'You've ruined it.'

'No I haven't. It looks fine now, as good as new.' Then Lionel added, 'Sorry.'

'You guys are just the pits. Here's your coffee. I'm off.'

'Bye, Edward.'

'Good luck, Edward,' and as the door closed behind him all of us, including Ruth, who had uttered these last words, erupted in uncontrollable laughter. Tears were running down my cheeks when the door opened and Prof. entered. He paused and looked at the three of us. 'Have I missed something?'

'Edward's last day, Prof.,' I said, surreptitiously wiping my eyes.

'Don't see what's so funny about that. Hmm. Not surprising no work ever gets done here.' The Prof. sat down. We were now in a difficult position, the whole academic team being trapped in the coffee room with the

204

Professor, a potentially volatile situation. For us all to file out together would have looked inexcusably rude. Lionel was first off the mark and, mumbling something about having to give a tutorial, got up to leave. Following his cue, before the diminutive one could put in her reason for leaving, Panther and I followed suit with a bright, 'Well, we'd better get back to work,' The feisty one was thus stuck in the company of the Prof. for at least fifteen minutes. As we left, we both gave her a wry smile. Her response was a glacial stare which chilled us to our very souls.

The three of us settled into the process of applying for consultant posts as gradually the whiteboard filled up with tunnels: some open or being dug, while some were closed, or caved in, as Lionel put it. When shortlisted, we attended interviews, and not infrequently were in competition for the same job. I was invited to apply for a post at the hospital in north London where I had begun my training and, after a disastrous interview, was not appointed.

Lionel, never one to do what was expected of him, declared his intention of disappearing off to Australia. I suspected that this was something to do with his on-off relationship with the lovely Shona who apparently blamed his behaviour, at least in part, on his peers, particularly me. When Lionel informed me of this, over a beer one night, I was outraged. 'Lionel, that's nonsense, and you know it!' I said.

'Maybe, but that's what the lovely Shona thinks.' Lionel smiled as he lifted his pint and directed it towards the left hand corner of his mouth.

'How on *earth* did she get that idea?'

'Well, to be honest, I may have been somewhat sparing with the truth, but after she got to hear about the trouser free episode and my antics with the diminutive feisty one, she got a trifle upset, so I had to think of some story to get myself off the hook and I immediately thought of you.' Lionel smiled as he placed his glass down unsteadily on the table.

'Lionel, you're an absolute bastard. I don't think I want to know what story you told her.'

'That's a good job because it was rather convoluted and I can't remember it myself. But the important thing is that it worked, and after I had explained that everything was your fault, the lovely Shona fell into my arms, saying that she'd obviously misjudged me.'

'Oh good. I'm pleased about that.'

'I should add that she did say some fairly uncomplimentary things about you though.' Lionel paused. 'The problem was I then got a bit carried away with the moment and I think I asked her to marry me.'

'What d'you mean, you *think*?' Gosh, Lionel. Why is it that your memory is so vague when it comes to important life events such as this?'

'Well, it's when I'm pissed, of course. Anyway, I must have proposed, because about half an hour later, when my mind came back into focus, the lovely Shona was extremely excited and talking about rings and churches and things. So, putting two and two together, I reckoned I must have proposed and she must have accepted. There was one proviso though.'

'Oh yes? And what might that have been?' I said, fearing that it might involve me.

'Well, she insisted that I put several thousand miles between myself, or should I say ourselves and you and the Panther.'

'Ridiculous, I hope you refused.'

'No. I agreed and applied for a job in Melbourne the next day. Grahame, I *had* to. It wasn't just that the lovely one wanted to put a significant distance between you and me; the feisty one was also beginning to show signs of affection towards me.'

'Gosh, that's harsh. What do you mean, "signs of affection?"'

'Well initially after the little unpleasantness of the trouserless episode she couldn't have been any nastier, which I could cope with, but after a while she started to be quite affectionate and to reminisce about the event with increasing fondness. I was beginning to panic. I was scared that she would order me to have sex with her, and I knew I wouldn't be able to refuse, particularly now she's completed the assertiveness course.'

'So, you're running away from the feisty one? That's quite pathetic.'

'Wouldn't you, if you could?'

'Absolutely.'

'So there you are, I'm off to the Antipodes in six weeks' time.'

'With the lovely one in tow.'

'Yes indeed.' Lionel's glass once again headed to the corner of his mouth.

'When are you getting married? I'll need to make sure I'm free.'

'Ah, well there's a bit of a problem there. We not going to get married until we're in Oz.'

'Why?'

'Well, to be honest, the lovely one didn't want either you or the Panther to be anywhere in the vicinity at that important moment in her life.'

Lionel smiled, blew a cloud of pipe smoke up to the ceiling of the bar and said, 'Well, I'm off to the chemo suite. I've booked a bed there tonight.'

'Beware the diminutive feisty one, and remember to set your alarm,' I advised as he headed unsteadily to the door.

Lionel departed for Australia, and within a few months the Panther was appointed to a prestigious post in the south-west of England, while I had been shortlisted for a consultant post in Edinburgh – or Auld Reekie, as Robert Burns had known it.

***

At the west end of Edinburgh's Georgian New Town, just fifty yards south of Princes Street lies Drumsheugh Gardens. This is a pleasant green enclave surrounded by what were once grand town houses, now mostly converted to offices and the occasional hotel. No. 11 was the headquarters of Lothian Health Board and it was here that the interviews for two consultant Oncologists were to be held. It was the fourth day of December; the cold streets were damp and glistening from the early morning drizzle, while the heady smell of hops – the reek – hung heavily in the stagnant air. Walking to my appointment, from the slightly run-down hotel in Royal Circus where I was staying, I passed through the financial heart of Scotland's capital city. I shared the busy pavements with newsvendors, insurance clerks, pretty office girls and bowler-hatted bankers. I jostled with businessmen and lawyers, their umbrellas tightly furled, briskly striding in and out of grey buildings with grand facades. Black cabs cruised the wide streets, or loitered outside hotels and offices, and in the early morning half-light their yellow FOR HIRE signs shone bright and welcoming. I detected the feel, the indescribable ambience of a capital city and felt somehow reassured and at home, almost as though I was back in London.

The dingy entrance to No. 11 hadn't been decorated for many years and smelt decidedly musty. Once inside, I discovered a hatch to my left and, after introducing myself to a lady who was stationed there, I was directed up a narrow flight of stairs to where there was a small landing. There, sellotaped to a door, was a sign written in blue felt-tip print stating simply INTERVIEWS, which I took to mean that this was the waiting room. I gingerly opened the door to discover eight other hopeful candidates sitting glumly around the periphery of this rather cramped room, all dressed in suits and looking decidedly ill-at-ease. I recognised several of them from previous such excursions and exchanged subdued greetings with those I knew, before I took the one remaining vacant seat.

From ten o'clock onwards, a pleasant middle-aged lady would enter our cell every half hour, and call out a name. Then, to a mumbled chorus – albeit not entirely sincere – of 'good luck', from the rest of us, one of our group would grudgingly leave the room. Then, for all but the two successful candidates, that whole process was destined to be repeated in some other location at a later date. Gradually, the numbers dwindled until it was my own turn.

'Doctor Howard?' asked the lady.

'That'll be me,' I said with a smile and with a final glance at those left in the waiting room I followed the lady back out to the landing and up a short flight of stairs. There she opened a door and I entered a large ornate Georgian drawing room. I barely registered the fine cornice and marble fireplace, as on my right was a long narrow table behind which were ranged, shoulder to shoulder, the panel of fifteen senior consultants. Opposite them was a solitary, lonely chair to which I was directed. I wondered briefly how many times I had been in such a position; taking the vacant chair opposite a gallery of inquisitors, and I was reminded of my interview at St Thomas' Hospital fifteen years before.

After brief introductions, I was asked a variety of questions which I answered to the best of my ability. My half hour up, I was formally thanked for attending and promptly ushered out. Outside in Drumsheugh Gardens, the sun had broken through the drab winter mist and I was in reasonably high spirits as I strolled the short distance to Princes Street. I headed for an attractive-looking pub I had identified earlier, simply called One Rutland Place, and there ordered the first of several beers. With two local candidates, it seemed unthinkable that I would be successful; but to my amazement I was. About a year after I had taken up my post, one of the members of the interview panel, a Professor of Surgery, confided in me that it had been the most acrimonious appointment committee that he'd ever sat on. He went on to say, 'But we got who we wanted in the end,' adding with a wry smile, 'but I won't say who *we* were!'

PART 4

TO PASTURES NEW

The handsome young man gazed enquiringly at me from the opposite side of my desk. It was nine years since my interview in Drumsheugh Gardens and I had settled into the busy, relentless routine that was being a teaching hospital consultant. I was in my Monday afternoon outpatient session designated specifically for men with testicular cancer, or 'ball boys' – as one of the trainees had labelled them. This intelligent looking, twenty five year old was one such patient. On first inspection he appeared like any other man with testicular cancer. He was clad in designer jeans and a T-shirt, over which he wore an expensive-looking brown leather jacket: indeed, he would not have looked out of place wandering around Jenner's department store in Princes Street. However, what made him stand out from the others in my clinic that afternoon was the fact that he was sporting decidedly non-designer handcuffs. In addition, from his left wrist hung a long chain attaching him to one of the two warders who were now sitting uneasily on either side of him. Not only was he well dressed but his personal appearance gave no hint of a villainous or violent nature. Short black hair topped a clean-shaven, comely face, and there was a strong smell of aftershave about his person.

He seemed gentle and friendly enough and so, secure in the knowledge that Sister Williams was present, I somewhat haughtily insisted that his handcuffs be removed, since I would need to examine him, and that the prison officers should leave the room to ensure patient confidentiality.

Once unfettered, he related, in a measured and educated voice, how he had discovered a lump in his testicle and subsequently he had undergone an operation to remove it. That had been just a week before. I glanced towards the ever-present Sister Williams, hovering discreetly near the door, ready to assist at any time. Although in her early sixties and small in stature, she had a certain presence, an aura that was more befitting a sumo wrestler than an outpatient nursing sister: she was not a woman to be trifled with. Although her presence was reassuring, as I listened to my patient's story, I found my gaze wandering around the room assessing possible escape routes and I began to question the wisdom of asking the warders, particularly the burly tattooed woman, to leave the room.

I was considering how difficult it would be for my patient to climb through the window when there came a quiet knock on the clinic room door. Sister Williams opened it a fraction. There, a nurse stood beckoning and my minder left the clinic, closing the door behind her. Now I was alone with the prisoner. I had no idea what his crime had been. It could have been something non-violent, like fraud or insider-trading but, for all I knew, he might have been convicted for the serial assault and murder of consultant oncologists. I began to feel distinctly uneasy and apprehensive.

'Right, Mr O'Riley, would you mind jumping on the couch, please, so that I can have a quick look at you?'

'No problem, Doc.'

I noted the scars on his arms at previous injection sites and made a mental note that venous access might be a problem if chemotherapy proved to be necessary. Over his left groin was a small surgical wound below which his scrotum had the bluish tinge of a resolving bruise. I concluded my examination as rapidly as possible. 'That's fine. Pop your things on again, please,' I said and returned to my desk where a few moments later, now fully dressed, he was once again seated opposite me.

'You know you've had a testicle removed and that it was swollen because it had a cancer in it. It's called a teratoma and the good news is that it is almost always curable.' I paused for a moment. He was looking at me in a slightly detached, uninterested way. 'It's possible that you won't need any further treatment at all, but that depends on whether or not the disease has spread. If it hasn't then we'll just follow you up closely, if it *has* spread you'll need some chemotherapy.' I paused again, 'Is that clear so far?'

'Yes, Doc. So what do we do now?'

'Well, we need to perform some further investigations: a scan and some blood tests, and I'll see you again with the results next week. If they're abnormal you'll need treatment.'

'Fine, Doc,' he paused for a moment, then looked directly at me. 'But I am going to be all right, aren't I?' Concern now registered on his face, the seriousness of the situation and the potential for needing treatment beginning to dawn on him.

'Yes. The outlook's excellent, either way,' I reassured him. The door opened and Sister entered. I tried not to look too relieved. 'Ah, Sister, we're just finishing. Could you ask the warders to come back in, please.' A moment later, chained and cuffed again, he was led back out into the waiting room. As the door closed I heaved a sigh of relief.

'Sister! What on earth did you do that for? You left me alone with a criminal, a desperado! He could have assaulted me, or taken me hostage …' I hesitated lost for words, '… or *anything*.'

'Oh, *Doctor* Howard, don't be so melodramatic.' She looked at me with that exasperated expression a mother displays to her naughty child. 'You were perfectly safe with him.'

'How can you be so sure? We've no idea what crimes he may have perpetrated. You know we're not allowed to ask. He could be a violent doctor-killer!'

'Don't be so ridiculous. He's in for drug offences and he's non-violent.'

'How do you know?'

'Oh, that's easy. I just said to the warders, "Drugs, I presume?" and they nodded!'

The following week Larry O'Riley was back in my clinic. On this occasion my moral qualms had abated

218

considerably and I decided that it would be quite acceptable for him to remain handcuffed and for the warders to stay in the room with him for the duration of the interview.

'Well, I'm afraid that the scan shows some enlarged lymph nodes in your abdomen and also some spread of the disease to your lungs. The other abnormality we've identified is that your tumour markers – those are the blood tests – are raised. Now there's nothing surprising about that but they are really quite high. Your cancer should still be curable but it does mean that you'll require treatment with chemotherapy.' As I paused for a moment I thought that at least his compliance should be good, remembering a drug addict I had recently treated whose life was so chaotic that he rarely attended when he was supposed to.

'The scan also showed some metal in your left thigh. Have you had an operation there?'

'No, Doc. That's a bread knife.'

'A bread knife?'

'Yeah. Not a whole one obviously, just the tip of one.' I looked up at him, my puzzled expression enough to prompt him to volunteer some further details.

'I was stabbed and the end of the knife broke off. Years ago that was and it's been there ever since.'

'Was it a fight?' As soon as I had said this I realised the stupidity of my question as it seemed safe to assume there was no other reason for inserting a breadknife into someone's thigh. I conjured up the picture of a desperate fight in some dark alley, like a scene from *West Side Story*.

'Well, not really. My girlfriend stabbed me one night when I arrived home pissed. She thought I'd been with another woman.' All this was stated in a matter-of-fact fashion as though such an incident was nothing out of the ordinary in any relationship. Firm but fair, I thought.

'Oh?' I said and deciding to change the subject and continue with the business of the interview.

'One of the side-effects of the treatment is that it will affect your sperm count. It should recover but we always advise storing a sperm sample prior to starting chemotherapy.'

'Okay, Doc. Whatever you say.'

'Under the circumstances it might be best if you produced a specimen when we admit you for your first cycle of treatment.'

'Be a bit difficult in these, Doc,' he said, looking down with a slight smile at his handcuffs. I glanced at the two warders. One was a pleasant, benign-looking man in his fifties, the other a burly woman. She was a fearsome-looking character, probably only in her third decade but prematurely aged by imbibing industrial quantities of alcohol and smoking upwards of forty cigarettes a day since she was a teenager. The tattoos down her arms seemed to depict scenes from the end of the world and visions of hell; her girth was twice that of her male colleague and on her makeup-free face she bore a visage that would have stopped an express train. This was not a woman to mess with, nor was she someone you would want to be handcuffed to while attempting to produce a sperm sample.

'What security measures will be necessary while Mr O'Riley is in hospital?' I enquired.

'He'll need to be handcuffed at all times and there will be one or two prison officers present night and day.'

'Okay. Well, we'll just have to sort something out when you're admitted.' I didn't want to go into the details of how a sperm sample could possibly be produced while being handcuffed to either of those two.

***

That evening, after my clinic, I drove from Edinburgh to West Lothian and it was with some trepidation that I steered my Alfa Romeo left, off the main road, to enter the three-quarter mile driveway that led to Riddell House. Passing through the ever-open, ivy-strewn wrought iron gates, I began to negotiate the numerous potholes in this narrow, meandering lane. To my right were mature but unkempt rhododendron bushes, some fifteen feet high, whereas on my left there was an unbroken vista across the gentle undulations of the West Lothian countryside. Among the bright reds and browns of the woodlands, where patches of dashing autumn colours still clung to the skeletal branches of beeches and sycamores, lay a farmland patchwork. There, stubbly yellow wheat fields scattered with rolls of autumn straw, nestled beside grassland on which cattle and sheep grazed peacefully. Half a mile or so further along the lane, the rhododendrons gave way to a small clearing on which stood two single-storey farm cottages, from the chimneys of which drifted the pleasing aroma of wood smoke. Then, after a gently sweeping right-hand turn, the lane snaked past a large, leafless oak tree before my tyres crunched on the large crescent-shaped expanse of gravel which lay directly in front of Riddell House itself.

I parked neatly in front of this two-storey Georgian mansion. Built solidly of freestone, it echoed the Palladian grandeur of many of the houses in Edinburgh's New Town. But this was a stately country house, once at the centre of several hundred acres of prime West Lothian farmland. After a brief glance at the reddening evening panorama, I entered what had once been an imposing vestibule. Now, just inside the door, where in days past a flunkey would have taken my hat and coat, stood a solitary Formica table on which were scattered information leaflets about the Foundation that now ran this Home for the benefit of its thirty residents, a mix of the young chronic sick and those suffering from cancer. Above the fireplace, where once a portrait would have hung, was a glum noticeboard listing nursing shifts for the month, along with the results of a long-past raffle. The floor was surfaced with fine red Victorian tiles, running down the middle of which was a strip of non-slip rubber to allow safe passage for wheelchairs and Zimmer frames. I passed through an impressive oak doorway and into a large sitting room dominated by a huge stone fireplace, now cold and empty.

Despite the absence of a fire, the room was warm and bright. Dotted around, seemingly at random, in seats or wheelchairs, were about a dozen residents. A collection of young and old: some knitting, some doing jigsaws and others gazing, unseeingly at the ever-present television. Joe was sitting in his wheel chair, as far away from the television as the geography of the room would allow. He had his back to it and was endeavouring to read a dog-eared paperback. As I passed he looked up.

'Evening, Joe,' I said with a smile.

'E-evening, Doc,' he replied in the hesitant and poorly articulated speech that is characteristic of those with certain neurological conditions.

'How are you today?' I always felt that this was a stupid and condescending question to ask a patient like Joe, whose condition betokened an inexorable, slow mental and physical decline until death, but somehow its very banality was also strangely reassuring and appropriate for both of us.

'Fine, Doc, thanks. Had q-quite a good day today. M-Managed to get out to sit in the sun for a while.' When the Home was opened Joe had been its first resident. An army regular, he had served in the Falklands with distinction, but then his career had been dramatically cut short at the tender age of thirty-five when he was diagnosed as having motor neurone disease. That had been eight years ago. Unable to manage at home, he had been admitted to hospital; his wife had left him and he had attempted suicide. The Home had proved to be his salvation. Here, he had his own room, a degree of privacy and even some responsibility as the most senior resident. He was the unofficial chair of an unofficial residents' committee.

'Good. Well done! See you later,' I said breezily and continued across the room towards the entrance to the conservatory where my meeting was to be held. This recent addition to the home had no plants in it – apart from those in small pots – but was used as a day-room, the extra space offering a modicum of privacy for those who called this mansion 'home'. The conservatory had now been vacated for a meeting of the House Committee and, although this was my first meeting as chairman, I had been involved with the Home in one role or another for several years. Having previously chaired the medical subcommittee, I was now nominally in charge of the eminent group of local gentry who voluntarily ran this institution.

I set my briefcase on the table and headed for the sandwiches where Jane was busily chatting to one of the committee members. 'Good evening, Matron. How are you?' Jane was a genuine matron. Not only was that her official title, one which for some misguided reason the NHS had abandoned years before, but she looked the part. As always, she was wearing a neatly pressed dark-blue uniform and an ornate, filigree silver nurse's buckle was at her waist, while on her feet were shiny, black, lace-up shoes. Her face creased into a smile. I wondered briefly how old she might be – probably in her early fifties, I estimated.

'Good evening, Doctor Howard. I'm fine, thank you, and yourself?'

'Fine, thanks, Matron, but slightly nervous about my first meeting as chairman,' I said with a smile.

'It'll be fine,' she said. 'There. Have a sandwich and an agenda. By the way, Martha phoned to say that she might be a bit late.'

I knew all the members of the committee, having previously sat on it, and indeed reported to it, as chair of the medical subcommittee. Sandwich in hand, I welcomed Cathy, the GP whose practice was responsible for the day-to-day medical care of the residents, and then greeted Siobhan, the wife of a wealthy local farmer and landowner. Siobhan was a handsome woman in her fifties, with expensive country clothes and a hairstyle to match. She ran a large household and her deep rich voice, with its impeccable Edinburgh accent, demanded instant attention and obedience. With a few further pleasantries to various members of the committee, I called the meeting to order.

After a brief prayer to ensure the success of the evening's proceedings, the business began. The committee received a series of reports: Matron's, Cathy's medical report, and that of the fundraiser amongst others, after which we discussed miscellaneous items of ongoing business. We had begun to debate the future of the derelict stable block when there came a timid knock on the door, following which it slowly opened; just a crack at first, and then wider, until there was just enough space for Martha's diminutive frame to slip through the gap and into the room.

'I'm *terribly* sorry I'm late.' She smiled and giggled nervously, her head tilted to the right, her hands clasped in front of her.

I stood up. 'Welcome, Martha. No problems, I hope?'

'No, it's just Mr Cobbler, Doctor Howard. I couldn't find him anywhere and didn't want to leave him out in the cold. He's got such a weak chest, you know?'

I didn't want the meeting to lose its momentum by digressing to the medical problems of Mr Cobbler, nor was I going to ask why her cat had such a ridiculous name. 'Fine. Please grab a seat. We were just discussing the stable block.' Martha advanced and with embarrassed smiles at all those seated around the table sat down, her handbag grasped firmly in her lap. She had grey rather than white hair with no attempt at colouring. Indeed there seemed little attempt at styling, as it hung around her face rather like a mop head. Her face was wrinkled, consistent with her years, and she wore a patterned dress which hung from her skinny shoulders as though from a coat hanger. For warmth she had donned a nondescript brown cardigan below which a glimpse of dark green woollen tights was visible. On her feet was a pair of brown, low-heeled sensible shoes. She had volunteered to work for the Foundation when the Home had first opened, even then admitting to being, 'seventy-two and a half years old, and nearing the end of my shelf-life.' She settled into her seat and then proceeded to smile directly at me for the rest of the evening.

'I think we should convert the buildings into two or three flats and rent the properties out.' Siobhan boomed out her proposal with an authority that indicated further discussion on the matter was unnecessary.

'The problem, Siobhan, is the cost. I don't know if you have seen the state of the outhouses recently. They're virtually derelict. They are only fit for demolishing.' This was George, a retired NHS manager. Well into his eighties, he had been in the vanguard of setting up the NHS in 1948. He was good value on the committee, offering sensible down-to-earth advice; but he had an unfortunate tendency to doze off, so if one needed his opinion on a topic it was wise to put it high up on the agenda. Sometimes even that didn't work, since he had been known to fall asleep during the opening prayers if they went on for too long.

'George, although I'm inclined to agree with you, unfortunately we can't do that, they are actually listed buildings.' This was business-like and informative, as one would expect from a successful retired lawyer. Having worked hard all his life, a mild heart attack had made Hamish rethink his priorities, so he sold his business, took early retirement and now split his time between the golf course and his chosen charity, which was Riddell House. He had been the inaugural chair of the House Committee, helping to set up the Home when the property had been bequeathed to the Foundation about five years earlier. As he was the previous chair of this committee, I had taken over from him and remained somewhat in awe of his reputation.

'Oh, is that right?' I said.

'Yes. I looked at that option several years ago and sadly that's the case. In fact the Foundation has a responsibility to maintain the fabric of the buildings and not let them deteriorate further.'

I summarized the discussion. 'Well, as I understand it, we can't knock them down and, if indeed we are supposed to maintain them, we may as well renovate

227

them so that we can raise some funds and make them work for us?'

'That's probably right, Grahame, but it would be a massive undertaking.' George was a cautious man.

'I agree with our chairman. That's what we should do.' Siobhan said this with a finality that helped me conclude the discussion. 'Right the first thing is get a report on the practicalities and possibly an estimate of cost.' I looked across the table, 'George, you've helped us in the past with building issues, could you get us a surveyor's report and an estimate?' George nodded agreement and we moved on.

'Now. Fundraiser's report please, Sheila.' I looked up from my agenda at our part-time fundraiser.

'Thank you, chairman. Well, it's been a fallow month I'm afraid. I received a cheque from the fire brigade for three hundred and fifteen pounds, forty-five pence, following a fundraising event, and I have had some meetings with local businesses about supporting the Home, but so far to no avail. I *do* think it would be helpful to have a focus for our fundraising, so a building project would be helpful from my point of view.'

'Thanks, Sheila. We all appreciate how hard fundraising is in the current climate. Any questions for Sheila?'

And so the meeting continued until I drew it to a close after about an hour and a half. The administrative affairs of Riddell House had been dealt with for another month.

***

'Grahame, I think the conundrum is an excellent one to unravel. It's very much caught on a rock and a hard place, you know.' We were standing in one of the long draughty corridors of the Cancer Centre and Abdul had accosted me on my way to the ward. He was trying to tell me about a patient, but as was so often the case he was talking in riddles and I hadn't the faintest idea what he was he was trying to get at.

'What exactly do you want me to do, Abdul?'

'Well, I think he is hanging in the balance, and we must leave no stone unturned in this particular scenario.' Abdul smiled at me, confident that he had now made himself crystal-clear.

I decided to be direct. 'Abdul, do you want me to see this patient?'

'Yes please, that would be good. As always, Grahame, you cut to the chase, you see.'

'That's fine, Abdul. Is he still an inpatient?'

'Yes, indeed. But …' his eyes widened and he looked up and down the corridor to make sure that he could not be overheard, '… he is on the *other* side.'

'The other side?'

'Yes. You know,' he dropped his voice to a whisper. 'He is in the Zoo.' Abdul was referring to the private hospital sometimes referred to as the Zoo due to its close proximity to that institution. For some reason, certain of my consultant colleagues were secretive about their private practice.

'That's fine. I'll see him tonight. Thanks, Abdul.' His dark face beamed. I knew from experience that the

229

best way to find out about a clinical problem was to see the patient for myself, since Abdul, although a delightful man, found it quite impossible to speak in plain English. He had qualified in Afghanistan where he still had family and had come to Edinburgh to train as a surgeon some ten years before. After several years of unsuccessful interviews he had finally been appointed to a consultant post just over a year ago.

He was a true gentleman, but his practice was rather chaotic and if something could be made more complicated than it needed to be, Abdul would do so. He was dark-skinned, as southern Afghans can be, with startling white teeth which dazzled when he smiled or laughed – which was often. His coarse, jet-black hair was cut short and on his upper lip he sported a well-trimmed moustache. He was slightly corpulent – or well-nourished as he preferred to be described – and he had obviously acquired most of his wardrobe at a time when he had been considerably slimmer. Hence he habitually left the top button of his gaudy shirts undone and from behind the loose knot of his tie a few chest hairs could usually be seen protruding. Over his abdomen, the tension on his shirt buttons was immediately apparent and not uncommonly there would be a gap through which one could glimpse an expanse of bulging stomach. Being a consultant in a major UK teaching hospital was the pinnacle of his dreams and he was very much aware of the significance of his achievement.

After work that evening, I drove the two miles from the Cancer Centre to the private hospital. What Abdul had referred to as a conundrum was in reality a straightforward case of bladder cancer. Abdul had performed a cystoscopy, confirmed the diagnosis and ordered investigations, the results of which were awaited. Then a decision would have to be made about the most appropriate treatment. I agreed to see the patient again in my clinic when those investigations had been completed.

***

'Candidate 610, please,' I called out to the small throng of six doctors waiting to be examined. A smartly-dressed, frightened-looking young woman extricated herself from their midst and I extended my hand as she approached. 'Are you number 610?' I asked. Having confirmed the candidate's identity and introduced myself I ushered her into the small cubicle where her *viva voce* examination was to be held.

'This is Doctor James,' I said, indicating the other examiner in the room. 'We will each ask you questions for twenty minutes.' I smiled, trying to put her at ease. Rickety room dividers had converted this basement room in the College into six rather fragile cubicles, each with its own door. Inside their rather stuffy interiors were three seats and on the wall opposite the doorway was a bank of X-ray light-boxes on which hung films demonstrating a range of different conditions. These small rooms had become rather stuffy during a long day of examining and now, at four o'clock, this was our penultimate candidate. Candidate 610 was a bright, intelligent-looking, attractive young woman and after she had settled herself into the vacant chair she turned to face me, a nervous smile on her face.

Soon after I had been appointed an examiner for the oncology final fellowship examination I had discovered that one did not have to be clever or erudite to assess a candidate's knowledge and ability. Simple questions were, in my opinion, adequate to discriminate between those who should pass and those who should not. I had distilled my questions down to their most basic, yet these could still uncover huge areas of ignorance in some candidates.

As always, I opened the questioning gently in an attempt to settle this pleasant young lady's nerves. She was clearly knowledgeable and both she and I soon began to relax. Towards the end of the twenty minutes, I asked her opinion on an X-ray and as she peered at a film in front of her I heard a gentle snoring sound. I looked across at my fellow-examiner and was appalled to find that he was sound asleep, his head nodding gently with each breath. We were examining for the final fellowship of the College, the ultimate hurdle for aspiring cancer doctors. It had been moulded and refined over many years by senior College officials to be a true and fair assessment of a candidate's capability, an exemplar of academic rigour. Central to this was the concept that there should, at all times, be two examiners present to ensure fairness and consistency. Now one of them had fallen soundly asleep.

I raised my voice slightly. 'And how would you treat this patient?' I asked, directing my question at my colleague as much as to the candidate in an attempt to

232

rouse him – but to no avail. Just then the half-time twenty-minute bell sounded. My fellow examiner, David, was rudely awakened, and after letting out a loud yell and nearly falling off his seat, promptly said, 'Good morning.' This otherwise admirable attempt to regain the initiative was addressed to me and not to the candidate.

'Thank you.' I smiled at the candidate. 'I'll pass you over to Doctor James now.'

After another twenty minutes the ordeal was over for this young lady. As the bell sounded the end of the session and she stood up to leave, I said, 'Well done,' shook her hand and ushered her out.

David and I now had ten minutes to agree our marks. 'Sorry about that, Grahame. Must have dozed off for a second, but she was okay, wasn't she?'

'Absolutely. I gave her straight 'B's for my session.'

'I'd agree with that,' he said with a wry smile. The marking complete and with a clear pass agreed, David and I wandered out of our cell to chat with the other examiners, before we interviewed the final candidates of the day. The door of the cubicle opposite us was still closed but was being rattled and shaken from within. After a moment there came a plea from inside. 'Can someone let us out please? The door's jammed.' David went to the door and tried without success to open it and even after more vigorous rattling and a judicious kick, the door remained resolutely closed.

Both of our trapped colleagues were female. 'Look, can someone get us out of here? I need the toilet,' said one.

'We're trying as hard as we can. But the door's completely jammed.' David was stifling a grin, and even I couldn't take the situation too seriously. 'Maybe we should leave you there till the end of the afternoon and try to get you out then?' I said smiling at the assembled group who had now gathered to proffer advice.

'Don't be bloody stupid, Grahame. Get us out.' There was now a noticeable tone of panic in the voice. 'I need the toilet!'

'Would it help if I chucked over an empty bottle?'

'Don't be such an arse, Grahame. Just get that door open.'

'We could slide a ruler under the door, that might help, I've seen it done in films?' No one was impressed with this suggestion from the newest member of the examination team, who then said brightly. 'Has anyone got a ladder?'

David looked at him in amazement, 'Good idea! Yes, I think I've got one in my pocket, let me just check.'

'Hurry up! I'm bursting!'

Realising that our humour was not being fully appreciated by the two incarcerated examiners, David and I decided on a more direct approach to solve the problem and charged the door. With a sharp, 'Stand back, we're coming in,' we both put our shoulders to the flimsy structure. The room dividers rattled then swayed and the door suddenly burst open depositing David and me unceremoniously on the floor.

As we started to disentangle ourselves Sue, in a desperate attempt to get to the toilet as quickly as possible, trod on David's head in the process, very nearly enucleating his left eye with her stiletto heel. Five minutes later, calm had been restored sufficiently to resume the serious and sombre process that was the final fellowship examination.

I introduced myself to one foreign trainee whom I recognized from several previous encounters. In fact, I had examined him so many times before that we were virtually on first name terms. 'Number, 237?'

'Yes, sir.'

'Hello, again. I'm Doctor Howard and this is Doctor James.' 'Poor man,' I thought. The exam was so much more difficult for those whose first language was not English. I ushered him into our cubicle where he took his seat, physically shaking.

'Now, settle down if you can and do try to relax.' I smiled broadly in what I hoped was a reassuring and benign fashion. His response was to wring his hands and squirm on his chair. I asked him a few simple questions which he answered in a sort of mantra; as though reading from a script, with little thought or intellect. My twenty minutes was running out and I was still unsure if this man should pass or fail. I needed a simple yet discriminating question and so described to him a straightforward clinical scenario where, in my opinion, a single test would resolve a diagnostic uncertainty.

'Right, I would like you to give me a single answer. If you had just *one* test you could do, what would it be?' I said, very slowly and succinctly.

He gave me an answer, but not the one I wanted.

'Okay,' I said, 'if you had *two* tests what would the second one be?' The same happened. As the bell rang, exasperated, I thought I would give him one last chance.

'Right, if you had *three* tests what would the third one be?' He thought for a while and then gave me the answer I was looking for.

'*Yes*!' I yelled. '*Well done*!' I sensed that David had very nearly burst into a round of applause.

Twenty minutes later, with the candidate gone, David said, 'Gosh, Grahame. That was like pulling teeth.' We agreed that, like the seasons, he would return again.

***

'Alastair, who's in the side-room?'

'Mr O'Riley, Doctor Howard.'

'Mr O'Riley? Remind me again?'

'At her Majesty's pleasure, half a bread knife in his thigh.'

'Ah yes! Of course. I remember him now.'

It was my weekly ward round and I was accompanied by my registrar, Alastair and Alison the houseman. Of course these were no longer their correct titles – they had been changed years before to meaningless acronyms which I could never remember – so to me they remained registrar and houseman: terms that I understood.

'How did his sperm banking go?' I asked.

'With difficulty, I think would be the correct description, Doctor Howard.' Alastair smiled.

236

'Did they unchain him?'

'Well, apparently he was accompanied by an awesome female warder.'

'I know the one,' I interrupted.

'And he complained that he couldn't do it with her in tow.'

'Oh, my hat! That was risky. It might have upset her. I for one wouldn't want to be in the vicinity if that happened! What did he do then?'

'Well apparently they checked the room out to make sure there was no way of escape, removed his handcuffs, locked him in the cubicle and said they would give him ten minutes!'

'And?'

'It seems he did the business.'

'Good. How's his treatment going?'

We discussed his management and then I led the way into the side-room. Larry O'Riley was lying on top of the bed dressed in jeans and a T-shirt, while his precious leather jacket hung securely from a coat hook near the door. A long chain ran from the handcuff on his right-hand wrist to a matching manacle worn by a male warder who sat reading a newspaper in the corner of the room. The second warder, whom Alastair had referred to as, 'that awesome woman,' was in the opposite corner concentrating intently on a television set which was showing a cartoon. Beside the bed was a drip-stand on which was a blue box with buttons and an LED display which every now and again let out a beeping sound for no apparent reason.

As I entered, the prisoner's gaze turned from the television towards me, and he gestured to the warder for the volume to be reduced. I noted that even in a hospital setting the warders had control of the remote.

'Mr O'Riley.' I shook his hand and there was a metallic clinking sound as the long chain rattled. He looked much as when I had seen him in the clinic except that he was now wearing a baseball hat. Like many such young men, he had shaved his head in anticipation of the inevitable hair loss associated with his chemotherapy.

'How are you getting on?' I asked.

'Fine, Doc. Thanks.'

I went through my normal procedure, repeating the details of the planned treatment and the potential side effects.

'How d'you know if the treatment's working, Doc?'

'We'll check your blood tests, the tumour markers, every week, and as long as they are going down then we know the treatment is working. At the end of four courses we'll repeat the scan.'

'And what if it doesn't work?'

'Well, we can change the drugs. Sometimes that's necessary.'

'Okay, Doc.'

'How are you finding the treatment so far?'

'To be honest, fine. I quite like it,' he turned and smiled at the awesome warder, 'it gets me out!'

'Good, I'll see you next week,' I said returning his grin.

I led the way out of the room, leaving our patient with his minders in the makeshift cell, and as I did so I heard the sound of *Tom and Jerry* return once more.

At the end of the ward round, Alastair turned to me. 'Doctor Howard, I had a call from Mr Abdul.'

'Oh yes?'

'Well, to be quite honest I'm not sure what he wanted, but it was something about a patient you had seen, a Mr Conundrum at the Zoo I think he said? Does that mean anything to you?'

'Don't worry, Alastair.' I laughed, 'I think I know what it's about. I'll give him a call.' I thanked the team and headed to my office where I picked up the phone. 'Abdul, how are you?'

'Very pleased, thank you, Grahame. And yourself?'

'Fine, I gather you called?'

'Yes. It's about that patient.' There was a slight pause, 'You know? The one on the other side.'

'Yes, I saw him last week and he's coming to my clinic on Friday.'

Abdul continued, 'I need to tell him the possibilities, what's high up the agenda, which way the wind blows so to speak. I was wondering if you could tell me.'

'I'll discuss all that with him on Friday.'

'Yes, but I need to give him the heads down before he's disgorged tonight, you see.' I agreed that would be helpful and we discussed the test results, concluding that the most appropriate treatment would be a combination of chemotherapy and radiotherapy.

'That's good. I'll be seeing him and will tell him what is on the cards and which way they have fallen.'

The following Friday I welcomed this sprightly, elderly man into my clinic room at the private hospital. He was neatly dressed, with his white hair carefully combed, and he looked comfortable, almost somewhat county in his Harris tweed jacket and cavalry-twill trousers. After introductions, I said, 'I believe Mr Abdul has explained the results of all the tests?'

'Well, yes. But to be perfectly frank, Doctor Howard, I didn't really understand what he was saying. It's probably my hearing, which is not as sharp as it used to be.' This delightful old gentleman was apologetic, blaming himself for his lack of understanding. I went through the treatment plan with him step by step, following which he appeared much more relaxed, and we agreed to start his chemotherapy the following week.

***

'Doctor Howard, would you be able to come to the Home after your clinic today? There are a couple of things I'd like to discuss.'

'Of course, Matron. I'll be there at about six o' clock.' I was in the habit of going to Riddell House most weeks after my clinic at nearby St John's Hospital, and thus it was that I found myself chatting with Matron over a cup of coffee that evening.

'I'm sorry to trouble you, Grahame, but there are a few things that I thought you should know about. Firstly, the good news! There has been some interest in the walled garden and the gardener's cottage.' This cottage had recently been refurbished and the Foundation had, for some time, been trying to rent it out. In addition, close by was a rather fine, but totally overgrown walled garden. In times long gone this had produced fresh fruit and vegetables for the kitchens of the Big Hoose, as Riddell House was known locally. Matron continued. 'The interested parties are ideal. They are two men who want to use the walled garden as a nursery with a view to developing a Plant Centre.'

'Excellent. They sound perfect. Let's get them in for a chat?'

'Well, there is a bit of a problem.'

'Oh, what's that?'

'Well, they're both called Jimmy.'

'Nothing wrong with being called Jimmy, is there?'

'No, but they're a *couple*.'

'A couple of what?'

Matron looked at me, exasperated, 'They're partners. They're *gay*.'

'Fine! That's even better, Matron. No women to deal with. A woman would probably have taken issue with the kitchen facilities. The two Jimmies sound ideal, so let's have then in for a chat.'

'Well, I don't have a problem with that either, but some members of the committee might not be happy with the proposal.'

'As far as I'm concerned, it's business, I don't care if they have two heads and tentacles; it's all income generation. Why don't we get them in for a chat and then ask Hamish his advice about the legalities and conveyancing issues?'

'Okay, that's fine by me. Thanks. Now the other thing. I'll have to deal with this myself but I thought you should know – I found the gardener in the airing cupboard yesterday.'

'*What*! Was he *dead*?'

'No, you fool! He was asleep.' Matron shook her head in recognition of my stupidity and then continued. 'Simon the under-gardener had said that he was a bit worried as he hadn't seen Billy all afternoon. So we made a search around the place but there was no sign of him. It was only at the shift change when we were getting some fresh linen out for the night that I heard a scream. One of the nurses had opened the cupboard and there, fast asleep, was Billy. The scream woke him up and he clambered out, apologising profusely.'

'For heaven's sake,' I said, 'I don't believe it. Have you been overworking him? I think the Foundation would take a dim view of one of their salaried employees being asleep in the airing cupboard?'

'Yes I agree, so I cautioned him that if there were any further misdemeanours he would be dismissed.'

'Seems sensible. Anything else, Matron?'

'Well, one thing. Chef's not turned up again, so it's sandwiches for dinner!'

***

'I'm not married, you know.'

I was puzzled. The man in sitting in front of me in my clinic at the cancer centre was in his mid-seventies and I had just explained to him that he needed a course of chemotherapy for his newly diagnosed bladder cancer.

'I'm not married,' he repeated before adding after a brief pause, '*yet*.'

My patient was a rather unprepossessing elderly man. His thinning dyed-black hair was combed over the top of his otherwise bald scalp, and even on this warm spring day he was wearing a grubby beige raincoat. I was not entirely surprised that this rather shabby, nondescript-looking man had not yet found a woman willing to share her life with him, but it appeared that *he,* at any rate, had not given up hope. He continued, 'I understand that this treatment can make you infertile?'

'Well, it's true that it can, and for younger men we routinely offer sperm storage,' I said, puzzled.

'It's still possible I might get married.' He peered at me in a slightly disconcertingly intense way and it suddenly dawned on me that this man was still hoping to meet a woman and have a family. I glanced down at his notes to check his date of birth: yes, he *was* seventy-four. It was true, I knew, that *some* men in their seventies find a new partner and father children, but for my money he wasn't going to be one of them.

'I believe you can store sperm?'

'Well, yes, but to be honest we don't normally do so in your age group.'

'If I'm going to have chemotherapy I would like to store some sperm.' This was a statement, not a request; and try as I might I could not dissuade him. Strictly speaking, I thought, he is fully entitled to this service.

I left the clinic room to make the arrangements for his treatment with Julie one of the specialist nurses. Having agreed the details of his chemotherapy I then added nonchalantly, 'Oh, and one other thing. He wants sperm storage.' She looked up at me, an expression of amazement on her face. 'I beg your pardon?'

'He wants sperm storage,' I said quietly.

'But he's *ancient*?'

'Yes, I *know* he's old but he says he still hopes to get married, have children and live happily ever after!'

'Lord knows what the infertility lab will make of this,' was all Julie could say as she bustled off to make the necessary arrangements.

We met later on in the day. 'Grahame, the lab were not at all happy about sperm storage for your seventy-four year old!' she smiled.

'Well, neither am I. But I don't think we have any choice. Will they do it?'

'Yes, but under duress. It's scheduled for tomorrow.'

The following week I was informed that he had attended but failed to produce a specimen.

'Doctor Howard.' Alastair caught me as I was unlocking my office first thing in the morning. 'Sorry to catch you before you've got your coat off but I was on call last night and I had the prison medical officer on the phone. He said that our bread-knife man was unwell.' I was immediately alarmed. 'How d'you mean – unwell?'

'Well, it sounds as though he might be septic. The timing's about right. I asked them to send him in urgently, but they refused.'

'They refused? That's not good enough. Did you tell them that he might die if he's not treated promptly?'

'Yes. The doctor was very helpful but the situation with the prison authorities is not the most straightforward. Anyway, they agreed to check his blood count and as expected he's neutropaenic.' Alastair was referring to the low white blood cell count often associated with chemotherapy. 'They've now agreed to get him over here as soon as possible.'

'How soon's that?'

'Well, I think it should be any time. They were actually very helpful when they realised the seriousness of the situation.'

'Thanks, Alastair. We haven't had a treatment-related death for eight years and I don't want one now,' I said grumpily. 'Let me know when he arrives, would you?'

It was another three hours before Alastair contacted me again. The news was not good. 'He's not at all well, Doctor Howard. He's shocked and septic.'

'Sounds like he should be on ITU?'

'He's on our ward at present but I've spoken to ITU warning them that we may need their help and one of their docs is coming over to see him.'

'Thanks. What treatment have you started?'

'The usual protocol: broad spectrum antibiotics and fluids, and I thought I'd give growth factors as well.'

'Good. I'll meet you on the ward in half an hour and we'll assess how he's doing.'

Larry O'Riley was a very different man from the one I had seen two weeks before. The chain was still there, as were the two warders, but he was lying on his bed panting; his head lolling forward, his face covered in sweat, his eyes sunken.

'Hello, Mr O'Riley.' He didn't even try to smile. It was all he could do to raise his eyes in my direction. Then between breaths he managed to whisper, 'Not so good this time, Doc.'

'Don't try to talk,' I said and then explained to him as briefly as I could what the problem was; that his blood count had been affected by the chemotherapy and that he now had an infection.

'Will I be all right, Doc?' he panted.

'We've started treatment and you should be fine.'

Although extremely unwell, he had detected the uncertainty and concern in my voice. 'Could I die, Doc?' His sunken eyes looked up from beneath his heavy lids.

'Well, this is a potentially serious situation. However, with this treatment you should be fine.'

'*But could I die*?' He was becoming slightly agitated, and there was no avoiding the question.

'Well it's *possible,* but with the treatment you're on you should recover fully.' I said. His eyes closed and he fell back on his pillow, too tired to say any more. The chain clinked.

I looked at his female warder. It was the same woman that I had met in the clinic about five weeks previously. 'I think it would be nice if you could unchain Mr O'Riley. Is that possible? He's not going anywhere and in this situation the handcuffs might well cause bruising.'

I was pleased therefore when, without the slightest hesitation, the tattooed lady singled out a key from a huge bunch attached to her belt and then carefully unlocked and removed the handcuffs with a tenderness that was palpable. She smiled at me, her face now soft and caring; and with a final, almost maternal glance at her charge, she returned to her chair in a corner of the room and resumed watching the silent television.

Our prisoner, Mr O'Riley, bread-knife man, was ill – seriously ill. His low blood count meant that he could not fight the infection he had acquired, and that he was liable to bruise and bleed very easily. His oxygen levels were low and he had a high temperature together with a low blood pressure, all the signs of septic shock, a potentially fatal condition.

'What d'you think about oxygen?' Alastair asked, referring to the recurring clinical problem of whether or not to administer oxygen to patients in this condition. When oxygen levels in the blood were low it was usually routine to administer it, but the problem with patients on this type of chemotherapy was that one of the prescribed drugs had the potential for causing severe lung damage. This risk, paradoxically, was hugely increased if oxygen were given – sometimes resulting the patient requiring ventilation and not uncommonly leading to death.

We discussed the pro and cons, agreeing to withhold oxygen for the time being but to review the situation at the end of the day.

Later that afternoon when my outpatient clinic had finished, we returned to the ward. If anything Larry was slightly worse.

'I think we'll have to risk a low concentration of oxygen. What do the ITU docs think?'

'They say that as long as his blood pressure is maintained he can stay on the ward.' Alastair then grinned. 'I suspect that's something to do with the fact that they've no vacant beds.'

'If he needs to be on ITU then they'll just have to find one. I'll negotiate with them if necessary. Do they know he's curable and that this is all reversible?'

'Yes. Couldn't be clearer. I presume we won't give him his bleomycin?'

'Absolutely. I think that's all we can do for now. Make sure the night team keep an eye on him and tell them I want to know if the situation changes.'

'Are you on call?'

'No, but I still want to be informed if he gets worse. I *don't* want a neutropaenic death.'

This situation was every oncologist's nightmare – a curable patient rendered seriously ill, potentially fatally so, by his treatment, a harsh reminder of how toxic our treatments could be. In treating those patients there was a delicate balance between success and failure. Reduce the intensity of the drugs and cure rates fell precipitately; maintain them and there was a significant risk of treatment-related deaths. And then there would be the problem of continuing his treatment when or if he recovered. He hadn't received anywhere near the required amount of therapy necessary to cure him.

That night I slept fitfully, and was pleased when my alarm awoke me without there having been a call during the night.

Back in the hospital, first thing next morning I donned my white coat and headed straight for the ward where I sought out Alastair. 'How's our prisoner?' I asked.

'Stable. Blood pressure is maintained, his temperature has dropped and oxygen saturation has improved.'

'On or off oxygen?'

'Off.'

'That's good. About as good as we can hope for right now. Well done.' We entered the side-room where our patient was lying asleep on his bed. His breathing was less laboured and his face was no longer covered in sweat. 'How are you feeling this morning?' I asked Larry quietly. His eyes opened and he slowly focused on me.

'Bloody awful, Doc, thanks.' There was a weak attempt at a smile. I grinned back and noted how the awesome warder was looking at her charge with genuine concern.

'I think you're just saying that, so the handcuffs don't go back on.' I grinned, glancing briefly at both the warders who smiled in return. I was now feeling more at ease because, although still very sick, Larry had improved slightly overnight and in this situation patients usually either recovered or died within hours.

'How's it goin', Doc?'

'So far, so good. You're not out of the woods yet but your condition has stabilised and you're doing well.' I glanced at the female warder and noted that her expression of concern had softened into one of relief.

'See you later.' I waved as I closed the door.

Outside, after discussing Larry's management, I said, 'You know, Alastair, I reckon you are wrong to call that delightful woman, "awesome". I think that underneath that stern exterior and those tattoos, there's another woman, all soft and cuddly, trying to get out?'

'D'you reckon, Doctor Howard? Would you risk annoying her to test out your theory?'

'Absolutely not.'

'By the way, Doctor Howard,' Alastair started to chuckle. 'I'm about to start a ninety-two year old man on chemotherapy. Do you want him to have sperm storage?'

'Very funny! Your chances of *ever* getting a job here have now fallen to zero.' I smiled and we stepped off the ward and headed for our weekly meeting to discuss newly-diagnosed patients and difficult clinical problems with our surgical colleagues.

'I think we should get started.' I was pleased to see that our chairman for the morning was the senior surgeon, Harold. Decisive and focused, his place in the chair meant that we would get through the business quickly, efficiently *and* on time. This so-called multidisciplinary meeting represented a huge advance in the consistency and efficiency of how we managed our patients. As well as oncologists like myself and our surgical colleagues, the whole clinical team including radiologists, pathologists, junior medical staff and specialist nurses were in attendance. There might be thirty or more people in the room, all potentially wanting to have their say on any particular case. Thus the success of these meetings was totally dependent on effective chairmanship. We tried to avoid having Abdul chair the meeting because when he did so it was an absolute disaster. No one had any idea what he was talking about or what decisions had been made and he would allow the discussion to wander aimlessly around the room.

'Right, chaps, we have sixty patients to discuss, so let's get going.' And so Harold opened the meeting. Fifteen minutes later, and with ten patients discussed, Abdul entered. As he made his way rather gingerly to the vacant seat in the front row on which he habitually sat, he acknowledged his colleagues with a nod and a wide smile. Harold paused briefly to welcome him. 'Good morning, Abdul.'

'Err-um. Good morning. So very sorry, er, to be late,' he muttered in his deep voice as he took his seat. He then started to shuffle noisily through the sheaf of papers that contained a brief résumé of the patients being discussed.

Harold continued, 'So we'll arrange a pelvic CT scan and then offer him radiotherapy if the disease is localised?' Harold looked around the room to be sure he had summarised the discussion accurately. There was no dissent. 'That's fine, all agreed. Now, next patient, Mr …'

'Err-um, shouldn't he have an operation surely? Why not?' An audible groan could be heard in the room as Abdul reopened the discussion.

Harold looked across the room to the source of this interruption. 'Abdul, he's got secondary spread.'

'No he hasn't. He should have surgery surely.'

'His bone scan is positive.'

'No it's not. It says "Bone scan normal" here.' Abdul prodded his sheaf of papers with his right index finger.

'No it's definitely positive; we've just reviewed the images.' Harold was beginning to show signs of exasperation as Abdul showed his sheet to his neighbour, pointing to the annotation he was referring to. There was some low muttering and then Abdul turned the page over.

'Sorry. Sorry, wrong patient. Page six, is it?'

'No, we're on page five, and likely to remain there unless we get a move on!'

'Sorry, sorry! It's Mr Williams, isn't it?'

'*No*! We were talking about Mr Smart on page five.'

'Sorry. Okay, yes. I'm there now. Sorry to have the wrong end of the sticky wicket, you know, but it's important to sort these potential wrinkles out, don't you think?' I glanced at our chairman and raised my eyebrows, *willing* him to continue.

'Sorry, Abdul, but we need to press on,' and Harold did so. Eventually we came to discuss Mr Williams and Abdul took it upon himself to summarise the background to the case.

'Err-um. Right now, we have in front of us Mr Williams with the normal bone scan, so you see he *should* have an operation.'

'Thanks, Abdul. Surgery is *one* option.' Harold looked around the room, eyebrows raised. Alastair took up the challenge, 'But he is seventy-eight, so wouldn't radiotherapy be a better option here?'

'Err-um, is he? No he's sixty. Who are we talking about now?'

'*Mr Williams*!' several of us said in unison.

'Oh yes. I see. Sorry. Err-um, he's older. Nevertheless, it's not that this means he cannot have the best treatment.'

'But there's no indication that surgery *is* better than radiotherapy!' I was becoming increasingly frustrated by this interminable debate, which tended to be repeated, week in and week out. Although there was absolutely no evidence to support his opinion, Abdul could not accept that his preferred treatment, surgery, was not the best option. He looked up at me with a hurt expression on his face, almost as if I had personally insulted him.

'Err, well, Grahame, I know your opinion, and that there's no evidence, but the surgery is the best one, isn't it?' He looked around the room for support. Most of the group had disengaged themselves completely from the discussion and were either looking out of the window or staring at the ceiling with glazed expressions on their faces while at least two were sound asleep.

Harold took control. 'No, Abdul, I think both modalities are equivalent and in this age-group I'd agree with Grahame that radiotherapy is the better option in this case.' There was no dissent and so Harold brought the discussion to a close, 'So, radiotherapy it is?'

Abdul looked puzzled. 'But if he were fit, and old ones are now often fit, he could have an operation?'

'Yes, but I think we're all agreed that surgery is not best here, Abdul. Right, I think we should move on.'

And Harold looked down at his papers. Abdul was not finished, however.

'But do we know how fit he is? Has anyone seen this man? It is misconstruing to say things about age just chronological, and not having seen the patient. He could be very fit as a fifty year.' Abdul paused briefly but not long enough to allow Harold to get the debate back on track.

'We should not cast aspirations without having eyeballed the man first.' Abdul looked up with a triumphant look in his eyes. He felt that he had eloquently demonstrated an important point about the clinical management of the elderly and although in some ways he was right, all he had succeeded in doing was to exasperate everyone else in the room. Having made his point and derailed the meeting, he believed he had now vindicated himself for his mistakes earlier in the proceedings, so he quietly dozed off, allowing Harold and the rest of us to finish the meeting without further interruption.

***

'Right. Good evening, everyone. Thank you for coming.' It was the Foundation's policy that prayers should be said at the start of our meetings. I looked across the table, 'Hamish. Would you be kind enough to say prayers, please?' I excluded myself from this duty as the only prayer I knew began: 'Thank you for what we are about to receive,' and I couldn't remember the rest. This seemed hardly appropriate when opening the house committee meeting at Riddell House so I delegated that responsibility to others. Hamish was good because he kept it short. If possible I avoided asking George as he took the duty very seriously and would often mumble on for ages, requesting divine assistance with each and every item on the agenda and prayers could take a significant amount of time, impinging on that available for the business of the meeting.

Prayers finished, Hamish opened the discussion about the proposed occupancy of the gardener's cottage. Half-way through there came the expected quiet knock, and Martha crept in, smiling and curtseying, 'Terribly sorry. It's Mr Cobbler again. He's got a chill.'

'That's fine, Martha. Do please take a seat.' I said and, once Martha was comfortably seated, Hamish continued: 'Well, I think the proposal to rent the cottage and the walled garden to these two gentlemen is an ideal solution, in that we'll have the income from the cottage, and the garden will be maintained at no cost to the Foundation. I commend it to the committee.' Hamish settled back in his seat.

'Thank you, Hamish. That was a very helpful summary. Are there any comments or questions?' I asked, looking around the table. There was a moment of silence then Siobhan looked up from her papers.

'Chairman, I'm a little concerned that their … er … lifestyle might not be appropriate for the Foundation?'

'Lifestyle, Siobhan?'

'Yes, these are two men. You know, living together.'

'Does anyone else have a problem with this?' I asked.

'I think it's rather nice.' Martha smiled and nodded her head. I suspected that she didn't have a clue as to what Siobhan was alluding.

'Well it may be quite "nice", Martha. But it's against God's will.' Siobhan's deep voice resonated around the conservatory.

'Oh! I didn't know God had an issue with gardeners?'

'No, Martha. The point is …' Siobhan hesitated then looked at me and raised her eyebrows, 'Ugh. Never mind.'

'Siobhan,' I said, 'your point is well taken but, unless the Foundation has guidelines prohibiting two members of the same sex from renting one of its properties, which (correct me if I'm wrong, Hamish)' and I glanced briefly at him, 'would, I believe, be discriminatory and illegal, we should just accept this as an ideal solution.' I paused. 'I have met the two Jimmies and they are really enthusiastic about their project.' There was silence. 'Well if there are no other comments, I propose that Hamish and I proceed with this. Thank you.'

'Sheila. Your report please?'

'Well, it's been a fallow month, chairman, but the good news is that I have accepted an offer of some old electrical equipment. A local company has donated all its old computers to us and I'm pleased to say that we now have a hundred desk-top computers and a few old electric kettles.' I was puzzled and looked at Matron, whose eyes rolled. I decided that I would not be the one to open this particular Pandora's Box and ask what on earth she was going to do with all those obsolete items but Siobhan had no such qualms.

'What on *earth* are you hoping to do with these, Sheila? They're probably obsolete and must be taking up a lot of space?'

'Well I imagine they are worth something, so I'm hoping to sell them on to local businesses.' Matron's eyes continued to roll and Siobhan groaned and said, 'Well, good luck!'

***

A few days later our prisoner had recovered sufficiently to be discharged back to the care of Her Majesty's Prison Service. Handcuffed once more, I explained to Larry and his minders that we would need to continue his treatment and indeed administer an extra course to compensate for the delay caused by his infection. As the little procession filed past me, the wardress caught my eye and smiled. 'Thanks for all you've done, Doctor.' I felt greatly moved by this unexpected aside.

'A pleasure,' I said, and found myself wondering about his family. Was he, like Joe in Riddell House, someone who had been abandoned by society; an organization becoming his substitute family. In Joe's case it had been the Foundation: the nurses, the cooks, the cleaners and the gardeners who had become his carers. Where was Larry's family? I asked myself. What had happened to the woman who stabbed him with a bread knife? I had seen no sign of her or indeed of any other visitors. Was the prison now his home and the warders his surrogate parents? Certainly there was a maternal streak a mile wide, in the tattooed and awesome one.

In fact Laurence Patrick O'Reilly – for that was the name on his birth certificate – had apparently enjoyed quite a privileged upbringing. Born in Dublin, he had moved with his parents to Edinburgh when he was just four years old. He was the rather late and unexpected only child of Mr and Mrs Sean O'Reilly. His father, a successful banker, was sixty and his mother in her late forties when he was born. By the time he was ten and a pupil at one of Edinburgh's best fee-paying schools, his father's behaviour had become rather erratic and he had made several ill-advised investments during an unstable period in the world's financial markets. Although no longer managing the assets of a large bank, he still behaved as if he were and, like so many gamblers, the more he lost the more he risked. The last straw for Mr O'Reilly senior was when his wife, to whom he was devoted, became ill. She developed a swollen abdomen, became jaundiced, was diagnosed as having widespread ovarian cancer and died six weeks later. The loss of his wife derailed the old man completely. On discovering his reckless behaviour, his bank took over as power of attorney just before he became bankrupt and, following a year or so of self-neglect, partly due to dementia and partly to grief, he died of influenza when Larry was only thirteen years old.

Not surprisingly, this was a most unsettling time for the young O'Riley. Orphaned, with his family home repossessed by the bank and having no assets of his own, he was unable to pay for his expensive education. However, the governors of the school acted in that great philanthropic tradition of the endowed Edinburgh academies and allowed him to remain, free of charge, as a boarder until he had completed his studies.

Larry was an intelligent young man with an enquiring mind, but the loss of both parents in such a short period of time had affected him deeply. He began to behave uncharacteristically, becoming belligerent and adversarial, his studies suffering as a result. It was just before his higher exams that he was caught smoking cannabis in the dormitory and was duly expelled, only being allowed back to sit his final exams. Under the circumstances he performed surprisingly well, gaining seven Highers at respectable grades.

On leaving school, the only remaining structure to Larry's life had gone. Now homeless and impecunious, he began to mix with others of the same ilk and his crepuscular world became that of the vagrant, the alcoholic and the drug addict. Being intelligent and well educated, he quickly took on a kind of ambassadorial role for his homeless friends, many of whom could neither read nor write. This was an activity which brought him to the attention of the authorities on more than one occasion. His tenacious defence of an alcoholic tramp, who had been brutally moved on by the police and subsequently died in custody, gained him a certain notoriety and indeed popularity with the press, as a kind of Robin Hood for the homeless. Nevertheless, his downward spiral continued for a further ten years and life on the streets led to many brushes with the law, as well as the bread knife incident following a brief relationship with a girl he had befriended.

Larry's social decline continued and after several warnings and court appearances for petty crime and possession of drugs he eventually received a custodial sentence for dealing in drugs and the assault of a traffic warden. That had been two years ago and, with maximum time off, he was due for release in some eighteen months.

Now he was back in his side-room, his jail away from jail, once more chained to his two minders. I had noticed that the male warder was seldom the same but, except for rare occasions, he was invariably accompanied by the awesome, tattooed woman who clearly had a soft spot for the young man.

'I'm pleased you've recovered from the infection but I'm afraid that doesn't mean there can be any let-up in your treatment.' Larry nodded his acknowledgement of this. 'We'll start another course today but in addition, to minimise the risk of further infection, we'll give you daily injections called growth factors to stimulate your bone marrow, as well as antibiotics.'

'That's fine, Doc. How's the treatment going in general?' Larry looked at me with an expression that was no longer uninterested, but penetrating and intelligent.

'It's going well. The infection you had needn't put us off track. Your tumour markers are still very high, but they are coming down nicely and there's no doubt you're responding.'

'What are the chances of curing me?'

I decided to make myself more comfortable and sat on the edge of his hospital bed. 'Overall, with this disease, more than ninety percent of patients are cured.' I said; then, after a brief pause, continued, 'but in your case it's lower because of the severity of the disease that you have and the fact that the tumour markers were very high.'

'So, what *are* the chances of curing me?'

'Well,' and I hesitated. 'If you read the books, they say that just over fifty percent of patients in your situation will be cured, but nowadays that figure should be nearer seventy percent.'

He didn't flinch but was thoughtful for some time and stared fixedly at the soundless cartoons on the television screen. 'You see, Doc, I've been thinking. I've made quite a mess of my life so far, but I've decided that when I get out I should do something *really* useful.' He turned his gaze from the television to look straight at me. 'What I want to do is to work for the homeless and the addicts on the street: the no-hopers. This prison sentence paradoxically has been good for me because without it I'd probably be dead by now. Being inside has meant that I've had to clean myself up, and getting cancer has made me reassess my life.' He stopped, expecting some response but none came from either of the warders.

'I have what is probably an unrivalled knowledge of what it's like to live on the streets and I'm lucky enough to have had an education which allows me to bridge the divide with the rest of Edinburgh society – so I think I could be a real help.'

This was the most Larry had ever said in one sentence since I'd first met him – possibly more than everything he'd said to me until then: a previously hidden insight into this very private man.

'Larry, I think that's an excellent idea. It's not for me to lecture you or advise on your lifestyle. My job is simply to treat and hopefully cure you. But you're right in saying that if you go back to your old lifestyle your prognosis, your chance of long-term survival, is far worse than it would be from your cancer.' After a pause I continued, 'Are you thinking of working for one of the charitable organisations.'

'Yes, but not one of the religious ones.'

'Why not?'

'They do *some* good work, but in my opinion religion is to blame for many of the ills of the world and for much human suffering. I would rather be associated with a secular organisation.'

The wardress butted in, 'Larry! You mustn't say that.'

'Why not, Agnes?'

So that was her name, I thought. She looked like an Agnes.

'Because that's … well, you shouldn't take God's name in vain.'

'But, Agnes, there isn't a God, not in the sense that you mean anyway.'

'Shush, you,' was all Agnes could muster in response.

'Interesting. I take it you're an atheist then?' I said.

'Yes. A determinist. I think Spinoza got it right.'

'But he didn't resolve the question of how you come to terms with your lack of self-destiny, so that you can embrace determinism and be content when *de facto* you have no control over your behaviour?'

'I know it's unresolved, but in my view the good life requires an acceptance of determinism, and it seems the best solution for now.'

'Cartesian theory seems to support the concept,' I added.

'Yes, in general, but some of Descartes' deductions seem a bit fatuous to me, though I'm no expert.' A smile crossed his face briefly. 'Agnes gets annoyed if I challenge the received wisdom.' He glanced at his wardress with affection, while she studiously stared at the silent cartoons on the television, then shrugged her shoulders and breathed out loudly with a huffing sound.

'Well, thanks, Doc. Let's get on with it.'

The following week Matron and I were having one of our ad hoc meetings at Riddell House.

'Grahame, Sheila has landed us with a room full of useless computers. She doesn't know one end of a p.c. from another and I've no idea what we're going to do with them all.'

'Not the best income-generating scheme in the history of the Foundation, I suspect. Anyway more to the point has anyone explained to Martha about the Gay Gordons, I mean the Wee Jimmies?'

'*No*! Leave her in peace. By the way, she said she had an announcement to make at the next meeting, I asked her what it was about but she blushed and said she would explain at the meeting, as it was a bit embarrassing.'

'My word, it's probably something to do with Mr Cobbler. Maybe he's got Mrs Cobbler pregnant. Shove it on the agenda, Matron'

'Now, what I really wanted to discuss is Billy. I have found out what the problem is. His wife has locked him out of their home, so he has nowhere to go at night and that's why we found him in the airing cupboard that evening.'

'Oh my hat, Matron! I know we're a charity, but this is ridiculous.'

'Well, I thought we could offer him accommodation here in the Home, for a small rental, until he sorts himself out. I checked with headquarters and they think it's the right thing to do. Are you happy with that?'

'That's fine, but I think there should be a time scale, say two months and then a review. We cannot have him taking up a room here indefinitely.'

'I agree, so can you inform the committee next week, please?'

The following week with prayers over, the House Committee were once more gathered in the conservatory, when there came the ever-predictable knock on the door. 'Come in, Martha, we were just debating the stable block. Is Mr Cobbler playing up again?'

'Just a little. Terribly sorry I'm late.'

Siobhan continued the point she had been making. 'Well, I for one am delighted that this is progressing and that the Foundation has agreed to renovate the stable block and convert it into two residences.'

'Yes. The Foundation has appointed an architect and a construction firm and work should commence in the New Year. I will of course keep you informed of progress.' I paused briefly. 'Now, Martha, I believe you have an announcement for us?' I looked at Martha who, as always, was beaming at me.

'Oh, thank you, chairman. Well, yes I have.' She let out a short giggle, 'Well, this is a bit embarrassing actually, at my age but,' she hesitated, 'well, I'm going to get married.' She looked, up smiling as always. 'There, I've said it.'

There was a stirring sound from around the table as chairs creaked, throats were cleared, and then came a loud clatter as Siobhan dropped her sandwich-laden plate. This in turn woke up George, who with a start almost fell off his chair. The whole committee looked at Martha in amazement. A spinster all her life, no one had expected this of her.

'Gosh!' said Siobhan. Then, realising that this was not the most appropriate response to such an announcement, she added, 'Well done, Martha,' in her deep resonant voice. There followed a complete silence while those around the table tried to think of something appropriate to say. It was clearly my role as chairman to relieve the tension so I overcame my personal surprise and said, 'Well, Martha. How absolutely wonderful! Congratulations.'

'You *are* a dark horse, Martha,' remarked Hamish who could barely contain his glee. 'So who's the lucky man?'

'Better late than never, I suppose.' Siobhan really seemed to have disengaged her brain. But none of this mattered one iota to Martha who just sat grinning benignly at one and all, her cheeks tinged with a hint of pink.

'Thank you all very much,' she said. 'The thing is, in view of my new responsibilities …' and here she giggled again, '… I've decided to stand down from this committee. I hope you don't mind?' She looked at me expectantly.

'Martha, I'm delighted. Not that you're standing down from the committee, of course, but delighted at your news.' Siobhan, realising that every time she opened her mouth something totally inappropriate came out, began to clap and the rest of us joined in heartily.

'I hope no one else is getting any similar ideas,' I said, and with that closed the meeting.

Afterwards Siobhan came up to me, 'Doctor Howard, I wonder if you would do me a favour.' She continued, 'I'm a member of the local WRI, and I was hoping you might come along to one of our meetings to give a short talk on cancer and perhaps answer a few questions?'

'I'd be delighted,' I replied, not knowing what I had let myself in for.

***

Back at the Cancer Centre, Larry initially responded well to his treatment. The next three courses proceeded uneventfully with no further episodes of sepsis and his tumour marker levels decreased rapidly, but when he was admitted for his fifth cycle the rate had slowed. I explained the results to him.

'What does that mean, Doc?' he asked.

'It's not unusual but it means that we should introduce new drugs. We need to get the markers down as low as possible.'

'Are they stronger drugs?'

'No, they're not stronger as such, they're just different drugs. And, before you ask, the side effects aren't any worse, in fact sometimes this new regimen is better tolerated than the one you've had so far.'

'Is it still every week?'

'No. Now this is where it really *is* different. I'm afraid you'll spend more time in hospital. Each course involves five days' treatment, then there's a gap of nine days at least after which we continue as soon as your blood count recovers. It's more intensive.'

'How many courses?'

'This may sound a bit fatuous, Larry, but as many as necessary,' I replied. 'Essentially, we continue until we get your markers down. We're looking at four courses *minimum*.' He said nothing, and I continued: 'On the plus side, your markers have come down a lot. One of them is normal, while the other one – which was very high at a quarter of a million – has now fallen to just under ten thousand but has stuck there and that's why we need to change the drugs.'

'What should the level be?'

'Just under five.'

'*Five*?'

'Yes, five.'

'Crumbs! That's still a long way to go?''

'Yes, but bear in mind that it's already gone down two hundred and forty thousand!'

'Okay, Doc. Let's get on with it.'

The change in treatment had the desired effect and the blood test resumed its downward trend, but the side effects became increasingly debilitating. As well as weight loss and a general deterioration in Larry's health, his bone marrow was taking longer and longer to recover between courses, resulting in delays. The one remaining abnormal tumour marker had fallen tantalisingly close to normal, but he was gradually becoming what some oncologists describe as, 'chemo-ed out'. The side effects of his treatment had built up to a degree where it was becoming more and more risky, potentially as dangerous as the disease itself. After three courses of the new regimen, his blood count eventually struggled up to a level where I thought it was adequate to give a further cycle.

'Well, Larry, your blood count's up enough for some more treatment,' I announced to him on the ward round. Agnes' face remained expressionless.

'Good, Doc.' Larry now looked the epitome of a cancer patient. He had lost all his hair, even that slight down or shadow which is present when men shave their head. This could not be mistaken for anything other than the effects of prolonged chemotherapy. He also had that greyish tinge to his skin, a combination of drug-induced discolouration and chronic mild anaemia. His face was thinner but if anything his smile had grown broader. Perversely, this diagnosis and the treatment had lifted his mood, given him a goal, a purpose, a distraction from the unremitting boredom of prison and the unrewarding association with others with whom he had so little in common, apart from law-breaking.

'What did the scans show?'

We had repeated these to see how the disease had responded and to assess whether or not surgery was likely to be necessary to remove any residual disease following his chemotherapy.

'A good response, Larry. Not complete, but good. The disease in your chest has totally disappeared. The enlarged nodes in your abdomen are much smaller but are still there. They are now about four centimetres in diameter compared to over ten when we started.'

'Does that mean I'll need an operation?'

'Possibly. Your marker is now down to one hundred. I think we should give you this course of treatment and see you with another scan in one month while performing weekly blood tests. Normally we like to see the blood test return to normal, but it may still drop after treatment.'

'Okay, Doc. Let's get on with it. Agnes will be pleased to finish the treatment. Won't you, Agnes?' Larry asked, smiling in her direction.

'Oh, Shush, you,' she responded warmly.

That final course of treatment very nearly killed Larry. His blood count crashed, he developed another serious infection and it was a further two and a half weeks before he had recovered sufficiently to be discharged. He was fully dressed and ready to leave when I caught up with him. The chain, his constant link with Agnes, rattled as we shook hands. His brown leather jacket, once so smart, now hung limply from his shoulders and his jeans fell in folds like rags from his hips and were held precariously in place by a belt drawn tight.

'Larry! So glad I've caught you,' I said. 'That's the last of the chemotherapy. We'll give you a rest now and I'll see you in the clinic in four weeks' time.'

'Thank God for that!' He looked at me, a faint smile on his lips. 'I don't think I could have coped with any more, Doc.'

'I don't think so either,' I concurred. 'We'll get your blood tests checked every week, repeat the scans and I'll see you with the results.' I patted him on the shoulder.

'Thanks, Doc,' he said, a slight smile briefly flickering across his face as he was led off the ward, the characteristic tinkle of his chain fading into the distance.

***

Some weeks later, having driven deep into the lush green farmlands of West Lothian, I found myself standing outside a wooden Scout hut, my spirits somewhat dampened by a light evening drizzle. Tentatively, I opened the half-glazed green door and peered into the gloomy interior. Standing within the bare wooden-floored room were about a dozen women fussing over trestle tables and chairs. As I entered, one of them looked up from the table she was dressing and on seeing me strode in my direction.

'You must be Doctor Howard.' This was more a statement than a question, and the subliminal message was: 'You'd better be Doctor Howard or there'll be hell to pay.' She reminded me of Miss Leeds, the Scout leader who had escorted me and about twenty other nine-year-old Cub Scouts, all the way from Norwich to Scotland and back with little more than a forked stick and a lot of tweed for assistance. The Empire was built on the backs of such women, I thought. When I admitted to being Doctor Howard, she grasped my hand and gently crushed it.

'I'm Molly, the chairman of this motley crew. Welcome! Now come and meet the gang.' The local WRI were indeed an interesting and varied group, entirely disparate in age, size and dress-sense. It's true there were a number of fearsome Molly-types and some expensive-looking Siobhan clones but, along with those rather frumpy stalwarts, were many specimens of flouncy perfumed femininity. With introductions completed and the room in order, my audience, who now numbered about twenty, took their seats in the body of the hall while I, along with the office-holders, took my place at a table in front of them.

'Good evening, ladies. I would like to welcome Doctor Howard to this meeting of the WRI.' An excited murmur buzzed around the room and with a smile I nodded my thanks to the chairwoman for her invitation. Although somewhat hearty and sturdy-looking, Molly was actually a youngish, handsome woman. A farmer's wife, I guessed, doing her bit for the community. She dropped her voice a trifle, glanced at me and whispered, 'We always start the meeting with our song.' Then, turning to her audience she said, 'Right, ladies, we shall now open the meeting with our anthem,' and in a wobbly soprano she started to sing. One by one, following her lead, the rest of the ladies joined in.

Although the pitch of their voices certainly went up and down I was unable to identify a melody as such. Similarly, the words – for words there were – were largely incoherent, but I did manage to decipher the odd one. The theme of the song seemed to be about crops and bad weather and there was something in the way of a refrain about feeding their men. I found the whole experience quite unsettling. I had given numerous talks to various audiences around the world but this had never happened to me before. I was the only male in the room and about twenty worthy ladies were tunelessly intoning something about the importance of keeping their men well-fed and happy. My uneasiness grew still stronger as I recalled my visit to a nearby bowling club some years before to receive a cheque. On that occasion some rather inebriated women had attempted to remove items of my clothing so that they could be auctioned for charity. But this was an entirely different breed of lady and as the song reached its tuneless climax I began to grin and had to look down at the floor. I knew that if I made eye-contact with any of these fine ladies I would have real difficulty in controlling my mirth.

When the echoes of their song gradually died away, I was invited to give my talk and when I had finished about half an hour later there was coughing, polite applause and the sound of creaking chairs as those who had fallen asleep suddenly awoke. The chairwoman asked if the audience had any questions and after the inevitable and slightly embarrassing silence Siobhan stood up and suggested that we should make smoking illegal. Naturally I supported her proposal and then sat down secure in the knowledge that within a very few minutes I would be sinking a well-earned pint – and having a cigarette.

'Well, if there are no more questions, it's time for our competition.' Molly then turned to me. 'Doctor Howard, before you go, we would appreciate it if you would judge the spoons.'

'I beg your pardon?'

'Judge the spoons.'

'*Judge the spoons*?' I tried not to sound too incredulous.

'Yes please. Every month, some of our members bring along a variety of spoons and we judge which is the best one.' My sense of unease returned; never in my wide travels had I been asked to judge any item of cutlery, spoon or otherwise, and I wasn't sure if I was entirely qualified to do so.

'Er, well, of course. But by what criteria am I judging them? Value or age or something?'

'Oh no, no! Nothing like that. Just choose which one you like best.' And so saying, Molly turned her attention to the body of the hall and announced, 'Right, ladies, Doctor Howard will now judge the spoons.'

I was then guided to a small table in one corner of the hall on which lay four spoons. Behind the table stood the proud owners, while the rest of the ladies gathered around, encircling and effectively trapping me. Each of the contenders looked at me with a mixture of pleading and apprehension as I lifted and inspected their particular offering. The first one was a Gift from Margate. It was a tea-caddy spoon, slightly tarnished and I knew its provenance since on the end of the handle was a shield neatly inscribed, 'A Gift from Margate.' Having given the spoon what I considered to be the attention it warranted, I moved on to the next. This one was a truly awful object which could have been lifted straight out of an army canteen. It was in fact a pudding spoon made of stainless steel, well-used and quite bent. I was totally at a loss as to what to say and so simply muttered, 'That's an interesting one!' and I detected a sharp intake of breath and a whispered, 'Oh, good!' from one of the four competitors. The third was a rather inconsequential teaspoon which for some presumably long-forgotten reason, had a 'K' inscribed on the handle; while the fourth was a solid silver teaspoon which carried an embossed RNLI insignia.

I knew I was about to upset at least three of the women in the room but everyone was now looking at me intently and a decision had to be made. I hesitated, pretending to be indecisive, before pronouncing, with what I hoped was adequate *gravitas,* 'Well it's a very difficult decision indeed, but, on balance, my choice is *this* one,' and I lifted up the silver RNLI spoon for all to see. There was a shriek of delight from the lady on my right and grudging congratulations from the three losers.

'Thank you, Doctor Howard.' Now we must let you go so that we can get on with the business of our meeting.' I tried to look disappointed and, to a gentle ripple of applause, was duly ushered out into the drizzle of the evening.

I was now in desperate need of a drink and drove at speed to the nearest hostelry where I had two pints in quick succession but it was only later, when I had put ten or more miles between me and the isolated Scout hut with its disappointed spoon owners, that I began to relax.

***

We were seated in a clinic room, between patients. 'How is Mr …?' Abdul paused and looked around the clinic room in which we were both sitting and then dropped his voice to a whisper. 'You know, from the other side.'

'He's tolerating his treatment very well.' I smiled at Abdul who as usual was wearing a broad grin. Two of his shirt buttons had come undone, exposing an impressive expanse of abdomen.

'When will you be wanting me to look into his bladder?' asked Abdul eagerly.

'Well, he's completed his chemotherapy and is now in the middle of his radiotherapy, so it will be several weeks before his treatment's completed. I'll drop you a line when he's finished.'

'Very good, I'll wait for the starting gun before I cross the tape as it were. Mustn't be too quick off the blocks.'

'Absolutely not, Abdul. That wouldn't do.'

The door then opened and a nurse ushered in an obese, elderly lady whom she directed to the chair opposite us. Abdul gave her one of his most welcoming smiles, 'Good evening, Mrs Maguire, and how are you today?'

'Well, Doctor Abdul, I'm very pleased with myself actually.' She leaned forward to emphasise what she was about to say, 'I've lost a stone.' This said, she gave Abdul a satisfied smile, crossed her arms and then sat back in her chair, a smug expression on her face.

Abdul's brow furrowed. 'Oh dear,' he said, 'where did you lose it?'

Our patient looked at Abdul in bemusement. 'How do you mean, where did I lose it?'

'Well, was it in the toilet?'

'What do you mean? I said I've lost a stone!'

'I know you've lost a stone. How big was it? It's very important that we should know, you see.'

I couldn't keep silent any longer. 'Abdul, I think Mrs Maguire means that she's lost a stone in weight.'

Abdul gave me a puzzled look, then slowly a broad smile of understanding crossed his face. 'Ah! In weight. Ah, I see now.' Then, nodding his head slowly he turned his attention back to our patient. 'Now, Mrs Maguire, that's a very big stone and must have been very painful. Did you keep it for us to see?'

As soon as I spotted him in the waiting room, I was pleased to see that Larry was looking a lot better. The ever-present Agnes ushered him into my clinic room and then sat quietly a chain's length away, while I explained to him the results of the most recent tests.

'The scans are much improved, but as I suspected there is still a significantly enlarged lymph node present in your abdomen which needs to be removed surgically.' He nodded, prepared for this news.

'What about the blood test, Doc?'

'Well, it hasn't gone back to normal. The last one was thirty-five. Now, although in an ideal world we would like to see it below five, for practical purposes I think we just have to accept that this is as low as it is going to go. It wouldn't be safe to give you any further chemotherapy and hopefully the test will continue to go down after the operation.

'Okay, Doc. Let's get on with it.'

I went into some details of the operation, explaining that it would have to be performed in Glasgow by a specialist surgeon, and then I raised my eyebrows to invite questions. There was a short silence before Agnes to my surprise cleared her throat and announced, 'So the treatment's failed then?'

'No! Not at all,' I countered. 'The blood test which indicates how much cancer there is has gone down a massive amount, although it's not quite returned to normal.' I looked at Agnes, then at Larry and back again. 'Moreover, the scans are much improved and it's not unusual to require an operation to remove residual disease.' I paused for a moment. 'This should be considered the final part of the treatment and hopefully it will be curative.'

'Hopefully?' asked Larry.

'Yes, hopefully. As you know, there are no guarantees.'

'Happy, Agnes?' Larry glanced sideways at her.

The chain rattled quietly. 'You know I have to report back to the Governor and tell him what's going on.' she said, slightly piqued. As I looked at her I noticed, among the visions of hell, and visible just below her rolled-up sleeve, a rather crude tattoo which simply read, *Liam R.I.P.* Her face was now stern, the deep lines set as though in concrete, and after a few further comments I accompanied them both out of the clinic room where the second warder was waiting to take Larry back to prison.

As I watched the two of them disappear down the clinic steps, Julie appeared beside me. 'How's he doing?' she asked.

'I'm not too happy, to be honest, but he's agreed to go for surgery. It's his only chance.'

'Must be very difficult going through all this while in prison?'

'Yes, it's bad enough when you're at home in the bosom of a caring family.'

'And he's got no family?' Julie looked up at me enquiringly.

'I don't think so. But he *has* got Agnes.'

'Agnes? Is that the woman who stabbed him.'

'No. That was a long time ago. Agnes is the wardress who accompanies him. She cares for him. A *lot.'*

'Truly?'

278

'Yes, a lot,' I repeated.

'I suppose she must, being chained to him all the time,' Julie laughed.

'Yes. They are quite attached to one another,' I agreed.

***

'Grahame. I'm sorry, but I really need your help with Billy and the two Jimmies.' Matron rarely contacted me outside our regular weekly meetings but here she was on the phone, sounding as though she was at the end of her tether, a distinct note of desperation in her voice.

'What's the problem, Matron?'

'Well, this issue has been going on for some time but has now come to a head, probably because Billy's living on site.'

'What's it all about?'

'To be honest, I think it's really about the Jimmies being gay, but Billy claims that they are taking over areas of the garden they shouldn't, and the Jimmies say that Billy's deliberately sabotaging their plant business.'

'Gosh! That's serious.'

'Yes, and they won't listen to me. I think it's because I'm a woman – so I'm afraid I need your help.'

'Crumbs! It must be serious if *you* can't deal with it, Matron.' I was genuinely surprised, as Matron would normally have been more than a match for two gays and a gardener.

'Well, yes. Jimmy senior actually said that they were thinking of moving out because of the harassment.'

'After all the problems we had renting out the cottage that would be disastrous. What does Billy have to say?'

'I think he feels that since he's an employee of the Foundation we will support him in any dispute with tenants. It came to a standoff yesterday, with a lot of shouting and swearing. There was nearly a fight, but Jimmy the younger was brandishing a hoe and, as it was two against one, Billy backed down.'

'Oh, my hat.'

'Grahame, I really would be most grateful if you could meet with them and bang their heads together. Get them to see some sense – if that's possible.'

'Okay, Matron. If you make it known that we are taking this seriously and set up some formal interviews; that might take the heat out of the situation. Could you do that?'

'Yes, I think that would be a good idea.'

'Fine, I'll come along after work one day soon and we can see the two Jimmies together, and then speak to Billy. It might help if you were there to see fair play. And by the way,' I added, 'no hoes or other gardening implements.'

And so it was that, about a week later, Matron and I walked the fifty yards from Riddell House along a tree-lined lane, past the beautifully-faded pastel pink brick of the walled garden, to the gardeners' cottage. It was late afternoon on a fine crisp early spring day and thick smoke billowed from the chimney of the small single-storey building. I followed Jane up the short path, edged by a carpet of snowdrops and crocuses, towards the open front door where the elder Jimmy was waiting. He was a short, slightly portly man with a refined English accent. He had once been a stockbroker but for reasons known only to himself, though no doubt related to his sexual orientation, he had radically changed his lifestyle when in his early forties. Sadly he had lost most of his savings in various unsuccessful artisanal ventures and was now essentially bankrupt. He had borrowed some money to buy the plant stock and basic equipment necessary to set up the business and for him this venture was a last throw of the dice. The Foundation had given him a lifeline with cheap accommodation and as much land as he needed at no extra cost.

The younger Jimmy hung back in the darkness of the small vestibule. Handsome and rather aesthetic-looking, he seemed more like an artist than a nurseryman, with his finely chiselled face, aquiline nose and long, straight dark-brown hair cascading to his shoulders. Over his checked shirt was an unbuttoned leather waistcoat, below which were faded-brown corduroy trousers with bald patches over the knees. To me these two characters looked like mature hippies, seventies drop-outs, and neither would have looked out of place in Camden Market on a Sunday. I shook hands with the elder Jimmy and for the first time entered the cosy, slightly shabby interior of their cottage. Inside it was dark and smoky but warm and comfortable. Old settees, the stuffing visible in places, were welcoming, if a trifle grubby. Two Labrador puppies scampered around our ankles.

'How are you settling in?' I asked.

'Very well, thank you, Doctor Howard. This situation is absolutely perfect for us. However, part of the attraction of living here is its isolation and we hoped that we would be left in peace to get on with things. We have had more that our fair share of harassment in the past. We just want to be left alone to set up our business. It's imperative that it succeeds.'

'Well, you know why Matron and I are here: we need to resolve this issue between yourselves and Billy the gardener.'

We listened to their version of events. Jimmy the elder did all the talking, occasionally referring to his friend for confirmation of some point or another. He was both passionate and genteel in his oratory, nearly moved to tears once or twice. I could only imagine the interaction between those two public school dropouts and Billy, the coarse, inarticulate West Lothian gardener. Afterwards, Matron and I readily accepted their invitation to be shown round the walled garden. This vast space, untended for three decades, had been completely overrun, yet nearly half had now been cleared ready for planting. Along the whole length of north wall ran a Victorian greenhouse. The cracked and missing panes and its once white wooden frame, now peeling and rotten in places, bore witness to years of neglect; but here too was evidence of restoration.

Matron and I finally made our farewells and wandered back to the Big House. 'They seem to be doing a rather good job, Matron. I'm impressed.'

'Yes. I agree. They're nice people and there can be no doubt that they work very hard.'

'And the rent?'

'Well, to be honest, they live a bit hand-to-mouth, and sometimes get behind, but it's always paid in the end, and it's better than the place lying empty.'

'Exactly. When am I seeing Billy?'

'Well, he's been a bit elusive and I haven't been able to pin him down to a time, but I'll give you a call as soon as I have arranged something.'

It was to be another week before I returned to the Home to meet with Billy. The apparent reason for the delay was that he wanted to write a report detailing his own version of the incident that had led to this fallout. As we settled in her office, Matron handed me a mug of tea along with the two sheets of grimy paper that constituted Billy's statement. On these soiled pages, ripped out of an exercise book and written in pencil, was a rather pathetic report running to three sides, probably the most Billy had written in his entire life. It started with an account of his personal circumstances: how his wife had locked him out of the marital home, and how the two Jimmies had taunted him. The final straw came when the Jimmies told him off for clearing the drive in front of the cottage and accused him of interfering with their front garden. I laid Billy's statement down on Jane's desk and looked at her quizzically.

'I know,' she said. 'Sad, isn't it?'

'Okay, let's see what he's got to say for himself.'

At Matron's invitation, Billy entered the room somewhat bashfully, sat down, bowed his head and stared at the floor. He was a small, wiry man, probably in his thirties, with angular, shrew-like facial features.

On his head was a dirty, woollen bobble-hat while he was clad in soiled overalls and heavy boots. His unshaven face was ingrained with dirt, most noticeably around his nostrils.

'Billy.' I said. 'Firstly, thank you for your written statement. That's been extremely helpful, and I'm sorry to hear of your personal circumstances. However, as you know, we're not here to discuss those.' Billy nodded without lifting his head and I continued. 'We need to solve the problem that has arisen between you and the tenants of the gardeners' cottage.'

'Aye!' he said, without looking up.

'I've spoken to them both and they say you deliberately interfered with their garden. I'd like to hear your version of events'

'Which bit o' the gairden?'

'The bit in front of the cottage.'

'That belongs to the Home.' Billy asserted. 'That's my job.'

'They claim it's their patch of land which comes with the cottage.'

'Nah. That's nae true.'

I looked at Matron and then back at Billy. His head was now in his hands and he was rubbing his eyes and when he eventually looked up they were moist and red. Usually a man of few words, he suddenly started to talk rapidly and without thought, his words jumbled and staccato, any pretence of self-control having disappeared.

'I cannae tak nae mair o't. My wife's pitten me oot and her new man's moved in. I've nae wye tae stay. The bairn only sees me at the weekend and if I lose this job I dinne ken what I'd do. Probably kill masel.' He looked at the floor and silent tears ran down his cheeks. I waited a moment, wondering what I might say for the best.

'Billy! Listen. No one's suggesting you'll lose your job. Matron, you can confirm that, can't you?'

'Doctor Howard's right, Billy. You've been given a warning after being found asleep in the airing cupboard, but so long as there aren't any further problems your job's not at risk.'

'Aye, guid. But I've got naewye to bide.'

Matron continued, 'Billy, you know you can live in the Home for as long as you need to, so you won't be out on the street.'

'Do you think there is any chance of making it up with your wife?' I asked.

'Nae chance, now she's got a new man.'

'Oh!'

'I just dinnae ken whit tae dae.'

The room fell silent. Billy sobbed quietly, I looked at the floor and Matron took a sip of tea from her mug. After a moment, with a glance at Jane, I turned to Billy.

'Right, Billy, I'm going to make a suggestion. I want you to listen. Okay?' He continued to stare at the floor. 'Are you listening?' He looked up and his red-rimmed eyes peered at me from his grimy, tear-stained face.

'Firstly, we have no intention of terminating your employment. Okay? Secondly, we have agreed that you can live here, in the Home, for as long as is necessary. Isn't that right, Matron?' She nodded. 'Now, with regard to the tenants, as far as I'm concerned the whole area

285

around their cottage is *their* property, rented from the Foundation. I think the only way so ensure there are no further problems is for you not to go beyond the gate that leads to the cottage. Will you agree to that?' As I said this I heard Jane's chair creak, but she said nothing.

'Nah, I cannae.'

'Why not?'

'Ma tools an' stuff are in the shed up the lane.'

'Get everything you need and bring them down to this side of the gate. Once that's done, you are not to go beyond there.' There was no response.

'Do you understand?' Still there was silence. 'Well?' Still no reply. 'Look, Billy, I'm afraid that if you don't agree we have a real problem.'

'What d'ye mean?'

At this juncture I was very unsure of my position and I had no idea if I had gone well beyond any authority I had. In fact, as chairman of a voluntary committee, I suspected that I had no real jurisdiction whatsoever over employees.

'Well, let's just say that it would be wise not to do so. I don't want any further friction between you and the two Jimmies.'

'If I agree, how can you stop them hasslin' me?'

'If you agree to this, I will go to the cottage immediately and tell them not to come beyond their side of the gate except for access.' Once again it occurred to me that I probably had no right to demand this, but I was now too deep in to withdraw. Billy nodded silently, 'Aye. Okay.'

'Good. One final thing. It's not my business, but I suggest you get some legal advice about your marriage and your house.' There was again no response. 'Do you have anything else you want to say to us?'

'Nah.'

'Very well. Thanks for coming in.' I smiled and stood up. As the door closed behind him, Matron sighed. 'What's the problem?' I asked.

'It'll never work!'

'Why ever not?'

'They're all as bad as one another, all three of them; and they're behaving like children.'

'So, putting clear blue water between them could defuse the situation.'

'Maybe.' Clearly Matron wasn't convinced, 'Thanks for coming anyway. I think that's all we can do for now.'

I strolled up the lane to the cottage to inform the two Jimmies of the deal.

'*What*! *We can't go past the gate*?'

'Well, you can. But only for access. Billy will stay on the other side of the gate once he has taken his tools away.'

They were far from happy. What had seemed to me to be a brilliant plan had simply upset both the parties concerned. Even Matron was convinced it would fail.

The flaw in my scheme was that I had not factored in the sheer puerility of the two factions. Matron had been spot-on when she'd said they were behaving like children but I was now committed to this plan and was determined it should work.

The following week I phoned to check on progress. 'How's it going, Matron? Is the demilitarized zone working?' I asked optimistically.

'Well, Grahame, you seem to have created a second front, a sort of No Man's Land across which brickbats are being thrown.'

'What d'you mean?'

'Well, they seem to be staying on their own side of the gate but they spend most of the day shouting at each other across the void.'

'Oh no!'

'And neither party is willing to move away just in case the other crosses the line. When Jimmy the elder turned away briefly to light a cigarette, Billy deliberately put one foot over the line and stamped it on the Jimmies' side in defiance.'

'I don't believe it. What happened?'

'Well he withdrew to his side of the line when the younger Jimmy rather menacingly took a trowel out of his trouser pocket.'

'Oh, my hat! Give it a while longer, Matron. See you next week for the house committee.'

'Evening, Joe.' As usual the Home's most senior resident was in his favourite place at the far end of the room away from the television. In front of him, on a tray balanced on the arms of his wheelchair, was a half-completed jigsaw.

'E-e-ev'nin', Doc.' His voice was more hesitant than usual and it took him longer to formulate his words.

'How's tricks?'

'Not too-oo bad, d-doc. Speech worse.' He took a deep breath, 'I gather our leader is v-visiting?'

'Yes, Joe. Her Ladyship is going to open the new stable block in a couple of months' time.'

'G-good. I-I-would like to meet her.'

'You will, Joe. I will personally introduce you as the first and indeed the longest-serving resident of Riddell House.'

'Thanks, Doc. I'd like that. I want to th-thank her for all that she does. If it wasn't for the Home, I'd be in some 'ospital somewhere. Wouldn't like that.'

'I agree. We're all looking forward to her visit. See you later, Jo. Now I'm off to my meeting.'

Half an hour later, Matron was drawing to the close of her report. 'Finally, I'm afraid we've had further problems with the chef. He was caught stealing food and I've had to dismiss him.'

Hamish, retired lawyer and previous chairman, had long been concerned about the honesty of the chef. 'Sadly, Matron,' he said, 'I'm not surprised and I think it's for the best. Have you been able to replace him?'

'Not yet, but we hope to have a new one start in a week or so. Until then we are just muddling along. I have to say that Martha has been a real star. When she heard of our dilemma she came along with her new husband – who used to be in the catering business – and they've prepared one meal each day for both the staff and the residents.' Matron looked briefly round the table and then, as there were no further questions, she continued: 'I am pleased to say that, although the stand-off between the two Jimmies and Billy continues, outright war seems to have been averted.' There was an audible chuckle from Hamish, which woke George who was sitting next to him.

'Is that right, Matron?' I asked, pleasantly surprised.

'Yes. Well, for now at any rate. And finally, I'm delighted to announce that her Ladyship has agreed to visit the home and formally open the renovated stable block.'

'Oh, good. I do hope members of the house committee will be invited to meet her,' Siobhan looked around the table for support. George, now wide-awake was the first to respond, 'Absolutely! I think we should put on a good show with a reception and a tour.'

'We should, of course, invite Martha,' added Matron.

There followed murmurs of support for this proposal from around the table.

'Matron, have we advertised the properties for rental yet?' Hamish, as always, got straight down to business.

'I'm pleased to say that the architect who designed the renovation wants one of the houses, and there has already been interest expressed in the other.'

'Excellent, her ladyship will be pleased to hear that, considering the investment the Foundation has made. Well done, Matron.' Hamish and the rest of the committee murmured their approval and soon after that I concluded the meeting. As it broke up and the members chatted and drifted away, Siobhan cornered me and over a sandwich said how much the WRI had enjoyed my presentation at their recent meeting. 'Pleasure, Siobhan.

An absolute pleasure. I hope I didn't upset anyone with my spoon-judging?'

'Of *course* you did! They take it very seriously. What a piece of nonsense that is. I think it dates back to medieval times. Come to think of it, most of the members do as well!' She chuckled and then moved away to speak to Jane about arrangements for our Founder's visit.

Two weeks later I dropped in to Riddell House after my clinic to see how the stand-off was going. Joe was stationed in the hallway, near the door, a place where you could often find him during the day when the weather was warm. 'Jo, I've got something for you.'

'H-Hi, Doc! C-Clinic finished?'

'Yes, another one down,' I smiled. 'How are you?'

'Okay, thanks. F-Finished the jigsaw, bloody thing! I spent *weeks* on it then at the end there was one piece missing. *One piece.* Shouldn't be allowed.'

I laughed. 'Never mind. There are plenty more to do.'

'No more for me I'm afraid. It's getting too difficult to control my hands.' He then demonstrated the extraordinary contortions he had to go through to insert a single piece of a jigsaw in its correct place.

'Here, Joe, I thought you might like this book. It's by Stephen Leacock and it's hilarious, Just watch that you don't laugh so much you have a heart attack!'

'Oh, t-thanks, Doc.' He smiled, then between fits of laughing and coughing he remarked, 'W-wouldn't it be i-ironic if I d-d-died laughing after eight years with motor n-neurone disease!'

'Don't do that for heaven's sake! You'd make the place look untidy.'

'No, We c-can't have that with her Ladyship coming, can we?' He looked at the slim volume I had brought for him. 'G-Good. It's nice and short.' Then he added quietly, 'I don't begin long books any more.'

I nodded with understanding. 'Right! I'm off to see Matron about affairs of state. Bye, Joe.'

As I entered Jane's office she smiled broadly. 'How's tricks, Matron?' I asked. 'All quiet on the Western Lothian Front?'

'It's amazing, Grahame. Suddenly they're the best of friends!'

'I don't believe it! What happened, Matron?'

'Well, I'm not entirely sure, and to be honest it's probably best I don't know. However it appears that the Jimmies took a huge risk and went to see Mrs Billy.'

'Crumbs! That was brave.'

'Yes, and apparently they told her in no uncertain terms how, as a result of her behaviour, not only had Billy gone off the rails but the fall-out was also putting their own fledgling business in jeopardy.'

'Gosh! Well done them!'

'Well, Grahame, it's what came next that's so amazing.' Jane took a sip of tea and then continued. 'It seems that Mrs Billy must have been concerned, because that weekend, when Billy went for his weekly visit, she invited him in. Unfortunately the new man was there and after a brief altercation Billy unceremoniously threw him through the front door, forgetting to open it first.'

'Oh, for heaven's sake!'

'Well, there's more! Instead of World War 3 breaking out, apparently Mrs Billy fell into his arms, said she'd made a terrible mistake and now he's moved back in.'

'That's great; but how has that helped with the Jimmy situation?'

'Well, it seems Billy got to hear about how the Jimmies had intervened on his behalf so he asked to meet them at Check Point Charlie – you know, in No Man's Land. Billy mumbled his thanks and they in turn asked if they could be of any further help. It was like *The Spy who came in from the Cold*. They gradually advanced into the middle of the demilitarized zone and shook hands. Then they began to apologise to one another. Jimmy senior said Billy could have some of their plants, and Billy offered to help with any heavy work with his tractor, and before you could say, "glasnost", they were the best of friends. Now they can't see enough of each other.'

I smiled. 'None so strange as folk, Matron.'

'Absolutely. I'm so very relieved it's been resolved since her Ladyship would have taken a dim view of grenades being lobbed across No Man's Land.'

***

'Are you sure there's an enlarged lymph node?' I quietly asked Janet, my fellow-examiner quietly, from behind the seated lady whose neck I was palpating.

'That's what it says here.' Janet checked her crib documenting the abnormalities to be found in patients taking part in the clinical exam for the final fellowship. As with the *viva-voce* exams, we worked in pairs but, instead of being sited in the College basement, these assessments took place in some of London's leading teaching hospitals. There, in return for modest travel expenses and as much tea as they could drink, patients with interesting symptoms and signs gathered to be examined by anxious and ever-hopeful candidates. We examiners had no prior knowledge of those patients and at the beginning of the day had only half an hour to develop an examining strategy based upon any abnormalities that we could detect. This was an inauspicious start.

'I can't feel any enlarged nodes at all. Here, you try.' Janet smiled at the patient, 'Do you mind if I feel your neck, Mrs Smith?'

'No. Not at all, luv.'

I stood aside to let Janet move to the back of the seated middle-aged lady who, according to the script, should have had several enlarged lymph nodes palpable on both sides of her neck. That would have provided perfect examination material by giving an opportunity to assess a candidate's clinical skills, as well as opening up numerous avenues for discussion about the differential diagnosis, possible investigations and treatment.

After a few moments expertly palpating Mrs Smith's neck, Janet looked puzzled. 'No. I agree there's nothing to feel.'

In order to clarify things I decided to cut to the chase and ask the person most likely to know – the patient.

'Mrs Smith,' I asked, 'it says here that you had some lumps in your neck. Is that true? It's just that we can't feel them.'

'That's because they've all gorn.' Mrs Smith beamed proudly at us both. 'I did 'ave huge lumps, massive they was, but they've all gorn away after the treatment, Doctor.' She paused for a moment, 'That's good, ain't it, Doctor?'

'It's very good for you,' I responded.

'But not so good for us!' I heard Janet whisper quietly.

'Do you have any lumps elsewhere?' I asked hopefully.

'No. Just in me neck, Doctor.'

'Where they've all gone away,' added Janet with a sigh. As we left the cubicle, she continued: 'Grahame, we have been given a completely normal lady for the examination. Brilliant, just *brilliant*!'

'Not an *ideal* case, I agree' I thought for a moment. 'I know. Perhaps we could ask the candidate to *pretend* that she had some lumps in her neck?'

'What do you mean?' Janet was puzzled.

'I think it might just work. It would go like this. "Doctor so and so, would you examine this lady's neck, please?" He would then say, "It feels normal to me."

295

"Absolutely! Well done," I'd agree. Then I'd say, "Now, I'd like you to pretend that she *does* have some lumps. Try again," and he'd say, "*Ah*, she has some lumps there." '

'Don't be such as ass,' said Janet, smiling ruefully at me.

'Well, Janet, we've landed a most interesting clinical case: *The Case of the Disappearing Lymph Nodes*. Pity for us that the treatment worked so quickly.'

Janet was thoughtful. 'It does leave us with a real problem as to what to ask the candidates.'

'Seriously, Janet, we can't use Mrs Smith as a clinical case, *unless* we tell the candidate the history and ask him to assess the response.'

'Not ideal. But possible. Let's just hope the other cases are better.' And so we set off to assess what the other cubicles held in the way of clinical signs.

For us examiners, the ideal case was someone with a clear clinical sign or condition, who spoke reasonable English and didn't mind several nervous candidates prodding their abdomens, or whatever part of their anatomy was of interest. In the past we had coped with demented and deaf patients but this was the first time we had been given a completely normal patient for the examination.

Several pairs of examiners were usually stationed at each hospital and therefore an interesting patient was at a premium, and each team would aim to be first to bag the patient with the best clinical signs. This often led to an unseemly rush across the ward or to the cubicle containing the prize case, and there could be jostling and even physical violence in an attempt to get there first.

The head examiner, Chris, indicated that further along the ward there was a man with a single hard lump on the left side of his face, below the ear.

'Any relevant clinical history?' asked Janet.

'Sadly, no. But I *was* thinking of hitting him on the nose so that it started to bleed, and then selling it as a case of nasopharyngeal cancer,' he smiled. Further along the ward were several patients with interesting lumps and bumps in various parts of their anatomy, accompanied by relevant X-rays and radiotherapy plans.

Being an examiner was almost as nerve-wracking as being the candidate, except for the fact that *we* couldn't fail. I recalled my own final fellowship exam many years before, when I was asked to do an indirect laryngoscopy on an elderly man.

'Look at this man's larynx, if you would.' I was instructed.

As the first candidate after the lunch break, I could detect the odour of expensive white wine on my examiner's breath.

I sat down in front of the patient, settled the head-mirror on my forehead, warmed the long thin laryngoscopy mirror in the spirit-burner and tested the temperature on the back of my hand in the prescribed fashion. I took hold of the patient's tongue and gently inserted the instrument into the back of his mouth and asked him to say, 'Aah.' I was hugely relieved when his upper throat opened up to reveal an excellent view of the larynx, which, apart from some slight redness, looked quite normal. I carefully withdrew the instrument.

'Did you get a view of the larynx?' one of the examiners asked.

'Yes, sir.'

'Good. Tell me what you saw.'

'Essentially I thought it looked normal. I couldn't see any lesions, although the left cord was possibly slightly erythematous,' I pronounced confidently.

'Excellent!' said the examiner, who then glanced at his colleague with a somewhat smug expression on his face. 'You see, George, we all think the larynx normal, apart from you.'

'But I only said it was slightly red. I never said there was any residual cancer.' George continued to defend himself and the two examiners argued quietly until we heard the bell announcing the end of the session. I imagined how much relief that bell must have brought to hundreds of candidates over the years.

It occurred to me that there were several factors wholly outside the candidates' control which could affect their chances of success. In addition to disagreements among the examiners, there were other variables such as the quality of the examiners' luncheon and whether or not they had argued with their wives that morning. Moreover, there was an ongoing debate about the best time of day to be examined. The received wisdom was that examiners were more hawkish in the morning, while by late afternoon they simply wanted to go home and were thus likely to be more relaxed about the occasional blunder perpetrated by a candidate. Now the roles were reversed and I was the examiner. I was determined to try to make this test less susceptible to the vagaries and whims of the examiner and time of day.

It was nine o'clock and the first candidates were waiting nervously at the entrance to the ward. Being chivalrous, I offered Janet the option of going first. 'Where d'you want to start?' I asked.

'I'll kick off with the abdomen on the left.'

'Okay, I'll probably move to the parotid, and then if necessary we could go to the completely normal lady, but only if we have to.'

Having agreed on this we took up our stations and, clipboards at the ready, sought out our first candidate of the day.

'Candidate 114, please,' I called out towards the shuffling, variegated group of young doctors. A nervous-looking young man, dark-skinned, with shiny, black neat hair and wearing an expensive, well-cut suit, stepped forward and confirmed his identity.

'I'm Doctor Howard,' I said warmly as I shook his hand. 'And this is Doctor …' I turned to where Janet had been standing just a moment before, but she had gone. I then spotted her walking briskly in the direction of the bed on which lay the patient with the interesting abdomen. Another pair of examiners were trying to beat her to this prize by executing a kind of pincer movement, but they were no match for Janet who was now travelling at speed. She reached the bed first where she halted, triumphantly guarding her trophy, while waiting for me and the candidate to catch up. I invited 114 to follow me and completed the introduction at the bedside.

Janet was looking decidedly pleased with herself and threw a smug glance at the other examiners who had veered off to another, less interesting case.

'Right! Would you please examine this man's abdomen?' she said. The candidate introduced himself to the patient, requested the necessary permission and proceeded to complete a competent abdominal examination. 'Have you found anything?' Janet asked after a few minutes.

'Yes I think he has a ...'

Janet indicated that he should wait until we had moved to a small side-room allocated to us for discussion, out of earshot of the patient.

'Okay, carry on. What did you find?'

'I think he looks slightly jaundiced and on examination of his abdomen he has a palpable enlarged liver.'

'Describe the liver, please.'

'It was hard and irregular, consistent with metastatic disease.'

'Okay. What else was abnormal?'

114 paused. 'That was all I found,' he said hesitantly.

'There is something else abnormal that you should have seen from the end of the bed.' I could see 114 beginning to panic and beads of sweat appeared on his brow as Janet continued. 'Come on! Something really obvious.'

114 thought for a while and then suddenly smiled, 'Oh! You mean the *scar*.'

'Yes! Absolutely. Tell me about it.'

'Sorry. I forgot.' 114's relief was tangible. 'Yes, he has a midline surgical scar.'

'Right. Putting all those findings together, what do you think is the most likely diagnosis?'

'An intra-abdominal cancer with liver secondaries.'

'What's the most likely primary?'

'A colorectal cancer.'

'Yes. Now what further investigations might you want to do?'

And so the questioning continued. When Janet had finished, I took our candidate back to the ward where he examined several other patients and, with some ten minutes remaining, I led 114 back to our room for some final questions.

'Now. Tell me about the man with the lump in his neck?' I asked.

'It was hard, fixed and felt malignant.'

'What do you think it was?' As Doctor 114 was about to answer, I heard a faint cry apparently emanating from an adjacent room. 'Can someone let me out, please?' I paused, puzzled, and then it came again a little louder, 'Is there anyone there? Can someone let me out, please?' I glanced at Janet who had been gazing listlessly out of the window. She was now looking intently at me as though I was to blame for this plaintive cry, as if for some unimaginable reason I had suddenly become a ventriloquist. Our candidate did not know how to respond to this unexpected intrusion and was wondering if it was part of the exam, some kind of intelligence test. He obviously felt that he should continue to answer the question as best he could, but the plea for help from next door had, quite unsurprisingly, adversely affected his concentration and he had now lost his train of thought. As he hesitated, there came another cry, still louder. 'Help! Can someone let me out please, I'm stuck.' This time I could detect a definite Welsh accent, and we could ignore it no longer.

'I'll go and see what that's all about,' said Janet as she stood up and headed for the door.

I looked at 114 and continued, 'Now, where were we? Oh yes, what do you think that lump was?'

'I think it was his parotid, and that he has a parotid cancer.'

'Good. What kind of parotid cancers are there?' By now both of us had regained some of our composure but just then, before he could reply, there came some muttering and a loud rattling sound from next door following which Janet re-entered the room. Her face was flushed and she wore a broad smile, 'Grahame,' she said, 'I think you'd better come next door,' and she hastily left the room once more.

'I'm sorry,' I said to the candidate, 'but would you excuse me for one moment.' I got up and entered the adjacent room which was a toilet. Opposite me, was a row of cubicles the doors of which were all open apart from one, from behind which came Huw's unmistakable Welsh lilt.

'Look, I'm awfully sorry, but I'm locked in, you see.'

'What is it about examiners and doors this year?' asked Janet, a bewildered expression on her face.

'Huw! Don't panic. We'll get you out.' I said in a firm but quietly confident voice. My tone, I thought, was appropriate to the occasion and designed to reassure any examiner who might be trapped in a toilet that salvation was close at hand.

'Oh good, Grahame, it's you. The bolt on the door has broken, the little knob's come off, you see, and I can't grip it. Do you have any pliers?'

'Let me check. No, amazingly, Huw, I don't seem to have any pliers about my person just now. I must have forgotten to pick them up this morning. How *stupid* of me. However, I'm sure Janet will have remembered to bring her pair of pliers with her.' I looked toward Janet who was kneeling on the floor convulsed with laughter.

'It's all very well you pair laughing, but I'm completely trapped in here!'

'We'll probably have to leave you there, Huw. Tell you what. I'll go and get you some food. Any preferences or would you like to see the menu?' Tears ran down my face.

'Don't be such as ass, Grahame. Just get me out of here, will you?'

'Okay, if you insist,' and, after a few moments fiddling with the lock on the outside of the door, it swung open allowing Huw to be released from his lavatorial incarceration, relief written all over his face.

'Thanks, chaps. Sorry about that. This little knob fell off, you see.'

'We don't want to know what happened to your little knob while you were in there, Huw,' said Janet between her guffaws.

'Too much information, Huw,' I added. 'Don't say another word or we'll lock you back in the karsi.'

After a brief pause to regain some degree of composure, Janet and I returned to where our candidate gazed at us with some bemusement as we settled back into our seats.

'Sorry about that,' I said, as though nothing out of the ordinary had occurred. 'One of our fellow examiners managed to lock himself in the toilet.' I looked at 114 with a slight smile, as if to imply that this sort of thing happened all the time. Our candidate just stared at me, stunned, his eyes wide open.

'All in a day's work for us examiners,' added Janet, choking back her laughter.

'Now,' I continued in a business-like way, 'you were telling me about the different type of cancer that might arise in a toilet – no, I mean in the parotid.'

* * *

The week after the examinations, back at the Cancer Centre, my secretary, Sue looked up from her desk – phone in hand. 'It's Matron from Riddell House, Doctor Howard. She was wondering if she might have a word with you.'

'Oh, no!' I said, 'I hope war hasn't broken out in West Lothian again.'

Sue looked puzzled. 'I beg your pardon?'

'Don't worry, Sue, you'll hear all about it on the news.' She looked at me, an expression of disbelief on her face. I smiled, 'Just joshing. Put her through to my office if you would, please.' I went next door, sat at my desk and picked up the phone. 'Matron,' I said, 'if the horticultural arms race has escalated, I'm not in.' After a pause I added, 'How can I help?'

'Sorry to trouble you, Grahame. No, it's nothing like that. I thought you would want to know that Joe died last night.'

I was shocked by this news and my light-heartedness instantly evaporated. Of course I knew he would die some time in the not too distant future. He had motor neurone disease after all and was deteriorating, but this was sudden and unexpected. Only two weeks before, we had talked of the Founder's forthcoming visit.

I was silent for some time. 'Oh, Matron, I'm so sorry. What happened? He seemed so fit the last time I spoke to him.'

'He became unwell two days ago when he developed a chest infection. Cathy came to see him and started him on antibiotics but by yesterday he had become much worse. He was unable to get out of bed and was quite cyanosed. I got Cathy back and she wanted him admitted to hospital immediately but he refused.'

I smiled to myself. 'Refused, did he?'

'Yes. Said he didn't want go into a hospital ever again, that Riddell House was his home and if he was going to die, he wanted to die here.'

'I'm not surprised. What happened then?'

'Well, once he had made that decision, he deteriorated quite rapidly and died in the early hours.'

'That's exactly what he would have wanted. He'd achieved his goal, his determination to stay out of

305

hospital and to die in what he considered to be his home. I hope he was comfortable?'

'Yes, he was very, very peaceful.'

'I don't suppose there were any family present?'

'Oh, yes! All of them.'

'*All* of them? I didn't think he had any, after his wife walked out on him.'

'Doctor Howard.' And there was a pause, 'You forget. *We* were his family.' I blinked the moisture out of my eyes and the phone fell silent for a moment before she continued. 'By the way, he asked me to make sure I returned the book you lent him.'

'Ah yes. I told him not to die laughing.'

'I beg your pardon?'

'Just a joke, Matron. A joke that Joe and I shared.'

***

There could be no doubting it, but nonetheless I examined the chest X-ray for some minutes longer, from different angles, and then held it up to the window. There were now several large round shadows in the lungs, indicating recurrent disease. It was only six months since Larry's operation to remove residual disease after his chemotherapy. It had gone very well – technically at any rate – as all the persistent masses had been successfully excised, but the omens had not been good, in that there was residual active cancer in the resected specimen and his blood tests had become abnormal again. I collected my thoughts and outlined a plan of management in my head. The first thing was to

306

perform further scans, repeat his blood tests and then decide what treatment options there were, although I knew those were now limited.

I stepped out into the waiting area. There he was, as always, chained to his alter ego. I didn't need to call his name; as soon as we made eye contact, he started to rise, almost dragging Agnes behind him, as if taking her for a walk. 'Come on, Agnes,' I heard him say. I held the door open as he chinked and clinked into the room and took the proffered seat. He glanced at the X-ray box where his film was displayed. 'How's the X-ray, Doc?' There was no way to lessen the impact and I suspected that Larry could see the abnormal shadows in his lungs just as well I could.

'Well, Larry, It's changed. Let me show you.' He stood up and moved closer to the screen. 'You see these round things?' He nodded. 'Well, they weren't there before and they're abnormal. I'm afraid that means the disease has recurred.' His face was expressionless while he continued to stare intently at the X-ray, yearning for it to be normal, hating it for what it meant.

'So it's come back, Doc?'

'Yes, I'm afraid it has.'

'So what do we do now?'

'The first thing is to see if there is any disease elsewhere, and that means repeating your scans. Then we'll have to discuss the treatment options.'

'There is some treatment then, Doc?' He looked at me intently.

'Yes, certainly. It's just not clear at this stage what would be best.'

'What's most likely?'

'Well, further chemotherapy probably, but radiotherapy can be helpful. It all depends on what your scans show.'

'But you said before that further chemotherapy wasn't possible?'

'At the end of your last period on chemotherapy, it was beginning to get risky and all your disease seemed to have responded, but the situation has changed, in that you now have active disease and we can use different drugs to minimise the side-effects. It's a question of risk versus benefit if you like, and the balance has now changed.'

'Can you cure me now, Doc?'

I hesitated, which of course said it all. Larry was an intelligent, well-educated young man. 'If I'm being honest, the aim of treatment now is to control the disease for as long as possible rather than to cure it. *But*,' I said, trying to find a positive note on which to finish, 'it *is* treatable and you should respond to further chemotherapy. 'It's just a question of how well, and for how long – which is very unpredictable.'

'Okay, Doc. Let's get on with it.'

His chain rattled as he got up to leave and, with Agnes in tow, her head bowed and her face grim, made his way to the door. It occurred to me that it was no longer clear who was chained to whom.

***

Bathed in the glorious early summer sunshine Matron and I were standing outside the front door of Riddell House. She was resplendent in matronly blue; her nurse's buckle was gleaming and her black shoes had a parade ground gloss. 'I know she won't like it but we are *not* wearing caps!'

'Her Ladyship *is* somewhat entrenched in her views about nurses' appearances,' I commented.

'You know I like my nurses to be well turned out, but if I insisted they wore caps they would walk out. It's as simple as that.'

'Well just tip me the wink when you are going to tell her and I'll step out of the ring!' I had donned my pinstripe suit for the occasion and we were both pacing about, slightly nervously, in front of the Home. A few minutes after ten o'clock, a small, rather battered Ford Fiesta drove on to the gravel and pulled up outside the main entrance. As it parked, I stepped forward and like a hotel doorman opened the passenger door and helped her Ladyship out of the car. Small and frail, she resembled a sparrow more than a woman who, with her combination of character, persuasiveness and sheer bloody-mindedness, had built up an empire of Homes across the UK to look after the sick and the lame. She was also a woman of few words. After a brief and business-like welcome, we ushered her into the main sitting room. I glanced at the space that would forever be Joe's, and wished that he could have been there, hammering in bits of jigsaw with his fist, frustrated by his failing body.

We strolled slowly about the room and introduced our Founder to members of staff and a selection of the patients.

'And who's this?' she asked wandering over to a seat by the conservatory. I looked at Matron, for we hadn't planted one of our selected patients in that location. I followed our visitor to where she was trying to engage in conversation with an elderly man in a three-piece suit who was sound asleep. It was George. While waiting for her Ladyship, he had taken a seat and then dozed off.

'I'm sorry to wake you,' she said politely, 'I must say you look *jolly* smart.' George was now half-awake and not entirely sure whether to own up that he was a member of the house committee who had fallen asleep, or to pretend to be a resident. He decided to be non-committal.

'Thank you, your Ladyship. One does one's best. It's kind of you to come and visit us.'

'It's a pleasure to see people like you who would otherwise have nowhere to go, being safe and cared for in the Home.'

George wondered what his wife might have to say about that and had half a mind to explain that he had a very nice home of his own, thank you very much, not to mention a wife who was more than capable of caring for him. But he was too polite to disagree, so he just smiled and said, 'It's very nice here.'

'What's wrong with this gentleman?' Her ladyship looked enquiringly at me. My immediate thought was to say that he had a severe case of narcolepsy.

'Well, actually George is here for a meeting,' I explained.

Her Ladyship looked slightly confused. 'How nice,' she said, then turning her attention back to George added, 'Can you walk?'

'With difficulty,' George replied with some degree of truth.

Having lost the gist of this conversation, her Ladyship decided to change the topic. 'Well, perhaps we should look at the new development now?' And so we escorted our visitor back into the warm sunlight across a small lawn to the renovated stable block. *En-route* there stood a line of people waiting to be introduced. We passed Billy and the Jimmies who were engaged in friendly conversation and then I introduced her to Martha.

'This is one of our house committee members who has just resigned in order to get married.' I explained. Martha smiled, curtseyed and then giggled as they shook hands.

'Well it's never too late, then?' Our founder smiled somewhat sardonically and moved along the line.

'And this is our fundraiser, Sheila, your Ladyship.'

'How is the fundraising going?' she asked.

'Well, it's been a fallow month, your Ladyship, but we were lucky enough to get a donation of over a hundred obsolete computers which should raise some funds.

'Oh, jolly well done.'

After a few words, some tea and sandwiches, it was all over. Her Ladyship was slightly surprised when

311

George, now fully alert, joined the rest of the committee in their farewells, but otherwise the visit passed without further incident.

**

'Well, I think we should begin the meeting, ladies and gentleman. Thank you all very much for coming.' I looked at George to ask him to say prayers, but he was already snoring gently. 'Hamish, would you be kind enough to start the meeting with prayers, please?'

'Certainly, Grahame.'

Prayers over, I asked Matron to present her report. After giving some bed-occupancy figures, she announced: 'We're still having problems with employing a chef. We have one part-time but still rely very much on Martha's good offices.'

'What happens when you have no cook?' George had woken up.

'We do whatever we can. Last night for example we simply had to send out for fish and chips.' Matron then paused for a moment. 'I know you will all be saddened to hear that Joe has passed away. He was the first resident to be admitted to the Home and had been here for nearly four years. He liked the Home so much that he decided not to go to hospital for treatment, preferring to die here.' A murmur of sympathy went round the table.

'On a brighter note I can report that Billy and the Jimmies are now the very best of friends. In fact, the nursery business is doing rather well. I am also pleased to announce that the stable block is occupied and the rental is being received.'

'Well done! Well done, Matron.' Hamish tapped the table in a gesture of applause.

'Thank you, Matron.' I said. 'Now, Sheila. Fundraisers report please.'

'Chairman, I'm afraid it's been a rather fallow month yet again. I don't suppose any members of the committee would like to buy a second-hand computer?' There was complete silence, apart from the gentle but audible snoring from George, who had drifted off again. She continued: 'But I do have some good news,' and she looked around the table excitedly. 'We have been bequeathed an elderly Morris Minor which should be worth a bob or two.' I didn't have to look – I could *hear* Matron's eyes rolling in their sockets.

'Thank you, Sheila. Well, good luck with that.' I looked around the table at the members of the committee, 'Well, if there's no further business we can close the meeting, Thank you all very much.'

And so another meeting of the house committee finished and the Foundation's business was concluded for a further month.

***

Larry's scans showed massive areas of recurrent disease in both his abdomen and chest, while his tumour markers were now nearly as high as they had been when he was first diagnosed. We agreed to try salvage chemotherapy with drugs to which he had not previously been exposed but, after a long-delayed second cycle, it was clear that he was not responding, and he was admitted two weeks later as an emergency after having had a seizure.

I knocked on the door of his side-room and entered. The change was remarkable. Larry still clung on to his leather jacket as though this was his last link with normality, an attempt to cling on to an existence he once had – life outside the two institutions that had become his world. The jacket was now about two sizes too large for him and his bald grey skull was partially covered by the collar. His face was asymmetric, the left side drooping, saliva dribbling from the corner of his mouth, and his wry attempt at a smile served only to emphasise the palsy. Already he was showing the signs of steroid therapy, his abdomen having become flabby and covered with the stretch marks more usually associated with pregnancy.

'Hi, Doc. Not so good, eh?'

'Hi, Larry.' I paused, pleased to see the lack of handcuffs, although Agnes was there in the corner of the room, still silently guarding her charge.

'What now?'

'Well, as you know, the scan shows that the disease has spread to your brain and that's why you had the seizure and have a weakness on one side of your face.' I stopped for a moment to allow him time to take in this information. 'Sadly, the drugs have failed to control the disease.' He looked at me questioningly. 'I think the best way to help control your symptoms would be a short course of radiotherapy to the brain. This should shrink the disease and stop you having any further seizures.'

Larry's speech was now slurred and tortuous, but there was still a hint of the old determination and a desire to press on, when he said, 'Let's gerr on with it then, Doc.'

He never recovered sufficiently to leave hospital. Although plans were made to transfer him to a nearby hospice, and all his restrictions were relaxed, Larry's deterioration was relentless. Although no longer chained to him, Agnes remained, ostensibly to guard him, but in reality to care. She seemed to be on duty all the time and, as Larry slowly faded, she took to not wearing her uniform. She never said, and I never asked, but I think this was her way of releasing him from custody. Now, unchained and with no uniformed guard, for the last few days of his life he had finally escaped from his past.

'How long, Doc?' Agnes had never asked this question before. She was, after all, his warder and not his next of kin. But now she had changed from guard to guardian and soon the now invisible chain connecting both of them would be sundered forever.

'You see …' and she glanced at the tattoo that I had noticed some months before, '… I had a son. Liam he was called. Died of a drugs overdose. Would have been Larry's age too.'

'Agnes,' I now called her by her name for the very first time. 'You can see as well as me how quickly he's deteriorating. He could die at any time.' I looked at her prematurely-lined face and gazed deep into her eyes before continuing, 'A few days at the most, I would imagine.'

Yet Larry, as always, was keen to get on with things and that night he struggled out of bed, collapsed and died. When the nurse came in for a routine check about an hour later she found him lying on the floor cradled in Agnes' arms. Silent tears ran down her face and stained her cheeks as she stared unseeingly at the wall.

'Grahame, Grahame!' There could be no mistaking Abdul's voice. I was already a few minutes late for my afternoon clinic and was in no mood for a nonsensical conversation. However, after the briefest of hesitations, I knew I couldn't ignore him so stopped and turned round. He was at the other end of the corridor, walking briskly towards me while waving vigorously. As he came closer his smile broadened and his teeth seemed to glow more brightly.

'Ah, Grahame. I am pleased to have attracted you.' He paused for a moment to catch his breath. 'Mr …' he glanced up and down the corridor and then, satisfied that we were alone, continued, 'you know, from the other side.'

'Yes, I remember. The conundrum,' I replied.

'That's right. I looked in his bladder yesterday at the zoo and it is good news. He is completely better.'

'That's really excellent!' I said. 'That *is* good news – thanks for telling me. Give him my regards next time you see him, would you?'

'Of course. I will keep you in touch.'

'You see, Abdul,' I looked him in the eye, 'there *are* alternatives to surgery.'

He smiled and shook his head, 'Yes, I know,' he replied, 'but they're just not as good.' His smile broadened and his teeth shone.

'Abdul, you're outrageous. You know there's no evidence whatsoever to support that statement!'

'No, I know, but the surgery is definitely the best.'

I decided to change the topic of our conversation. 'By the way, do you remember Larry?'

'The prisoner whose scans we reviewed; bread knife in his thigh?'

'Yes, that's right. Sadly, he died last night.'

'I am not surprised,' Abdul said in a matter of fact fashion, 'he had a lot of disease and huge markers, didn't he?'

'Well, that's true, but he was *potentially* curable and it's always disappointing to lose one of the ball boys.'

Abdul tilted his head slightly and for once his smile faded, 'Of course, but you see, Grahame, you always want to eat your cake and have it all at the same time.' He raised an index finger to emphasise his point. 'You cannot win always the war, without cracking some eggs for the omelette, you see.'

For once I thought that perhaps, just perhaps, I did understand what Abdul was saying. 'Yes, Abdul, I think you may have a point. But it's nice to win a battle every now and then.' I clapped him on the back. 'Now I must get to my clinic. See you later.'